LLEWELLYN'S

2015

MOON SIGN

BOOK

Llewellyn's 2015 Moon Sign Book®

ISBN 978-0-7387-2686-1

Cover design by Kevin R. Brown
Cover illustrations: Scrolls: iStockphoto.com/4468602/ANGELGILD
     Moon: iStockphoto.com/12271763/Magnilion
     Banner: iStockphoto.com/23088297/David Goh
Editing by Nicole Nugent
Stock photography models used for illustrative purposes only and may not endorse or represent the book's subject.
Copyright 2014 Llewellyn Worldwide Ltd. All rights reserved.
Typography owned by Llewellyn Worldwide Ltd.

Any Internet references contained in this work are current at publication time, but the publisher cannot guarantee that a specific location will continue to be maintained.

Astrological data compiled and programmed by Rique Pottenger. Based on the earlier work of Neil F. Michelsen.

You can order Llewellyn annuals and books from *New Worlds*, Llewellyn's catalog. To request a free copy of the catalog, call toll-free 1-877-NEW-WRLD, or visit our website at www.llewellyn.com.

Llewellyn Publications is a registered trademark of Llewellyn Worldwide Ltd.
2143 Wooddale Drive, Woodbury, MN 55125-2989 USA
Moon Sign Book® is registered in U.S. Patent and Trademark Office.
Moon Sign Book is a trademark of Llewellyn Worldwide Ltd. (Canada).
Printed in the USA

Llewellyn Publications
A Division of Llewellyn Worldwide Ltd.
2143 Wooddale Drive
Woodbury, MN 55125-3989
www.llewellyn.com

Printed in the United States of America

Table of Contents

What's Different About the Moon Sign Book?

Readers have asked why *Llewellyn's Moon Sign Book* says that the Moon is in Taurus when some almanacs indicate that the Moon is in the previous sign of Aries on the same date. It's because there are two different zodiac systems in use today: the tropical and the sidereal. *Llewellyn's Moon Sign Book* is based on the tropical zodiac.

The tropical zodiac takes 0 degrees of Aries to be the Spring Equinox in the Northern Hemisphere. This is the time and date when the Sun is directly overhead at noon along the equator, usually about March 20–21. The rest of the signs are positioned at 30-degree intervals from this point.

The sidereal zodiac, which is based on the location of fixed stars, uses the positions of the fixed stars to determine the starting point of

0 degrees of Aries. In the sidereal system, 0 degrees of Aries always begins at the same point. This does create a problem though, because the positions of the fixed stars, as seen from Earth, have changed since the constellations were named. The term "precession of the equinoxes" is used to describe the change.

Precession of the equinoxes describes an astronomical phenomenon brought about by the Earth's wobble as it rotates and orbits the Sun. The Earth's axis is inclined toward the Sun at an angle of about 23½ degrees, which creates our seasonal weather changes. Although the change is slight, because one complete circle of the Earth's axis takes 25,800 years to complete, we can actually see that the positions of the fixed stars seem to shift. The result is that each year, in the tropical system, the Spring Equinox occurs at a slightly different time.

Does Precession Matter?

There is an accumulative difference of about 23 degrees between the Spring Equinox (0 degrees Aries in the tropical zodiac and 0 degrees Aries in the sidereal zodiac) so that 0 degrees Aries at Spring Equinox in the tropical zodiac actually occurs at about 7 degrees Pisces in the sidereal zodiac system. You can readily see that those who use the other almanacs may be planting seeds (in the garden and in their individual lives) based on the belief that it is occurring in a fruitful sign, such as Taurus, when in fact it would be occurring in Gemini, one of the most barren signs of the zodiac. So, if you wish to plant and plan activities by the Moon, it is helpful to follow *Llewellyn's Moon Sign Book*. Before we go on, there are important things to understand about the Moon, her cycles, and their correlation with everyday living. For more information about gardening by the Moon, see page 61.

Weekly Almanac

Your Guide to Lunar Gardening & Good Timing for Activities

But it's also important to lean on the spade from time to time, and marvel at the extraordinariness of spring, epitomised by the miracle of the bulb.

~Eileen Campbell

January

December 28–January 3

You are not tied to any past mistake unless you lash yourself to it.

*~*Guy Finley

Date	Qtr.	Sign	Activity
Dec 25, 11:07 pm– Dec 28, 1:35 am	1st	Pisces	Plant grains, leafy annuals. Fertilize (chemical). Graft or bud plants. Irrigate. Trim to increase growth.
Dec 30, 5:56 am– Jan 1, 12:09 pm	2nd	Taurus	Plant annuals for hardiness. Trim to increase growth.
Jan 3, 8:08 pm– Jan 4, 11:53 pm	2nd	Cancer	Plant grains, leafy annuals. Fertilize (chemical). Graft or bud plants. Irrigate. Trim to increase growth.

The term *superfoods* has come into vogue in the last decade, making its first appearance in the late Nineties. There is no firm definition, but many of these foods are fruits and vegetables that a home garden can grow! The information for these profiles is culled from various print and online sources, but it should not be taken as a substitute for medical advice of any kind.

		JANUARY				
S	M	T	W	T	F	S
				1	2	3
4	5	6	7	8	9	10
11	12	13	14	15	16	17
18	19	20	21	22	23	24
25	26	27	28	29	30	31

January 4–10 ☋

*I might repeat to myself slowly and soothingly, a list of
quotations beautiful from minds profound—if I can remember
the damn things.*

~DOROTHY PARKER

Date	Qtr.	Sign	Activity
Jan 4, 11:53 pm–Jan 6, 6:03 am	3rd	Cancer	Plant biennials, perennials, bulbs, and roots. Prune. Irrigate. Fertilize (organic).
Jan 6, 6:03 am–Jan 8, 5:58 pm	3rd	Leo	Cultivate. Destroy weeds and pests. Harvest fruits and root crops for food. Trim to retard growth.
Jan 8, 5:58 pm–Jan 11, 6:57 am	3rd	Virgo	Cultivate, especially for medicinal plants. Destroy weeds and pests. Trim to retard growth.

A main aim of many "diets" or eating plans is to increase the
intake of fruits and vegetables. The USDA recommends that
half your meal plate be covered in fruits or vegetables—2.5 to
3 cups for adults. Use the following food and plant profiles as
inspiration for your shopping cart and garden plans. Read on for
a quick glossary of terms commonly used to describe why these
fruits and vegetables are so good for you.

2014 © svry Image from BigStockPhoto.com

○

January 4
11:53 pm EST

JANUARY

S	M	T	W	T	F	S
				1	2	3
4	5	6	7	8	9	10
11	12	13	14	15	16	17
18	19	20	21	22	23	24
25	26	27	28	29	30	31

January 11–17

Time is the most valuable thing man can spend.

~THEOPHRASTUS

Date	Qtr.	Sign	Activity
Jan 13, 6:44 pm–Jan 16, 3:01 am	4th	Scorpio	Plant biennials, perennials, bulbs, and roots. Prune. Irrigate. Fertilize (organic).
Jan 16, 3:01 am–Jan 18, 7:04 am	4th	Sagittarius	Cultivate. Destroy weeds and pests. Harvest fruits and root crops for food. Trim to retard growth.

Foods that provide *anti-inflammatory* effects are good because they reduce swelling, pain, and tenderness. In fact, most pain relievers work by reducing inflammation. This is particularly helpful for those suffering with chronic pain, arthritis, or heart conditions.

Phytonutrients are the chemicals that protects a plant from things like fungi, germs, and bugs—and they can help protect your body from threats as well. *Flavonoids* and *carotenoids* are two types of phytonutrient.

_____

_____

_____

_____

January 13
4:46 am EST

JANUARY

S	M	T	W	T	F	S
				1	2	3
4	5	6	7	8	9	10
11	12	13	14	15	16	17
18	19	20	21	22	23	24
25	26	27	28	29	30	31

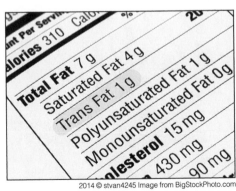

January 18–24 ～～～

Discipline is where beauty and soulfulness meet.

~VICTORIA MORAN

Date	Qtr.	Sign	Activity
Jan 18, 7:04 am– Jan 20, 7:59 am	4th	Capricorn	Plant potatoes and tubers. Trim to retard growth.
Jan 20, 7:59 am– Jan 20, 8:14 am	4th	Aquarius	Cultivate. Destroy weeds and pests. Harvest fruits and root crops for food. Trim to retard growth.
Jan 22, 7:48 am– Jan 24, 8:31 am	1st	Pisces	Plant grains, leafy annuals. Fertilize (chemical). Graft or bud plants. Irrigate. Trim to increase growth.

Many of the foods featured in these pages provide sources of *"good fat"* (unsaturated fat), which can improve "good cholesterol" levels (HDL, or the bottom number in your cholesterol reading). Other healthy foods inhibit "bad cholesterol" (LDL, or the top number in your reading). Good cholesterol helps fight the buildup of bad cholesterol in your arteries and veins. Consult your doctor to find out what your particular cholesterol goals should be.

2014 © Yastremska Image from BigStockPhoto.com

January 20
8:14 am EST

JANUARY

S	M	T	W	T	F	S
				1	2	3
4	5	6	7	8	9	10
11	12	13	14	15	16	17
18	19	20	21	22	23	24
25	26	27	28	29	30	31

∼∼∼ January 25–January 31

*Where'er I roam, whatever realms to see, my heart
untravell'd fondly turns to thee.*   ∼OLIVER GOLDSMITH

Date	Qtr.	Sign	Activity
Jan 26, 11:37 am– Jan 26, 11:48 pm	1st	Taurus	Plant annuals for hardiness. Trim to increase growth.
Jan 26, 11:48 pm– Jan 28, 5:36 pm	2nd	Taurus	Plant annuals for hardiness. Trim to increase growth.
Jan 31, 2:09 am– Feb 2, 12:41 pm	2nd	Cancer	Plant grains, leafy annuals. Fertilize (chemical). Graft or bud plants. Irrigate. Trim to increase growth.

*A*ntioxidants prevent the oxidation of other molecules, which produces *free radicals*—these can cause chemical reactions that result in cell damage or cell death. *Polyphenols* are a class of antioxidants that may reduce inflammation and slow the progression of degenerative heart diseases and cancers.

Foods that *regulate blood sugar* prevent glucose spikes and dips and aid in the prevention and management of diabetes, one of the most common chronic health issues in America.

*January 26
11:48 pm EST*

JANUARY

S	M	T	W	T	F	S
				1	2	3
4	5	6	7	8	9	10
11	12	13	14	15	16	17
18	19	20	21	22	23	24
25	26	27	28	29	30	31

2014 © viperagp Image from BigStockPhoto.com

February

February 1–7

Man is the only animal that blushes. Or needs to.

~MARK TWAIN

Date	Qtr.	Sign	Activity
Jan 31, 2:09 am– Feb 2, 12:41 pm	2nd	Cancer	Plant grains, leafy annuals. Fertilize (chemical). Graft or bud plants. Irrigate. Trim to increase growth.
Feb 3, 6:09 pm– Feb 5, 12:46 am	3rd	Leo	Cultivate. Destroy weeds and pests. Harvest fruits and root crops for food. Trim to retard growth.
Feb 5, 12:46 am– Feb 7, 1:44 pm	3rd	Virgo	Cultivate, especially for medicinal plants. Destroy weeds and pests. Trim to retard growth.

Plants that are eligible for container growing are noted as such in their profile. However, large plants simply will not thrive or produce good yields if grown in too small a container—in most cases, a container of at least 5 gallons should be used for food crops. Plants suitable for smaller containers include lettuces, greens, herbs, tomatoes, carrots, and peppers.

February 3
6:09 pm EST

2014 © Suchat Siriboot Image from BigStockPhoto.com

FEBRUARY

S	M	T	W	T	F	S
1	2	3	4	5	6	7
8	9	10	11	12	13	14
15	16	17	18	19	20	21
22	23	24	25	26	27	28

〜〜 **February 8–14**

An apple a day keeps the doctor away.

Date	Qtr.	Sign	Activity
Feb 10, 2:05 am–Feb 11, 10:50 pm	3rd	Scorpio	Plant biennials, perennials, bulbs, and roots. Prune. Irrigate. Fertilize (organic).
Feb 11, 10:50 pm–Feb 12, 11:46 am	4th	Scorpio	Plant biennials, perennials, bulbs, and roots. Prune. Irrigate. Fertilize (organic).
Feb 12, 11:46 am–Feb 14, 5:24 pm	4th	Sagittarius	Cultivate. Destroy weeds and pests. Harvest fruits and root crops for food. Trim to retard growth.
Feb 14, 5:24 pm–Feb 16, 7:13 pm	4th	Capricorn	Plant potatoes and tubers. Trim to retard growth.

The old saying actually has a kernel of truth—apples contain polyphenols, fiber for digestion, and can help regulate blood sugar. There are nearly endless varieties of apples available; if you don't like one, try others! Some types can be expensive off-season, so consider buying in bulk and canning applesauce of your favorite kinds—it's probably the simplest food to can in a water bath. Planting an apple tree is a great long-term food investment, and their foliage is beautiful in spring and fall. Zones 3–8.

February 11
10:50 pm EST

FEBRUARY

S	M	T	W	T	F	S
1	2	3	4	5	6	7
8	9	10	11	12	13	14
15	16	17	18	19	20	21
22	23	24	25	26	27	28

2014 © wishfaery Image from BigStockPhoto.com

February 15–21

*A person, be it gentleman or lady, who has not pleasure in a
good novel, must be intolerably stupid.*   ~JANE AUSTEN

Date	Qtr.	Sign	Activity
Feb 14, 5:24 pm– Feb 16, 7:13 pm	4th	Capricorn	Plant potatoes and tubers. Trim to retard growth.
Feb 16, 7:13 pm– Feb 18, 6:47 pm	4th	Aquarius	Cultivate. Destroy weeds and pests. Harvest fruits and root crops for food. Trim to retard growth.
Feb 18, 6:47 pm– Feb 20, 6:13 pm	1st	Pisces	Plant grains, leafy annuals. Fertilize (chemical). Graft or bud plants. Irrigate. Trim to increase growth.

The apricot is a small tree that is related to the plum. (A pluot is a cross between an apricot and a plum.) Apricots contains beta-carotene for the eyes, fiber for digestion, antioxidants, potassium, Vitamins A and C, and iron. This perennial tree is slightly hardier than the peach tree, but the blossoms are vulnerable to spring frosts. Its spring flowers are a lovely white. Zones 4–9.

*February 18
6:47 pm EST*

2014 © Nitr Image from BigStockPhoto.com

			FEBRUARY			
S	M	T	W	T	F	S
1	2	3	4	5	6	7
8	9	10	11	12	13	14
15	16	17	18	19	20	21
22	23	24	25	26	27	28

February 22–February 28

Most of the shadows of this life are caused by our standing in our own sunshine.   ~Ralph Waldo Emerson

Date	Qtr.	Sign	Activity
Feb 22, 7:28 pm– Feb 24, 11:54 pm	1st	Taurus	Plant annuals for hardiness. Trim to increase growth.
Feb 27, 7:50 am– Mar 1, 6:34 pm	2nd	Cancer	Plant grains, leafy annuals. Fertilize (chemical). Graft or bud plants. Irrigate. Trim to increase growth.

Fresh asparagus is a traditional spring treat—cooked until crisp-tender and sprinkled with lemon juice is a favorite. This plant contains antioxidants and anti-inflammatories, as well as Vitamins A and C. Count yourself lucky if you know of an established asparagus patch! As a perennial vegetable, asparagus takes years to produce large yields, but it will continue to do so for many years to come, making it great for folks who will be in one place for the long haul. Containers may be used, but they must be quite large. Zones 4–8.

February 25
12:14 pm EST

February

S	M	T	W	T	F	S
1	2	3	4	5	6	7
8	9	10	11	12	13	14
15	16	17	18	19	20	21
22	23	24	25	26	27	28

2014 © Handmade Pictures Image from BigStockPhoto.com

March

March 1–7

Art is the desire of man to express himself, to record the reactions of his personality to the world he lives in.

~Amy Lowell

Date	Qtr.	Sign	Activity
Mar 27, 7:50 am–Mar 1, 6:34 pm	2nd	Cancer	Plant grains, leafy annuals. Fertilize (chemical). Graft or bud plants. Irrigate. Trim to increase growth.
Mar 5, 1:05 pm–Mar 6, 7:52 pm	3rd	Virgo	Cultivate, especially for medicinal plants. Destroy weeds and pests. Trim to retard growth.

One of the most well-known sources of "good" fat is the avocado. This fruit can also prevent prostate cancer and strokes. It's great sliced up on sandwiches or salads, or use its creamy texture to make an egg salad without mayo. Getting an avocado pit to grow roots is a fun experiment for kids, but avocadoes grown as house plants will most likely never bear fruit—though they are still pretty plants to have around. Zones 9–11.

○
March 5
1:05 pm EST

March

S	M	T	W	T	F	S
1	2	3	4	5	6	7
8	9	10	11	12	13	14
15	16	17	18	19	20	21
22	23	24	25	26	27	28
29	30	31				

March 8–14

There is peace and a strength and a sweet sympathy to be found in a walk by the side of the sea.

~ANITA McLEAN WASHINGTON

Date	Qtr.	Sign	Activity
Mar 9, 9:10 am–Mar 11, 7:30 pm	3rd	Scorpio	Plant biennials, perennials, bulbs, and roots. Prune. Irrigate. Fertilize (organic).
Mar 11, 7:30 pm–Mar 13, 1:48 pm	3rd	Sagittarius	Cultivate. Destroy weeds and pests. Harvest fruits and root crops for food. Trim to retard growth.
Mar 13, 1:48 pm–Mar 14, 2:40 am	4th	Sagittarius	Cultivate. Destroy weeds and pests. Harvest fruits and root crops for food. Trim to retard growth.
Mar 14, 2:40 am–Mar 16, 6:14 am	4th	Capricorn	Plant potatoes and tubers. Trim to retard growth.

Bananas are famous as a great provider of potassium, which can ease muscle cramps. (Potassium also regulates blood sugar and balances fluids in the body.) Bananas are also a good source of fiber, and they are extremely portable and great for the lunch bag or box. This treelike biennial can reach 25 feet in height and does not do well in containers. Zones 9B–11.

_____

_____

_____

_____

March 13, 1:48 pm EDT
Daylight Saving Time
begins March 8, 2:00 am

MARCH

S	M	T	W	T	F	S
1	2	3	4	5	6	7
8	9	10	11	12	13	14
15	16	17	18	19	20	21
22	23	24	25	26	27	28
29	30	31				

2014 © silentgunman Image from BigStockPhoto.com

March 15–21 ♈

Love is a great beautifier.

~Louisa May Alcott

Date	Qtr.	Sign	Activity
Mar 14, 2:40 am– Mar 16, 6:14 am	4th	Capricorn	Plant potatoes and tubers. Trim to retard growth.
Mar 16, 6:14 am– Mar 18, 6:58 am	4th	Aquarius	Cultivate. Destroy weeds and pests. Harvest fruits and root crops for food. Trim to retard growth.
Mar 18, 6:58 am– Mar 20, 5:36 am	4th	Pisces	Plant biennials, perennials, bulbs, and roots. Prune. Irrigate. Fertilize (organic).
Mar 20, 5:36 am– Mar 20, 6:28 am	1st	Pisces	Plant grains, leafy annuals. Fertilize (chemical). Graft or bud plants. Irrigate. Trim to increase growth.

Basil is one of the easiest of the superfood plants to grow and use, and even apartment dwellers can have great success with it. The leaves contain flavonoids that ward off cancer. Use a large harvest for fresh pesto or snip fresh leaves over nearly any dish. Basil is hard to dry, but you can easily keep your plant indoors in a container for year-round use. Pinch off flowers and buds to encourage leaf production. Zones 4–10.

March 20
5:36 am EDT

March

S	M	T	W	T	F	S
1	2	3	4	5	6	7
8	9	10	11	12	13	14
15	16	17	18	19	20	21
22	23	24	25	26	27	28
29	30	31				

2014 © rtsubin Image from BigStockPhoto.com

March 22–28

Sweet spring, full of sweet days and roses, a box where sweets compacted lie.
~GEORGE HERBERT

Date	Qtr.	Sign	Activity
Mar 22, 6:40 am– Mar 24, 9:23 am	1st	Taurus	Plant annuals for hardiness. Trim to increase growth.
Mar 26, 3:45 pm– Mar 27, 3:43 am	1st	Cancer	Plant grains, leafy annuals. Fertilize (chemical). Graft or bud plants. Irrigate. Trim to increase growth.
Mar 27, 3:43 am– Mar 29, 1:48 am	2nd	Cancer	Plant grains, leafy annuals. Fertilize (chemical). Graft or bud plants. Irrigate. Trim to increase growth.

Beet lovers will almost always tell you that their vegetable has gotten a bad rap for no good reason. Beets contain betalines and vitamins A, B, B2, and C. The most common preparation of beets is to roast them, to bring out their natural sweetness (yes, sweetness!) and allow the skins to slip right off. Try other colors of beets for variety—red, orange, and even striped. Like most root crops, this hardy plant prefers loose soil, and it can do well in containers. Zones 2–10.

_____

_____

_____

_____

March 27
3:43 am EDT

MARCH

S	M	T	W	T	F	S
						1
2	3	4	5	6	7	
8	9	10	11	12	13	14
15	16	17	18	19	20	21
22	23	24	25	26	27	28
29	30	31				

2014 © tdietrich Image from BigStockPhoto.com

April

March 29–April 4

By speaking of our misfortunes, we often relieve them.

~Pierre Corneille

Date	Qtr.	Sign	Activity
Mar 27, 3:43 am– Mar 29, 1:48 am	2nd	Cancer	Plant grains, leafy annuals. Fertilize (chemical). Graft or bud plants. Irrigate. Trim to increase growth.
~~Apr 3, 3:07 am–~~ Apr 4, 8:06 am	~~2nd~~	~~Libra~~	Plant annuals for fragrance and beauty. Trim to increase growth.

Which contains more Vitamin C, an orange or a bell pepper? It's the bell pepper! These colorful vegetables also contain anti-oxidants and can help maintain healthy cholesterol levels and ward off diabetes. Peppers do well in containers of adequate size, and spraying the leaves with Epsom salt water when blooms appear can really boost your yield. Go for whatever colors please the eye, they're all great for you. Zones 1–11.

2014 © Martina_L Image from BigStockPhoto.com

○
April 4
8:06 am EDT

APRIL

S	M	T	W	T	F	S
		1	2	3	4	
5	6	7	8	9	10	11
12	13	14	15	16	17	18
19	20	21	22	23	24	25
26	27	28	29	30		

April 5–11

Again the blackbirds sing; the streams wake, laughing, from their
winter dreams; and tremble in the April showers the tassels of the
maple flowers.   ~JOHN GREENLEAF WHITTIER

Date	Qtr.	Sign	Activity
Apr 5, 3:04 pm– Apr 8, 1:08 am	3rd	Scorpio	Plant biennials, perennials, bulbs, and roots. Prune. Irrigate. Fertilize (organic).
Apr 8, 1:08 am– Apr 10, 8:47 am	3rd	Sagittarius	Cultivate. Destroy weeds and pests. Harvest fruits and root crops for food. Trim to retard growth.
Apr 10, 8:47 am– Apr 11, 11:44 pm	3rd	Capricorn	Plant potatoes and tubers. Trim to retard growth.
Apr 11, 11:44 pm– Apr 12, 1:44 pm	4th	Capricorn	Plant potatoes and tubers. Trim to retard growth.

B erries can satisfy your sweet tooth and deliver a health boost. Cranberries help with yeast infections and tooth issues, while blueberries fight fat and heart disease. Raspberries provide potassium. Blueberries require acidic soil; zones 3–7. Raspberry canes can be invasive (containers can help), so cut back ruthlessly each fall and remove suckers during summer. Zones 4–8.

April 11
11:44 pm EDT

APRIL

S	M	T	W	T	F	S
			1	2	3	4
5	6	7	8	9	10	11
12	13	14	15	16	17	18
19	20	21	22	23	24	25
26	27	28	29	30		

2014 © sailorr Image from BigStockPhoto.com

April 12–18 ♈

Sweet April! Many a thought is wedded unto thee, as hearts are wed. ∼HENRY WADSWORTH LONGFELLOW

Date	Qtr.	Sign	Activity
Apr 11, 11:44 pm– Apr 12, 1:44 pm	4th	Capricorn	Plant potatoes and tubers. Trim to retard growth.
Apr 12, 1:44 pm– Apr 14, 4:12 pm	4th	Aquarius	Cultivate. Destroy weeds and pests. Harvest fruits and root crops for food. Trim to retard growth.
Apr 14, 4:12 pm– Apr 16, 5:00 pm	4th	Pisces	Plant biennials, perennials, bulbs, and roots. Prune. Irrigate. Fertilize (organic).
Apr 16, 5:00 pm– Apr 18, 2:57 pm	4th	Aries	Cultivate. Destroy weeds and pests. Harvest fruits and root crops for food. Trim to retard growth.
Apr 18, 5:31 pm– Apr 20, 7:28 pm	1st	Taurus	Plant annuals for hardiness. Trim to increase growth.

Broccoli is another vegetable that often gets an undeserved "yuck," but it can regulate the bowels and blood sugar, promote eye and heart health, and provide vitamins A, B2, and C. Go for a crisp-tender steam rather than a mushy boiled version for better flavor, or roast alongside other fall veggies. Broccoli plants like cooler temperatures and will grow in containers. Zones 3+.

2014 © oksix Image from BigStockPhoto.com

April 18
2:57 pm EDT

APRIL

S	M	T	W	T	F	S
			1	2	3	4
5	6	7	8	9	10	11
12	13	14	15	16	17	18
19	20	21	22	23	24	25
26	27	28	29	30		

April 19–25

Ah, month that comes with rainbow crowned, and golden
shadows dressed—constant to her inconstancy, and faithful
to unrest.   ~ALICE CARY

Date	Qtr.	Sign	Activity
Apr 18, 5:31 pm–Apr 20, 7:28 pm	1st	Taurus	Plant annuals for hardiness. Trim to increase growth.
Apr 23, 12:25 am–Apr 25, 9:13 am	1st	Cancer	Plant grains, leafy annuals. Fertilize (chemical). Graft or bud plants. Irrigate. Trim to increase growth.

If you've only tried canned brussels sprouts, you haven't really tried brussels sprouts. Trust us. These green bundles support a healthy circulatory system and can help prevent cancer. Trim and halve the larger sprouts, then sauté until tender with a bit of oil and sea salt. Cook a few slices of bacon, then use the drippings for sautéing the sprouts; crumble the bacon over the top before serving. This hardy crop is best harvested after a frost. Strip the plant's lower leaves to encourage larger sprouts. Can be grown in large containers; Zones 4–7.

_____

_____

_____

_____

April 25
7:55 pm EDT

APRIL

S	M	T	W	T	F	S
			1	2	3	4
5	6	7	8	9	10	11
12	13	14	15	16	17	18
19	20	21	22	23	24	25
26	27	28	29	30		

May
April 26–May 2

Do not do an immoral thing for moral reasons!

~THOMAS HARDY

Date	Qtr.	Sign	Activity
Apr 30, 10:03 am– May 2, 9:47 pm	2nd	Libra	Plant annuals for fragrance and beauty. Trim to increase growth.
May 2, 9:47 pm– May 3, 11:42 pm	2nd	Scorpio	Plant grains, leafy annuals. Fertilize (chemical). Graft or bud plants. Irrigate. Trim to increase growth.

Cabbage is another veggie that actually contains more Vitamin C than the orange. It also helps the body detox and may prevent Alzheimer's. The most popular cabbage dishes is the obvious: cole slaw. Experiment with varieties and recipes to find your favorite: creamy, crunchy, sweet, or tangy. This hardy plant is susceptible to worms, so keep a close watch on your crop for chewed leaves or telltale brown streaks. Hand-pick worms on sight and use row covers for larger infestations. Wasps and birds are natural predators. Suitable for containers; Zones 3+.

			MAY			
S	M	T	W	T	F	S
					1	2
3	4	5	6	7	8	9
10	11	12	13	14	15	16
17	18	19	20	21	22	23
24	25	26	27	28	29	30
31						

2014 © Handmade Pictures Image from BigStockPhoto.com

May 3–9

*Art is not a handicraft, it is the transmission of feeling the
artist has experienced.*   ~LEO TOLSTOY

Date	Qtr.	Sign	Activity
May 2, 9:47 pm– May 3, 11:42 pm	2nd	Scorpio	Plant grains, leafy annuals. Fertilize (chemical). Graft or bud plants. Irrigate. Trim to increase growth.
May 3, 11:42 pm– May 5, 7:13 am	3rd	Scorpio	Plant biennials, perennials, bulbs, and roots. Prune. Irrigate. Fertilize (organic).
May 5, 7:13 am– May 7, 2:16 pm	3rd	Sagittarius	Cultivate. Destroy weeds and pests. Harvest fruits and root crops for food. Trim to retard growth.
May 7, 2:16 pm– May 9, 7:22 pm	3rd	Capricorn	Plant potatoes and tubers. Trim to retard growth.
May 9, 7:22 pm– May 11, 6:36 am	3rd	Aquarius	Cultivate. Destroy weeds and pests. Harvest fruits and root crops for food. Trim to retard growth.

Canteloupe and honeydew are the orange and green staples of many fruit salads. Canteloupe has an alkaline effect that balances the body's pH level; honeydew's green color provides zeaxanthin for eye health. Both melons like sun and dry feet but have spotty seed germination. Large containers; Zones 4–11.

_____

_____

_____

_____

○
May 3
11:42 pm EDT

MAY

S	M	T	W	T	F	S
					1	2
3	4	5	6	7	8	9
10	11	12	13	14	15	16
17	18	19	20	21	22	23
24	25	26	27	28	29	30
31						

2014 © annolovisa Image from BigStockPhoto.com

May 10–16

As I turn my attention to my garden, I am filled with gratitude
for this moment in the year when all is fresh and new.

~VERONICA RAY

Date	Qtr.	Sign	Activity
May 9, 7:22 pm– May 11, 6:36 am	3rd	Aquarius	Cultivate. Destroy weeds and pests. Harvest fruits and root crops for food. Trim to retard growth.
May 11, 6:36 am– May 11, 10:53 pm	4th	Aquarius	Cultivate. Destroy weeds and pests. Harvest fruits and root crops for food. Trim to retard growth.
May 11, 10:53 pm– May 14, 1:13 am	4th	Pisces	Plant biennials, perennials, bulbs, and roots. Prune. Irrigate. Fertilize (organic).
May 14, 1:13 am– May 16, 3:02 am	4th	Aries	Cultivate. Destroy weeds and pests. Harvest fruits and root crops for food. Trim to retard growth.
May 16, 3:02 am– May 18, 12:13 am	4th	Taurus	Plant potatoes and tubers. Trim to retard growth.

Speaking of germination issues, we come to the carrot, provider of Vitamin A for the eyes and to cleanse the liver. Carrots like loose, sandy soil; it's easy to create the right environment in a pot. Since germination is so slow and spotty, it's best to seed like crazy and thin to the proper spacing when plants are a few inches tall. Good in containers; Zones 3+.

2014 © edu1971 Image from BigStockPhoto.com

◑

May 11
6:36 am EDT

MAY

S	M	T	W	T	F	S
					1	2
3	4	5	6	7	8	9
10	11	12	13	14	15	16
17	18	19	20	21	22	23
24	25	26	27	28	29	30
31						

May 17–23

Sweet is the breath of morn, her rising sweet with charm of earliest birds.

~John Milton

Date	Qtr.	Sign	Activity
May 16, 3:02 am–May 18, 12:13 am	4th	Taurus	Plant potatoes and tubers. Trim to retard growth.
May 18, 12:13 am–May 18, 5:27 am	1st	Taurus	Plant annuals for hardiness. Trim to increase growth.
May 20, 9:56 am–May 22, 5:42 pm	1st	Cancer	Plant grains, leafy annuals. Fertilize (chemical). Graft or bud plants. Irrigate. Trim to increase growth.

Broccoli's common companion, cauliflower, packs nearly as much punch as its green cousin. Cauliflower contains vitamins A, B, B2, and C, as well as 60mg folate per raw cup—an essential mineral for pregnant women. This Brassica likes cool temperatures and can be blanched (shaded) for extra tenderness. When the heads are a few inches wide, simply gather the leaves at the top of the plant and secure with twine or a clothespin. Mash cooked cauliflower for an alternative to mashed potoatoes. Grows in containers; Zones 3+.

May 18
12:13 am EDT

May

S	M	T	W	T	F	S
					1	2
3	4	5	6	7	8	9
10	11	12	13	14	15	16
17	18	19	20	21	22	23
24	25	26	27	28	29	30
31						

May 24–30

*All that happens is as usual and familiar as the rose in spring
and the crop in summer.* ~MARCUS AURELIUS ANTONIUS

Date	Qtr.	Sign	Activity
May 27, 5:42 pm– May 30, 5:34 am	2nd	Libra	Plant annuals for fragrance and beauty. Trim to increase growth.
May 30, 5:34 am– Jun 1, 2:39 pm	2nd	Scorpio	Plant grains, leafy annuals. Fertilize (chemical). Graft or bud plants. Irrigate. Trim to increase growth.

Cherry trees comes in two varieties: sweet and sour. Both kinds contain beta carotene and can improve memory. They're also a natural source of melatonin. Sweet cherries are more finicky to grow than sour varieties, but don't be put off by the term—sour cherries can still make a wonderful snack if they are left to fully ripen on the tree, plus they are self-pollinating (unlike sweet cherries). Mulch to maintain even moisture, especially as the fruits are ripening, to prevent splitting. Cherry juice is a great way to consume cherries as well—mix it with soda water to cut down on the pucker-factor. Sour: Zones 3–6. Sweet: Zones 5–7.

May 25
1:19 pm EDT

2014 © annolovisa Image from BigStockPhoto.com

			MAY			
S	M	T	W	T	F	S
					1	2
3	4	5	6	7	8	9
10	11	12	13	14	15	16
17	18	19	20	21	22	23
24	25	26	27	28	29	30
31						

June

May 31–June 6

*Good advice is almost certain to be ignored, but that's no
reason not to give it.*

~AGATHA CHRISTIE, AS MISS MARPLE

Date	Qtr.	Sign	Activity
May 30, 5:34 am–Jun 1, 2:39 pm	2nd	Scorpio	Plant grains, leafy annuals. Fertilize (chemical). Graft or bud plants. Irrigate. Trim to increase growth.
Jun 2, 12:19 pm–Jun 3, 8:50 pm	3rd	Sagittarius	Cultivate. Destroy weeds and pests. Harvest fruits and root crops for food. Trim to retard growth.
Jun 3, 8:50 pm–Jun 6, 1:02 am	3rd	Capricorn	Plant potatoes and tubers. Trim to retard growth.
Jun 6, 1:02 am–Jun 8, 4:16 am	3rd	Aquarius	Cultivate. Destroy weeds and pests. Harvest fruits and root crops for food. Trim to retard growth.

Cucumbers are a common plant for first-time gardeners, and they tend to be prolific producers. Cucumbers provide several vitamins (B, C, B2) and can help rehydrate the body. Pick them small for the best flavor, and leave those skins on to get the most vitamin content. This tender crop can be grown in pots, and even vertically if you are space-challenged. Zones 4+.

○
June 2
12:19 pm EDT

JUNE

S	M	T	W	T	F	S
	1	2	3	4	5	6
7	8	9	10	11	12	13
14	15	16	17	18	19	20
21	22	23	24	25	26	27
28	29	30				

2014 © stokkete Image from BigStockPhoto.com

June 7–13

If I have seen further... it is by standing upon the shoulders of giants.

~SIR ISAAC NEWTON

Date	Qtr.	Sign	Activity
Jun 6, 1:02 am– Jun 8, 4:16 am	3rd	Aquarius	Cultivate. Destroy weeds and pests. Harvest fruits and root crops for food. Trim to retard growth.
Jun 8, 4:16 am– Jun 9, 11:42 am	3rd	Pisces	Plant biennials, perennials, bulbs, and roots. Prune. Irrigate. Fertilize (organic).
Jun 9, 11:42 am– Jun 10, 7:14 am	4th	Pisces	Plant biennials, perennials, bulbs, and roots. Prune. Irrigate. Fertilize (organic).
Jun 10, 7:14 am– Jun 12, 10:16 am	4th	Aries	Cultivate. Destroy weeds and pests. Harvest fruits and root crops for food. Trim to retard growth.
Jun 12, 10:16 am– Jun 14, 1:51 pm	4th	Taurus	Plant potatoes and tubers. Trim to retard growth.

Eggplant is another food that draws automatic groans, but this vitamin-packed vegetable can help you lose weight, prevent cancer, and maintain healthy skin. Google "eggplant parmesan" for a delicous alternative to the sometimes-guilty chicken dish, or shred eggplant into any red sauce for a sneaky serving. Although susceptible to cold (no fridge for these guys!), eggplants can remain on the plant until you're ready to use them. Suitable for containers; Zones 4–10.

2014 © sweetpepper Image from BigStockPhoto.com

June 9
11:42 am EDT

JUNE

S	M	T	W	T	F	S
		1	2	3	4	5	6
7	8	9	10	11	12	13
14	15	16	17	18	19	20
21	22	23	24	25	26	27
28	29	30				

June 14–20

Judges and senates have been bought for gold; esteem and love were never to be sold.   ∼ALEXANDER POPE

Date	Qtr.	Sign	Activity
Jun 12, 10:16 am– Jun 14, 1:51 pm	4th	Taurus	Plant potatoes and tubers. Trim to retard growth.
Jun 14, 1:51 pm– Jun 16, 10:05 am	4th	Gemini	Cultivate. Destroy weeds and pests. Harvest fruits and root crops for food. Trim to retard growth.
Jun 16, 6:51 pm– Jun 19, 2:23 am	1st	Cancer	Plant grains, leafy annuals. Fertilize (chemical). Graft or bud plants. Irrigate. Trim to increase growth.

Grapefruits can be eaten to help prevent arthritis, control cholesterol levels, and ease the common cold. Most folks only know this as a raw fruit eaten at breakfast or mixed in fruit salads, but it can be cut in half, sprinkled with a touch of sugar, and broiled for a healthy dessert. *Beware that some drugs, statins in particular, interact with grapefruit. Consult your pharmacist before adding grapefruit to your diet!* This perennial tree doesn't grow well in containers. Zones 7+, but best in Zones 9+.

June 16
10:05 am EDT

JUNE

S	M	T	W	T	F	S
	1	2	3	4	5	6
7	8	9	10	11	12	13
14	15	16	17	18	19	20
21	22	23	24	25	26	27
28	29	30				

2014 © Artesia Wells Image from BigStockPhoto.com

June 21–27

When I play with my cat, who knows if I am not a pastime to her more than she is to me?

~MICHEL EYQUEM DE MONTAIGNE

Date	Qtr.	Sign	Activity
Jun 24, 1:41 am– Jun 24, 7:03 am	1st	Libra	Plant annuals for fragrance and beauty. Trim to increase growth.
Jun 24, 7:03 am– Jun 26, 1:57 pm	2nd	Libra	Plant annuals for fragrance and beauty. Trim to increase growth.
Jun 26, 1:57 pm– Jun 28, 11:21 pm	2nd	Scorpio	Plant grains, leafy annuals. Fertilize (chemical). Graft or bud plants. Irrigate. Trim to increase growth.

Grapes contain phytonutrients, but the exact phytonutrients vary with the type of grape. Mix up which types of grapes you eat to get the best nutritional effect. Eat grapes as a simple snack or mix them in with chicken salad or a green salad. This perennial vine can be grown in containers of large size. Zones 2–10, depending on variety.

June 24
7:03 am EDT

2014 © Xilius Image from BigStockPhoto.com

JUNE

S	M	T	W	T	F	S
		1	2	3	4	5	6
7	8	9	10	11	12	13
14	15	16	17	18	19	20
21	22	23	24	25	26	27
28	29	30				

July

June 28–July 4

Work as if you were to live a hundred years; pray as if you were to die tomorrow.   ~Benjamin Franklin

Date	Qtr.	Sign	Activity
Jul 1, 5:11 am– Jul 1, 10:20 pm	2nd	Capricorn	Graft or bud plants. Trim to increase growth.
Jul 1, 10:20 pm– Jul 3, 8:21 am	3rd	Capricorn	Plant potatoes and tubers. Trim to retard growth.
Jul 3, 8:21 am– Jul 5, 10:23 am	3rd	Aquarius	Cultivate. Destroy weeds and pests. Harvest fruits and root crops for food. Trim to retard growth.

Green beans are full of antioxidants to help your circulatory systems, plus vitamins A, B, B2, and C. You'll find that fresh, organically grown beans need less seasoning than conventional or canned beans. Pole beans are climbers that produce continuously (perfect for fresh eating), while bush varieties grow to about 2 feet high and will produce one or more "waves" of ripe beans all at once (perfect for freezing). Zones 3+, suitable for containers.

○
July 1
10:20 pm EDT

	July					
S	M	T	W	T	F	S
				1	2	3	4
5	6	7	8	9	10	11
12	13	14	15	16	17	18
19	20	21	22	23	24	25
26	27	28	29	30	31	

July 5–11 ♋

For old as I am, and old as I seem, my heart is full of youth.

~MARTIN FARQUHAR TUPPER

Date	Qtr.	Sign	Activity
Jul 3, 8:21 am– Jul 5, 10:23 am	3rd	Aquarius	Cultivate. Destroy weeds and pests. Harvest fruits and root crops for food. Trim to retard growth.
Jul 5, 10:23 am– Jul 7, 12:38 pm	3rd	Pisces	Plant biennials, perennials, bulbs, and roots. Prune. Irrigate. Fertilize (organic).
Jul 7, 12:38 pm– Jul 8, 4:24 pm	3rd	Aries	Cultivate. Destroy weeds and pests. Harvest fruits and root crops for food. Trim to retard growth.
Jul 8, 4:24 pm– Jul 9, 3:49 pm	4th	Aries	Cultivate. Destroy weeds and pests. Harvest fruits and root crops for food. Trim to retard growth.
Jul 9, 3:49 pm– Jul 11, 8:16 pm	4th	Taurus	Plant potatoes and tubers. Trim to retard growth.
Jul 11, 8:16 pm– Jul 14, 2:14 am	4th	Gemini	Cultivate. Destroy weeds and pests. Harvest fruits and root crops for food. Trim to retard growth.

Greens pack myriad punches, and they generally fall into the categories of cool crops (spring or fall—mustard greens, turnip greens, and kale) or hot crops (summer—collards and swiss chard). Sauté chopped greens in sesame oil and top with toasted sesame seeds, or flavor with a chopped slice or two of bacon. Suitable for containers; Zones 3–9.

July 8
4:24 pm EDT

JULY

S	M	T	W	T	F	S
			1	2	3	4
5	6	7	8	9	10	11
12	13	14	15	16	17	18
19	20	21	22	23	24	25
26	27	28	29	30	31	

July 12–18

Quarrels would not last long if the fault were only on one side.

~François, Duc de La Rochefoucauld

Date	Qtr.	Sign	Activity
Jul 11, 8:16 pm–Jul 14, 2:14 am	4th	Gemini	Cultivate. Destroy weeds and pests. Harvest fruits and root crops for food. Trim to retard growth.
Jul 14, 2:14 am–Jul 15, 9:24 pm	4th	Cancer	Plant biennials, perennials, bulbs, and roots. Prune. Irrigate. Fertilize (organic).
Jul 15, 9:24 pm–Jul 16, 10:15 am	1st	Cancer	Plant grains, leafy annuals. Fertilize (chemical). Graft or bud plants. Irrigate. Trim to increase growth.

Sweet, sticky honey doesn't immediately strike most as a health food, but it is a great alternative to processed white sugar. Use it to sweeten tea, top whole-grain toast, or add flavor to oatmeal or plain Greek yogurt. Honey can help prevent cancer and heart disease, as well as regulate blood glucose and aid digestion. Beekeeping is a complex endeavor, so you are likely better off finding local honey at your farmers' market or independent grocer. *See page 290 for information on local honey and immunity.*

_____

_____

_____

_____

●

July 15
9:24 pm EDT

JULY

S	M	T	W	T	F	S
			1	2	3	4
5	6	7	8	9	10	11
12	13	14	15	16	17	18
19	20	21	22	23	24	25
26	27	28	29	30	31	

2014 © Nitr Image from BigStockPhoto.com

July 19–25 ♌

It is not enough to have a good mind. The main thing is to use it well.

~René Descartes

Date	Qtr.	Sign	Activity
Jul 21, 9:23 am–Jul 23, 10:07 pm	1st	Libra	Plant annuals for fragrance and beauty. Trim to increase growth.
Jul 23, 10:07 pm–Jul 24, 12:04 am	1st	Scorpio	Plant grains, leafy annuals. Fertilize (chemical). Graft or bud plants. Irrigate. Trim to increase growth.
Jul 24, 12:04 am–Jul 26, 8:24 am	2nd	Scorpio	Plant grains, leafy annuals. Fertilize (chemical). Graft or bud plants. Irrigate. Trim to increase growth.

The small kiwi fruit contains phytonutrients, Vitamin C, and a good amount of fiber. You can skip the fuzzy skin entirely; cut in half and use a spoon to scoop out the flesh. Kiwi's bright-green color is perfect in summer fruit salads. These perennial plants come in male and female varieties, and you need both in order to produce fruit. The ones found in grocery stores are the "common" type, grown in Zones 7–9. The "hardy" type will grow in Zones 4–7. This vinelike plant is not suitable for containers.

July 24
12:04 am EDT

			July			
S	M	T	W	T	F	S
			1	2	3	4
5	6	7	8	9	10	11
12	13	14	15	16	17	18
19	20	21	22	23	24	25
26	27	28	29	30	31	

2014 © lesyanovo Image from BigStockPhoto.com

♏ August

July 26–August 1

Money is a great servant and a terrible master.

~DEBRA MOFFITT

Date	Qtr.	Sign	Activity
Jul 24, 12:04 am– Jul 26, 8:24 am	2nd	Scorpio	Plant grains, leafy annuals. Fertilize (chemical). Graft or bud plants. Irrigate. Trim to increase growth.
Jul 28, 2:47 pm– Jul 30, 5:40 pm	2nd	Capricorn	Graft or bud plants. Trim to increase growth.
Jul 31, 6:43 am– Aug 1, 6:36 pm	3rd	Aquarius	Cultivate. Destroy weeds and pests. Harvest fruits and root crops for food. Trim to retard growth.
Aug 1, 6:36 pm– Aug 3, 7:24 pm	3rd	Pisces	Plant biennials, perennials, bulbs, and roots. Prune. Irrigate. Fertilize (organic).

Lemons and limes have long been used to improve digestion and constipation (squeezed into a glass of hot water), reduce fever (lemon juice in water), and promote healthy hair and skin (used both topically and consumed). Lemons and limes can make plain old water palatable to folks who don't care for the taste, and lemonade and limeade are refreshing alternatives to soda on hot days. These perennial trees can be grown in large containers; Zones 8–10.

○

July 31
6:43 am EDT

AUGUST

S	M	T	W	T	F	S
						1
2	3	4	5	6	7	8
9	10	11	12	13	14	15
16	17	18	19	20	21	22
23	24	25	26	27	28	29
30	31					

2014 © caterpillar Image from BigStockPhoto.com

August 2–8

I love to hear the crickets sing, late on summer night. I hear them as I go to sleep, and everything seems right.

~ANITA MCLEAN WASHINGTON

Date	Qtr.	Sign	Activity
Aug 1, 6:36 pm– Aug 3, 7:24 pm	3rd	Pisces	Plant biennials, perennials, bulbs, and roots. Prune. Irrigate. Fertilize (organic).
Aug 3, 7:24 pm– Aug 5, 9:29 pm	3rd	Aries	Cultivate. Destroy weeds and pests. Harvest fruits and root crops for food. Trim to retard growth.
Aug 5, 9:29 pm– Aug 6, 10:03 pm	3rd	Taurus	Plant potatoes and tubers. Trim to retard growth.
Aug 6, 10:03 pm– Aug 8, 1:40 am	4th	Taurus	Plant potatoes and tubers. Trim to retard growth.
Aug 8, 1:40 am– Aug 10, 8:08 am	4th	Gemini	Cultivate. Destroy weeds and pests. Harvest fruits and root crops for food. Trim to retard growth.

Mangos can aid digestion, boost immunities, and even support a healthy libido! Slice a section off the top and bottom of the fruit and hold it in place with a corn cob skewer. Use a vegetable peeler for the skin, then slice the flesh away from the central pit. This perennial tree cannot be grown in pots; Zones 10–11.

August 6
10:03 pm EDT

2014 © volff Image from BigStockPhoto.com

AUGUST

S	M	T	W	T	F	S
						1
2	3	4	5	6	7	8
9	10	11	12	13	14	15
16	17	18	19	20	21	22
23	24	25	26	27	28	29
30	31					

August 9–15

Accuse not Nature, she hath done her part; do thee but thine.

~JOHN MILTON

Date	Qtr.	Sign	Activity
Aug 8, 1:40 am– Aug 10, 8:08 am	4th	Gemini	Cultivate. Destroy weeds and pests. Harvest fruits and root crops for food. Trim to retard growth.
Aug 10, 8:08 am– Aug 12, 4:52 pm	4th	Cancer	Plant biennials, perennials, bulbs, and roots. Prune. Irrigate. Fertilize (organic).
Aug 12, 4:52 pm– Aug 14, 10:53 am	4th	Leo	Cultivate. Destroy weeds and pests. Harvest fruits and root crops for food. Trim to retard growth.

Ever heard of a mangosteen? Probably not, but don't fret. This fruit grows on large tropical trees. Only the white inside of the red or purple fruit is edible. The white portion is about 2 inches, while the entire fruit is close to 3 inches. Since foreign fresh mangosteens cannot be imported due to pest issues, finding them in grocery stores is rare; if you spot them, treat yourself! Mangosteens provide immunities and polyphenols. Simply score the shell with a knife and pry it open to enjoy the raw fruit. Zones 11–12.

August 14
10:53 am EDT

AUGUST

S	M	T	W	T	F	S
						1
2	3	4	5	6	7	8
9	10	11	12	13	14	15
16	17	18	19	20	21	22
23	24	25	26	27	28	29
30	31					

August 16–22

Science is simply common sense at its best.

~THOMAS HUXLEY

Date	Qtr.	Sign	Activity
Aug 17, 4:23 pm– Aug 20, 5:24 am	1st	Libra	Plant annuals for fragrance and beauty. Trim to increase growth.
Aug 20, 5:24 am– Aug 22, 3:31 pm	1st	Scorpio	Plant grains, leafy annuals. Fertilize (chemical). Graft or bud plants. Irrigate. Trim to increase growth.
Aug 22, 3:31 pm– Aug 22, 4:41 pm	2nd	Scorpio	Plant grains, leafy annuals. Fertilize (chemical). Graft or bud plants. Irrigate. Trim to increase growth.

Three mushroom varieties make the superfoods list. Portabellas include potassium and antioxidants; shiitakes boost immunities; and morels have potassium and B vitamins, and they support liver function. Mushrooms can be a great non-meat source of protein. Eat them fresh if you don't like the texture of canned mushrooms. Kits are now commonly available for easily home-growing mushrooms, and you can often grow such mushrooms indoors. Zones 1–11.

◐

August 22
3:31 pm EDT

AUGUST

S	M	T	W	T	F	S
						1
2	3	4	5	6	7	8
9	10	11	12	13	14	15
16	17	18	19	20	21	22
23	24	25	26	27	28	29
30	31					

2014 © Nitr Image from BigStockPhoto.com

♍ August 23–29

One must not always think so much about what one should
do, but rather what one should be. ~MEISTER ECKHART

Date	Qtr.	Sign	Activity
Aug 25, 12:22 am– Aug 27, 4:03 am	2nd	Capricorn	Graft or bud plants. Trim to increase growth.
Aug 29, 4:51 am– Aug 29, 2:35 pm	2nd	Pisces	Plant grains, leafy annuals. Fertilize (chemical). Graft or bud plants. Irrigate. Trim to increase growth.
Aug 29, 2:35 pm– Aug 31, 4:33 am	3rd	Pisces	Plant biennials, perennials, bulbs, and roots. Prune. Irrigate. Fertilize (organic).

Nectarines, though technically a subspecies of peach, are smaller and slightly redder than peaches, and they have no fuzz. They're generally a little smaller and sweeter than a peach as well, and they contain two times the Vitamin A! These perennial tree fruits also have lutein, beta-carotene, and Vitamin C and can help prevent some types of cancer. Zones 5–8.

_____

_____

_____

_____

○
August 29
2:35 pm EDT

AUGUST

S	M	T	W	T	F	S
						1
2	3	4	5	6	7	8
9	10	11	12	13	14	15
16	17	18	19	20	21	22
23	24	25	26	27	28	29
30	31					

2014 © Alexlukin Image from BigStockPhoto.com

September ♍
August 30–September 5

*Twilight's mystery is so sweet and holy, just because it ends
in starry night.*
~ADELAIDE A. PROCTER

Date	Qtr.	Sign	Activity
Aug 29, 2:35 pm– Aug 31, 4:33 am	3rd	Pisces	Plant biennials, perennials, bulbs, and roots. Prune. Irrigate. Fertilize (organic).
Aug 31, 4:33 am– Sep 2, 5:02 am	3rd	Aries	Cultivate. Destroy weeds and pests. Harvest fruits and root crops for food. Trim to retard growth.
Sep 2, 5:02 am– Sep 4, 7:48 am	3rd	Taurus	Plant potatoes and tubers. Trim to retard growth.
Sep 4, 7:48 am– Sep 5, 5:54 am	3rd	Gemini	Cultivate. Destroy weeds and pests. Harvest fruits and root crops for food. Trim to retard growth.
Sep 5, 5:54 am– Sep 6, 1:40 pm	4th	Gemini	Cultivate. Destroy weeds and pests. Harvest fruits and root crops for food. Trim to retard growth.

Nuts and seeds are commonly found in trail mixes and health bars, and for good reason: they contain healthy fats, support brain function, and provide a natural energy boost. Try almonds, cashews, walnuts, hemp seeds, pumpkin seeds, and chia seeds for variety. Sprinkle nuts and seeds on oatmeal and yogurt.

2014 © Nitr Image from BigStockPhoto.com

◑
*September 5
5:54 am EDT*

SEPTEMBER

S	M	T	W	T	F	S
		1	2	3	4	5
6	7	8	9	10	11	12
13	14	15	16	17	18	19
20	21	22	23	24	25	26
27	28	29	30			

♍ September 6–12

For all sad words of tongue or pen, the saddest are these: "It might have been"!

~JOHN GREENLEAF WHITTIER

Date	Qtr.	Sign	Activity
Sep 5, 5:54 am– Sep 6, 1:40 pm	4th	Gemini	Cultivate. Destroy weeds and pests. Harvest fruits and root crops for food. Trim to retard growth.
Sep 6, 1:40 pm– Sep 8, 10:36 pm	4th	Cancer	Plant biennials, perennials, bulbs, and roots. Prune. Irrigate. Fertilize (organic).
Sep 8, 10:36 pm– Sep 11, 9:56 am	4th	Leo	Cultivate. Destroy weeds and pests. Harvest fruits and root crops for food. Trim to retard growth.
Sep 11, 9:56 am– Sep 13, 2:41 am	4th	Virgo	Cultivate, especially for medicinal plants. Destroy weeds and pests. Trim to retard growth.

Olive oil is a well-known alternative to vegetable oil. Pressed from whole olives (a superfood in their own right), the oil is a staple of the Mediterranean diet. It contains good fat, fatty acid, and polyphenols. Use extra-virgin olive oil in raw preparations, as in quick salad dressings and on pasta. Use regular olive oil to cook with, as in sautéing vegetables or making kale or vegetable chips in the oven. This perennial tree can be grown in the right container; Zones 8–10.

SEPTEMBER

S	M	T	W	T	F	S
		1	2	3	4	5
6	7	8	9	10	11	12
13	14	15	16	17	18	19
20	21	22	23	24	25	26
27	28	29	30			

2014 © Olga Krig Image from BigStockPhoto.com

September 13–19 ♍

Life is a jest; and all things show it. I thought so once; but
now I know it.   ~JOHN GAY

Date	Qtr.	Sign	Activity
Sep 11, 9:56 am– Sep 13, 2:41 am	4th	Virgo	Cultivate, especially for medicinal plants. Destroy weeds and pests. Trim to retard growth.
Sep 13, 10:41 pm– Sep 16, 11:43 am	1st	Libra	Plant annuals for fragrance and beauty. Trim to increase growth.
Sep 16, 11:43 am– Sep 18, 11:32 pm	1st	Scorpio	Plant grains, leafy annuals. Fertilize (chemical). Graft or bud plants. Irrigate. Trim to increase growth.

Many people reach for the orange juice at the first sign of a cold. Oranges contain a good dose of Vitamin C, and they can help you avoid diabetes, kidney stones, arthritis, and digestive issues. Oranges are best eaten plain or in a simple fruit salad—my favorite recipe is topped with a lime-honey-poppyseed dressing. And nothing beats fresh-squeezed orange juice! There are even specific types of oranges grown just for juicing. Some varieties of this perennial tree can be grown in containers; Zones 8–10.

September 13
2:41 am EDT

2014 © annolovisa Image from BigStockPhoto.com

SEPTEMBER

S	M	T	W	T	F	S
		1	2	3	4	5
6	7	8	9	10	11	12
13	14	15	16	17	18	19
20	21	22	23	24	25	26
27	28	29	30			

September 20–26

O, sir! I must not tell my age. They say women and music
should never be dated.   ~OLIVER GOLDSMITH

Date	Qtr.	Sign	Activity
Sep 21, 8:33 am– Sep 23, 1:51 pm	2nd	Capricorn	Graft or bud plants. Trim to increase growth.
Sep 25, 3:43 pm– Sep 27, 3:29 pm	2nd	Pisces	Plant grains, leafy annuals. Fertilize (chemical). Graft or bud plants. Irrigate. Trim to increase growth.

The papaya fruit (or pawpaw to some Brits) was first cultivated in southern Mexico and Central America. The green to
golden yellow fruit can grow to be 6 to 18 inches long! It contains
antioxidants and can ease heart disease and inflammation. To eat,
cut the fruit in half lengthwise and scoop out the seeds. Eat the
flesh with a spoon or melon baller, or remove the skin with a vegetable peeler and slice the flesh. This tree can grow to be 30 feet
tall and thus cannot be grown in containers; Zones 10–12.

_____

_____

_____

_____

September 21
4:59 am EDT

SEPTEMBER

S	M	T	W	T	F	S
		1	2	3	4	5
6	7	8	9	10	11	12
13	14	15	16	17	18	19
20	21	22	23	24	25	26
27	28	29	30			

October ♎

September 27–October 3

I saw an angel in the marble and carved until I set him free.

~MICHAELANGELO

Date	Qtr.	Sign	Activity
Sep 25, 3:43 pm– Sep 27, 3:29 pm	2nd	Pisces	Plant grains, leafy annuals. Fertilize (chemical). Graft or bud plants. Irrigate. Trim to increase growth.
Sep 27, 10:51 pm– Sep 29, 2:57 pm	3rd	Aries	Cultivate. Destroy weeds and pests. Harvest fruits and root crops for food. Trim to retard growth.
Sep 29, 2:57 pm– Oct 1, 4:03 pm	3rd	Taurus	Plant potatoes and tubers. Trim to retard growth.
Oct 1, 4:03 pm– Oct 3, 8:22 pm	3rd	Gemini	Cultivate. Destroy weeds and pests. Harvest fruits and root crops for food. Trim to retard growth.
Oct 3, 8:22 pm– Oct 4, 5:06 pm	3rd	Cancer	Plant biennials, perennials, bulbs, and roots. Prune. Irrigate. Fertilize (organic).

Peanut butter is an excellent source of non-meat protein, good fats, potassium, and fiber. But watch the portion sizes! Eat a tablespoon with fruit or whole-grain toast, or add to breakfast smoothies. Peanuts are an annual ground crop. Zones 5+.

2014 © Yastremska Image from BigStockPhoto.com

○
September 27
10:51 pm EDT

OCTOBER

S	M	T	W	T	F	S
				1	2	3
4	5	6	7	8	9	10
11	12	13	14	15	16	17
18	19	20	21	22	23	24
25	26	27	28	29	30	31

♎ October 4–10

Earth is all in splendor drest; queenly fair, she sits at rest,
while the deep, delicious day dreams its happy life away.

~Margaret E. Sangster

Date	Qtr.	Sign	Activity
Oct 3, 8:22 pm– Oct 4, 5:06 pm	3rd	Cancer	Plant biennials, perennials, bulbs, and roots. Prune. Irrigate. Fertilize (organic).
Oct 4, 5:06 pm– Oct 6, 4:31 am	4th	Cancer	Plant biennials, perennials, bulbs, and roots. Prune. Irrigate. Fertilize (organic).
Oct 6, 4:31 am– Oct 8, 3:50 pm	4th	Leo	Cultivate. Destroy weeds and pests. Harvest fruits and root crops for food. Trim to retard growth.
Oct 8, 3:50 pm– Oct 11, 4:45 am	4th	Virgo	Cultivate, especially for medicinal plants. Destroy weeds and pests Trim to retard growth.

Fresh peas provide a sweetness and texture that is simply unmatched by processed versions. Peas are good for your blood glucose, regularity, and bone health (Vitamin K). They also have Vitamins A, B, and C and fiber, and can benefit those with heart disease. This cool-weather crop likes to climb, so plant it along a fence or trellis. Suitable for containers; Zones 3–11.

October 4
5:06 pm EDT

OCTOBER

S	M	T	W	T	F	S
				1	2	3
4	5	6	7	8	9	10
11	12	13	14	15	16	17
18	19	20	21	22	23	24
25	26	27	28	29	30	31

October 11–17

*There are gains for all our losses, there are balms for all
our pain.*   ～ANONYMOUS, "LOST"

Date	Qtr.	Sign	Activity
Oct 8, 3:50 pm– Oct 11, 4:45 am	4th	Virgo	Cultivate, especially for medicinal plants. Destroy weeds and pests. Trim to retard growth.
Oct 12, 8:06 pm– Oct 13, 5:38 pm	1st	Libra	Plant annuals for fragrance and beauty. Trim to increase growth.
Oct 13, 5:38 pm– Oct 16, 5:18 am	1st	Scorpio	Plant grains, leafy annuals. Fertilize (chemical). Graft or bud plants. Irrigate. Trim to increase growth.

Pineapple is a tropical perennial that takes up to three years to produce fruit. It is good for your gums and eye health, and it can ease arthritis pain. Fresh pineapple is worth the peeling hassle every now and again. Choose a heavy fruit with a strong scent, and store it upside down before cutting to evenly distribute the juices. Cut 1/2 inch off the top and bottom. Take many vertical slices off the sides to peel away the hard skin and "eyes." Then cut the mass in quarters lengthwise and remove the tough core. This perennial can be grown in large containers; Zones 9–11.

*October 12
8:06 pm EDT*

OCTOBER

S	M	T	W	T	F	S
				1	2	3
4	5	6	7	8	9	10
11	12	13	14	15	16	17
18	19	20	21	22	23	24
25	26	27	28	29	30	31

2014 © thanavut Image from BigStockPhoto.com

♏ October 18–24

Autumn wins you best by this, its mute appeal to sympathy for its decay.

~ROBERT BROWNING

Date	Qtr.	Sign	Activity
Oct 18, 2:52 pm– Oct 20, 4:31 pm	1st	Capricorn	Graft or bud plants. Trim to increase growth.
Oct 20, 4:31 pm– Oct 20, 9:38 pm	2nd	Capricorn	Graft or bud plants. Trim to increase growth.
Oct 23, 1:18 am– Oct 25, 2:22 am	2nd	Pisces	Plant grains, leafy annuals. Fertilize (chemical). Graft or bud plants. Irrigate. Trim to increase growth.

Plums grow on medium-sized trees (usually pruned to under 20 feet) in many areas of the United States. The fruits are about 1–3 inches with a single hard pit. Eating plums can benefit your heart, glucose levels, bones, memory, and digestive regularity. There are many varieties of plum, so ask your local nursery which types do best in your area. Which plum you plant will also determine how sweet your fruits are and what color they will be. Zones 4–9, depending on type.

_____

_____

_____

_____

◐

October 20
4:31 pm EDT

OCTOBER

S	M	T	W	T	F	S
				1	2	3
4	5	6	7	8	9	10
11	12	13	14	15	16	17
18	19	20	21	22	23	24
25	26	27	28	29	30	31

October 25–31 ♏

If you want to make a wise man happy—improve yourself!

~IDRIES SHAH

Date	Qtr.	Sign	Activity
Oct 23, 1:18 am– Oct 25, 2:22 am	2nd	Pisces	Plant grains, leafy annuals. Fertilize (chemical). Graft or bud plants. Irrigate. Trim to increase growth.
Oct 27, 2:07 am– Oct 27, 8:05 am	2nd	Taurus	Plant annuals for hardiness. Trim to increase growth.
Oct 27, 8:05 am– Oct 29, 2:24 am	3rd	Taurus	Plant potatoes and tubers. Trim to retard growth.
Oct 29, 2:24 am– Oct 31, 5:09 am	3rd	Gemini	Cultivate. Destroy weeds and pests. Harvest fruits and root crops for food. Trim to retard growth.
Oct 31, 5:09 am– Nov 2, 10:48 am	3rd	Cancer	Plant biennials, perennials, bulbs, and roots. Prune. Irrigate. Fertilize (organic).

Pomegranate made a splash as a health food several years ago. This perennial tree produces fruit that is good for your blood pressure, can reverse plaque buildup in arteries, and prevent breast, prostate, and lung cancers. Search the Internet for videos on how to best release the fleshy seeds from their outer shell, then enjoy over cereal or yogurt. (You can swallow or spit out the insides of the seeds as you wish.) Zones 7–10.

2014 © chunumunu Image from BigStockPhoto.com

○
October 27
8:05 am EDT

OCTOBER

S	M	T	W	T	F	S
				1	2	3
4	5	6	7	8	9	10
11	12	13	14	15	16	17
18	19	20	21	22	23	24
25	26	27	28	29	30	31

♏ November

November 1–7

Procrastination is the thief of time.   ∽EDWARD YOUNG

Date	Qtr.	Sign	Activity
Oct 31, 5:09 am– Nov 2, 10:48 am	3rd	Cancer	Plant biennials, perennials, bulbs, and roots. Prune. Irrigate. Fertilize (organic).
Nov 2, 10:48 am– Nov 3, 7:24 am	3rd	Leo	Cultivate. Destroy weeds and pests. Harvest fruits and root crops for food. Trim to retard growth.
Nov 3, 7:24 am– Nov 4, 9:22 pm	4th	Leo	Cultivate. Destroy weeds and pests. Harvest fruits and root crops for food. Trim to retard growth.
Nov 4, 9:22 pm– Nov 7, 10:14 am	4th	Virgo	Cultivate, especially for medicinal plants. Destroy weeds and pests Trim to retard growth.

Pie isn't the only way to enjoy pumpkin, which contains Vitamin A, carotenoids, and fiber. Try pumpkin pancakes, breakfast pumpkin muffins, or roasted pumpkin with a touch of brown sugar and butter. For eating (as opposed to carving), bigger isn't always better. To grow pumpkin, you'll need a large area away from other winter squashes. Don't let the pumpkins frost or remain too wet, and don't break their stems when picking. This annual can be grown from large containers; Zones 4+.

November 3, 7:24 am EST
Daylight Saving Time ends
November 1, 2:00 am

NOVEMBER

S	M	T	W	T	F	S
1	2	3	4	5	6	7
8	9	10	11	12	13	14
15	16	17	18	19	20	21
22	23	24	25	26	27	28
29	30					

2014 © syaber Image from BigStockPhoto.com

November 8–14 ♏

*Let others hail the rising sun: I bow to that whose course
is run.*

~DAVID GARRICK

Date	Qtr.	Sign	Activity
Nov 9, 11:02 pm– Nov 11, 12:47 pm	4th	Scorpio	Plant biennials, perennials, bulbs, and roots. Prune. Irrigate. Fertilize (organic).
Nov 11, 12:47 pm– Nov 12, 10:14 am	1st	Scorpio	Plant grains, leafy annuals. Fertilize (chemical). Graft or bud plants. Irrigate. Trim to increase growth.
Nov 14, 7:21 pm– Nov 17, 2:24 am	1st	Capricorn	Graft or bud plants. Trim to increase growth.

Nothing says "health food" like a big green salad. Start yours with Romaine lettuce, which is high in protein, Omega-3, and various vitamins and minerals. Romaine is relatively easy to grow and can be succession seeded indoors for year-round harvests. Keep your seeds moist and in good sunlight and avoid hot temperatures, which will cause your plant to "bolt" or go to seed. Each plant needs about a foot of space to grow. Harvest a few leaves at a time or the entire head. Good in containers; Zones 4–9.

*November 11
12:47 pm EST*

NOVEMBER

S	M	T	W	T	F	S
1	2	3	4	5	6	7
8	9	10	11	12	13	14
15	16	17	18	19	20	21
22	23	24	25	26	27	28
29	30					

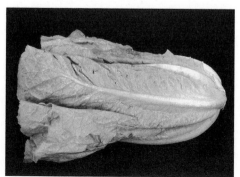

2014 © crspix Image from BigStockPhoto.com

♏ November 15–21
Where the willingness is great, the difficulties cannot be great.
~NICCOLÒ MACHIAVELLI

Date	Qtr.	Sign	Activity
Nov 14, 7:21 pm–Nov 17, 2:24 am	1st	Capricorn	Graft or bud plants. Trim to increase growth.
Nov 19, 7:21 am–Nov 21, 10:12 am	2nd	Pisces	Plant grains, leafy annuals. Fertilize (chemical). Graft or bud plants. Irrigate. Trim to increase growth.

Spinach is another great salad base. High in iron, fiber, and Vitamins A, B2, and C, spinach doesn't have to be the slimy canned kind that Popeye downed. Use it in salads, pasta dishes, or with scrambled eggs or omelettes. Spinach is a cool-season green that pairs especially well with strawberries, which ripen about the same time in most locations. Plant spinach from fresh seed each year in early spring and early fall. Spinach is likely to bolt over 80 degrees F. Keep a few sizeable leaves to "feed" the plant as you cut away outer leaves for eating. Suitable for containers; Zones 3–9.

November 19
1:27 am EST

NOVEMBER

S	M	T	W	T	F	S
1	2	3	4	5	6	7
8	9	10	11	12	13	14
15	16	17	18	19	20	21
22	23	24	25	26	27	28
29	30					

2014 © Dutchlight Netherlands Image from BigStockPhoto.com

November 22–28 ♐

Music is the art of thinking with sounds.

~JULES COMBARIEU

Date	Qtr.	Sign	Activity
Nov 23, 11:26 am–Nov 25, 12:15 pm	2nd	Taurus	Plant annuals for hardiness. Trim to increase growth.
Nov 25, 5:44 pm–Nov 27, 2:27 pm	3rd	Gemini	Cultivate. Destroy weeds and pests. Harvest fruits and root crops for food. Trim to retard growth.
Nov 27, 2:27 pm–Nov 29, 7:47 pm	3rd	Cancer	Plant biennials, perennials, bulbs, and roots. Prune. Irrigate. Fertilize (organic).

Strawberries are good for your immunity, eyes, cholesterol levels, and for preventing heart attacks and cancers. They also help fight signs of aging from sun damage! Strawberry plants can be invasive, though, so give careful thought to where you plant and how you can keep the runners from taking over. Harvests are generally in late spring to early summer, but you can easily freeze extra fruit for off-season smoothies. This perennial does well in containers of suitable size; Zones 4–8.

2014 © jvolodina Image from BigStockPhoto.com

○
November 25
5:44 pm EST

NOVEMBER

S	M	T	W	T	F	S
1	2	3	4	5	6	7
8	9	10	11	12	13	14
15	16	17	18	19	20	21
22	23	24	25	26	27	28
29	30					

December
November 29–December 5

It is better to hide ignorance, but it is hard to do this when we relax over wine. ∼HERACLITUS

Date	Qtr.	Sign	Activity
Nov 27, 2:27 pm– Nov 29, 7:47 pm	3rd	Cancer	Plant biennials, perennials, bulbs, and roots. Prune. Irrigate. Fertilize (organic).
Nov 29, 7:47 pm– Dec 2, 5:09 am	3rd	Leo	Cultivate. Destroy weeds and pests. Harvest fruits and root crops for food. Trim to retard growth.
Dec 2, 5:09 am– Dec 3, 2:40 am	3rd	Virgo	Cultivate, especially for medicinal plants. Destroy weeds and pests. Trim to retard growth.
Dec 3, 2:40 am– Dec 4, 5:34 pm	4th	Virgo	Cultivate, especially for medicinal plants. Destroy weeds and pests. Trim to retard growth.

Sweet potatoes are a great way to consume the orange part of the produce rainbow if you don't care for carrots. High in iron, magnesium, and Vitamins A, B6, C, and D, sweet potatoes are a good carb that can aid in weight loss. This very tender crop must be started from existing potatoes, or potato slips. Cure sweet potatoes in dry heat before storing. Suitable for large containers; Zones 9–11, or Zones 5–9 with help staying warm and dry.

December 3
2:40 am EST

DECEMBER

S	M	T	W	T	F	S
		1	2	3	4	5
6	7	8	9	10	11	12
13	14	15	16	17	18	19
20	21	22	23	24	25	26
27	28	29	30	31		

December 6–12

What passion cannot music raise and quell?

~JOHN DRYDEN

Date	Qtr.	Sign	Activity
Dec 7, 6:26 am– Dec 9, 5:25 pm	4th	Scorpio	Plant biennials, perennials, bulbs, and roots. Prune. Irrigate. Fertilize (organic).
Dec 9, 5:25 pm– Dec 11, 5:29 am	4th	Sagittarius	Cultivate. Destroy weeds and pests. Harvest fruits and root crops for food. Trim to retard growth.
Dec 12, 1:46 am– Dec 14, 7:59 am	1st	Capricorn	Graft or bud plants. Trim to increase growth.

The tomato is a staple in most home gardens, and for good reason. They are versatile in the kitchen and in health perks from a phytochemical called lycopene: helping manage diabetes and the effects of smoking; benefiting the heart, skin, eyes, and bones; and warding off cancers. Transplant tomatoes deeply to encourage additional root growth, stake them early on to prevent damage, and remove suckers to improve yields. Ask your garden center for varieties best suited to your goals: sauce, salsa, or slicers for salads. Suitable for containers; Zones 3–12.

December 11
5:29 am EST

2014 © Sanja Kosanovic Image from BigStockPhoto.com

DECEMBER

S	M	T	W	T	F	S
		1	2	3	4	5
6	7	8	9	10	11	12
13	14	15	16	17	18	19
20	21	22	23	24	25	26
27	28	29	30	31		

December 13–19

I have discovered that all human evil comes from this, man's being unable to sit still in a room.   ~Blaise Pascal

Date	Qtr.	Sign	Activity
Dec 12, 1:46 am– Dec 14, 7:59 am	1st	Capricorn	Graft or bud plants. Trim to increase growth.
Dec 16, 12:45 pm– Dec 18, 10:14 am	1st	Pisces	Plant grains, leafy annuals. Fertilize (chemical). Graft or bud plants. Irrigate. Trim to increase growth.
Dec 18, 10:14 am– Dec 18, 4:26 pm	2nd	Pisces	Plant grains, leafy annuals. Fertilize (chemical). Graft or bud plants. Irrigate. Trim to increase growth.

And now for that epitome of summer, the watermelon! Watermelon contains Vitamin C, antioxidants, and anti-cancer properties. Watermelons come in yellow and orange varieties as well as red, so try a new color to provide new interest in this old favorite. Like most melons, this plant likes lots of sun, space, and dry feet (don't let the roots get too wet). Suitable for containers; Zones 3–11.

December 18
10:14 am EST

DECEMBER

S	M	T	W	T	F	S
		1	2	3	4	5
6	7	8	9	10	11	12
13	14	15	16	17	18	19
20	21	22	23	24	25	26
27	28	29	30	31		

December 20–26

Love begins at home. ~MOTHER TERESA OF CALCUTTA

Date	Qtr.	Sign	Activity
Dec 20, 7:13 pm– Dec 22, 9:31 pm	2nd	Taurus	Plant annuals for hardiness. Trim to increase growth.
Dec 25, 12:27 am– Dec 25, 6:12 am	2nd	Cancer	Plant grains, leafy annuals. Fertilize (chemical). Graft or bud plants. Irrigate. Trim to increase growth.
Dec 25, 6:12 am– Dec 27, 5:31 am	3rd	Cancer	Plant biennials, perennials, bulbs, and roots. Prune. Irrigate. Fertilize (organic).

Dried fruits can also provide unique nutritional benefits, in addition to making the fruit easier to store. Raisins, simply dried grapes, pack a higher level of antioxidants. Sprinkle them in salads or over cereal, but watch the serving size to avoid consuming too much sugar—¼ cup is all you need. Prunes are dried plums with the pit removed. And they're not just for relieving constipation (though that is the first thing most folks think of). Prunes regulate blood sugar and lower cholesterol, while having a low glycemic index and a nice dose of potassium.

December 25
6:12 am EST

DECEMBER

S	M	T	W	T	F	S
		1	2	3	4	5
6	7	8	9	10	11	12
13	14	15	16	17	18	19
20	21	22	23	24	25	26
27	28	29	30	31		

2014 © Scis65 Image from BigStockPhoto.com

December 27–January 2, 2015

The stars are forth, the moon above the tops of the snow-
shining mountains—beautiful!   ∼LORD BYRON

Date	Qtr.	Sign	Activity
Dec 25, 6:12 am–Dec 27, 5:31 am	3rd	Cancer	Plant biennials, perennials, bulbs, and roots. Prune. Irrigate. Fertilize (organic).
Dec 27, 5:31 am–Dec 29, 1:58 pm	3rd	Leo	Cultivate. Destroy weeds and pests. Harvest fruits and root crops for food. Trim to retard growth.
Dec 29, 1:58 pm–Jan 1, 1:41 am	3rd	Virgo	Cultivate, especially for medicinal plants. Destroy weeds and pests. Trim to retard growth.

Fermented foods are generally loved or hated, and strongly so. Cabbage is fermented into two different superfoods: kimchi and sauerkraut. Kimchi is a spicy Korean side dish that contains many beneficial digestive enzymes. (Kimchi can also be made out of vegetables other than cabbage.) Sauerkraut is a traditional European condiment or side dish. The fermenting process produces natural probiotics that aid digestion. Make sure to check labels for words like *raw*, *alive*, or *unpasteurized* if you are buying it from the store, however—shelf-stable brands are heated, killing the good bacteria.

DECEMBER

S	M	T	W	T	F	S
		1	2	3	4	5
6	7	8	9	10	11	12
13	14	15	16	17	18	19
20	21	22	23	24	25	26
27	28	29	30	31		

2014 © lenka Image from BigStockPhoto.com

Gardening by the Moon

Today, people often reject the notion of gardening according to the Moon's phase and sign. The usual nonbeliever is not a scientist but the city dweller who has never had any real contact with nature and little experience of natural rhythms.

Camille Flammarion, the French astronomer, testifies to the success of Moon planting, though:

"Cucumbers increase at Full Moon, as well as radishes, turnips, leeks, lilies, horseradish, and saffron; onions, on the contrary, are much larger and better nourished during the decline and old age of the Moon than at its increase, during its youth and fullness, which is the reason the Egyptians abstained from onions, on account of their antipathy to the Moon. Herbs gathered while the Moon increases are of great efficiency. If the vines are trimmed at night when the Moon is in the sign of the Lion, Sagittarius, the Scorpion, or the Bull, it will save them from field rats, moles, snails, flies, and other animals."

Dr. Clark Timmins is one of the few modern scientists to have conducted tests in Moon planting. Following is a summary of his experiments:

Beets: When sown with the Moon in Scorpio, the germination rate was 71 percent; when sown in Sagittarius, the germination rate was 58 percent.

Scotch marigold: When sown with the Moon in Cancer, the germination rate was 90 percent; when sown in Leo, the rate was 32 percent.

Carrots: When sown with the Moon in Scorpio, the germination rate was 64 percent; when sown in Sagittarius, the germination rate was 47 percent.

Tomatoes: When sown with the Moon in Cancer, the germination rate was 90 percent; but when sown with the Moon in Leo, the germination rate was 58 percent.

Two things should be emphasized. First, remember that this is only a summary of the results of the experiments; the experiments themselves were conducted in a scientific manner to eliminate any variation in soil, temperature, moisture, and so on, so that only the Moon sign is varied. Second, note that these astonishing results were obtained without regard to the phase of the Moon—the other factor we use in Moon planting, and which presumably would have increased the differential in germination rates.

Dr. Timmins also tried transplanting Cancer- and Leo-planted tomato seedlings while the Cancer Moon was waxing. The result was 100 percent survival. When transplanting was done with the waning Sagittarius Moon, there was 0 percent survival. Dr. Timmins' tests show that the Cancer-planted tomatoes had blossoms twelve days earlier than those planted under Leo; the Cancer-planted tomatoes had an average height of twenty inches at that time compared to fifteen inches for the Leo-planted; the first ripe tomatoes were gathered from the Cancer plantings eleven days ahead of the Leo plantings; and a count of the hanging fruit and its size and weight shows an advantage to the Cancer plants over the Leo plants of 45 percent.

Dr. Timmins also observed that there have been similar tests that did not indicate results favorable to the Moon planting theory. As a scientist, he asked why one set of experiments indicated a positive verification of Moon planting, and others did not. He checked these other tests and found that the experimenters had not followed the geocentric system for determining the Moon sign positions, but the heliocentric. When the times used in these other tests were converted to the geocentric system, the dates chosen often were found to be in barren, rather than fertile, signs. Without going into a technical explanation, it is sufficient to point out that geocentric and heliocentric positions often vary by as much as four days. This is a large enough differential to place the Moon in Cancer, for example, in the heliocentric system, and at the same time in Leo by the geocentric system.

Most almanacs and calendars show the Moon's signs heliocentrically—and thus incorrectly for Moon planting—while the *Moon Sign Book* is calculated correctly for planting purposes, using the geocentric system. Some readers are confused because the *Moon Sign Book* talks about first, second, third, and fourth quarters, while other almanacs refer to these same divisions as New Moon, first quarter, Full Moon, and fourth quarter. Thus the almanacs say first quarter when the *Moon Sign Book* says second quarter.

There is nothing complicated about using astrology in agriculture and horticulture in order to increase both pleasure and profit, but there is one very important rule that is often neglected—use common sense! Of course this is one rule that should be remembered in every activity we undertake, but in the case of gardening and farming by the Moon, if it is not possible to use the best dates for planting or harvesting, we must select the next best and just try to do the best we can.

This brings up the matter of the other factors to consider in your gardening work. The dates we give as best for a certain activity apply to the entire country (with slight time correction), but in your section of the country you may be buried under three feet of snow on a date we say is good to plant your flowers. So we have factors of weather, season, temperature, and moisture variations, soil conditions, your own available time and opportunity, and so forth. Some astrologers like to think it is all a matter of science, but gardening is also an art. In art, you develop an instinctive identification with your work and influence it with your feelings and wishes.

The *Moon Sign Book* gives you the place of the Moon for every day of the year so that you can select the best times once you have become familiar with the rules and practices of lunar agriculture. We give you specific, easy-to-follow directions so that you can get right down to work.

We give you the best dates for planting, and also for various related activities, including cultivation, fertilizing, harvesting, irrigation, and getting rid of weeds and pests. But we cannot tell you exactly when it's good to plant. Many of these rules were learned by observation and experience; as the body of experience grew, we could see various patterns emerging that allowed us to make judgments about new things. That's what you should do, too. After you have worked with lunar agriculture for a while and have gained a working knowledge, you will probably begin to try new things—and we hope you will share your experiments and findings with us. That's how the science grows.

Here's an example of what we mean. Years ago Llewellyn George suggested that we try to combine our bits of knowledge about what to expect in planting under each of the Moon signs in order to benefit from several lunar factors in one plant. From this came our rule for developing "thoroughbred seed." To develop thoroughbred seed, save the seed for three successive years from plants grown by the correct Moon sign and phase. You can plant in the first quarter phase and in the sign of Cancer for fruitfulness; the second year, plant seeds from the first year plants in Libra for beauty; and in the third year, plant the seeds from the second year plants in Taurus to produce hardiness. In a similar manner you can combine the fruitfulness of Cancer, the good root growth of Pisces, and the sturdiness and good vine growth of Scorpio. And don't forget the characteristics of Capricorn: hardy like Taurus, but drier and perhaps more resistant to drought and disease.

Unlike common almanacs, we consider both the Moon's phase and the Moon's sign in making our calculations for the proper timing of our work. It is perhaps a little easier to understand this if we remind you that we are all living in the center of a vast electromagnetic field that is the Earth and its environment in space. Everything that occurs within this electromagnetic field has an effect on everything else within the field. The Moon and the Sun are the most important of the factors affecting the life of the Earth, and it is their relative positions to the Earth that we project for each day of the year.

Many people claim that not only do they achieve larger crops gardening by the Moon, but that their fruits and vegetables are much tastier. A number of organic gardeners have also become lunar gardeners using the natural rhythm of life forces that we experience through the relative movements of the Sun and Moon. We provide a few basic rules and then give you day-by-day guidance for your gardening work. You will be able to choose the best dates to meet your own needs and opportunities.

Planting by the Moon's Phases

During the increasing or waxing light—from New Moon to Full Moon—plant annuals that produce their yield above the ground. An annual is a plant that completes its entire life cycle within one growing season and has to be seeded each year. During the decreasing or waning light—from Full Moon to New Moon—plant biennials, perennials, and bulb and root plants. Biennials include crops that are planted one season to winter over and produce crops the next, such as winter wheat. Perennials and bulb and root plants include all plants that grow from the same root each year.

A simpler, less-accurate rule is to plant crops that produce above the ground during the waxing Moon, and to plant crops that produce below the ground during the waning Moon. Thus the old adage, "Plant potatoes during the dark of the Moon." Llewellyn George's system divided the lunar month into quarters. The first two from New Moon to Full Moon are the first and second quarters, and the last two from Full Moon to New Moon the third and fourth quarters. Using these divisions, we can increase our accuracy in timing our efforts to coincide with natural forces.

First Quarter

Plant annuals producing their yield above the ground, which are generally of the leafy kind that produce their seed outside the fruit. Some examples are asparagus, broccoli, brussels sprouts, cabbage, cauliflower, celery, cress, endive, kohlrabi, lettuce, parsley, and spinach. Cucumbers are an exception, as they do best in the first quarter rather than the second, even though the seeds are inside the fruit. Also plant cereals and grains.

Second Quarter

Plant annuals producing their yield above the ground, which are generally of the viney kind that produce their seed inside the fruit. Some examples include beans, eggplant, melons, peas, peppers, pumpkins, squash, tomatoes, etc. These are not hard-and-fast divisions. If you can't plant during the first quarter, plant during the second, and vice versa. There are many plants that seem to do equally well planted in either quarter, such as watermelon, hay, and cereals and grains.

Third Quarter

Plant biennials, perennials, bulbs, root plants, trees, shrubs, berries, grapes, strawberries, beets, carrots, onions, parsnips, rutabagas, potatoes, radishes, peanuts, rhubarb, turnips, winter wheat, etc.

Fourth Quarter

This is the best time to cultivate, turn sod, pull weeds, and destroy pests of all kinds, especially when the Moon is in Aries, Leo, Virgo, Gemini, Aquarius, and Sagittarius.

The Moon in the Signs

Moon in Aries

Barren, dry, fiery, and masculine. Use for destroying noxious weeds.

Moon in Taurus

Productive, moist, earthy, and feminine. Use for planting many crops when hardiness is important, particularly root crops. Also used for lettuce, cabbage, and similar leafy vegetables.

Moon in Gemini

Barren and dry, airy and masculine. Use for destroying noxious growths, weeds, and pests, and for cultivation.

Moon in Cancer

Fruitful, moist, feminine. Use for planting and irrigation.

Moon in Leo

Barren, dry, fiery, masculine. Use for killing weeds or cultivation.

Moon in Virgo

Barren, dry, earthy, and feminine. Use for cultivation and destroying weeds and pests.

Moon in Libra

Semi-fruitful, moist, and airy. Use for planting crops that need good pulp growth. A very good sign for flowers and vines. Also used for seeding hay, corn fodder, and the like.

Moon in Scorpio

Very fruitful and moist, watery and feminine. Nearly as productive as Cancer; use for the same purposes. Especially good for vine growth and sturdiness.

Moon in Sagittarius

Barren and dry, fiery and masculine. Use for planting onions, seeding hay, and for cultivation.

Moon in Capricorn

Productive and dry, earthy and feminine. Use for planting potatoes and other tubers.

Moon in Aquarius

Barren, dry, airy, and masculine. Use for cultivation and destroying noxious growths and pests.

Moon in Pisces

Very fruitful, moist, watery, and feminine. Especially good for root growth.

A Guide to Planting

Plant	Quarter	Sign
Annuals	1st or 2nd	
Apple tree	2nd or 3rd	Cancer, Pisces, Virgo
Artichoke	1st	Cancer, Pisces
Asparagus	1st	Cancer, Scorpio, Pisces
Aster	1st or 2nd	Virgo, Libra
Barley	1st or 2nd	Cancer, Pisces, Libra, Capricorn, Virgo
Beans (bush & pole)	2nd	Cancer, Taurus, Pisces, Libra
Beans (kidney, white, & navy)	1st or 2nd	Cancer, Pisces
Beech tree	2nd or 3rd	Virgo, Taurus
Beets	3rd	Cancer, Capricorn, Pisces, Libra
Biennials	3rd or 4th	
Broccoli	1st	Cancer, Scorpio, Pisces, Libra
Brussels sprouts	1st	Cancer, Scorpio, Pisces, Libra
Buckwheat	1st or 2nd	Capricorn
Bulbs	3rd	Cancer, Scorpio, Pisces
Bulbs for seed	2nd or 3rd	
Cabbage	1st	Cancer, Scorpio, Pisces, Taurus, Libra
Canes (raspberry, blackberry, & gooseberry)	2nd	Cancer, Scorpio, Pisces
Cantaloupe	1st or 2nd	Cancer, Scorpio, Pisces, Taurus, Libra
Carrots	3rd	Cancer, Scorpio, Pisces, Taurus, Libra
Cauliflower	1st	Cancer, Scorpio, Pisces, Libra
Celeriac	3rd	Cancer, Scorpio, Pisces
Celery	1st	Cancer, Scorpio, Pisces
Cereals	1st or 2nd	Cancer, Scorpio, Pisces, Libra
Chard	1st or 2nd	Cancer, Scorpio, Pisces
Chicory	2nd or 3rd	Cancer, Scorpio, Pisces
Chrysanthemum	1st or 2nd	Virgo
Clover	1st or 2nd	Cancer, Scorpio, Pisces

Plant	Quarter	Sign
Coreopsis	2nd or 3rd	Libra
Corn	1st	Cancer, Scorpio, Pisces
Corn for fodder	1st or 2nd	Libra
Cosmos	2nd or 3rd	Libra
Cress	1st	Cancer, Scorpio, Pisces
Crocus	1st or 2nd	Virgo
Cucumber	1st	Cancer, Scorpio, Pisces
Daffodil	1st or 2nd	Libra, Virgo
Dahlia	1st or 2nd	Libra, Virgo
Deciduous trees	2nd or 3rd	Cancer, Scorpio, Pisces, Virgo, Libra
Eggplant	2nd	Cancer, Scorpio, Pisces, Libra
Endive	1st	Cancer, Scorpio, Pisces, Libra
Flowers	1st	Cancer, Scorpio, Pisces, Libra, Taurus, Virgo
Garlic	3rd	Libra, Taurus, Pisces
Gladiola	1st or 2nd	Libra, Virgo
Gourds	1st or 2nd	Cancer, Scorpio, Pisces, Libra
Grapes	2nd or 3rd	Cancer, Scorpio, Pisces, Virgo
Hay	1st or 2nd	Cancer, Scorpio, Pisces, Libra, Taurus
Herbs	1st or 2nd	Cancer, Scorpio, Pisces
Honeysuckle	1st or 2nd	Scorpio, Virgo
Hops	1st or 2nd	Scorpio, Libra
Horseradish	1st or 2nd	Cancer, Scorpio, Pisces
Houseplants	1st	Cancer, Scorpio, Pisces, Libra
Hyacinth	3rd	Cancer, Scorpio, Pisces
Iris	1st or 2nd	Cancer, Virgo
Kohlrabi	1st or 2nd	Cancer, Scorpio, Pisces, Libra
Leek	2nd or 3rd	Sagittarius
Lettuce	1st	Cancer, Scorpio, Pisces, Libra, Taurus
Lily	1st or 2nd	Cancer, Scorpio, Pisces
Maple tree	2nd or 3rd	Taurus, Virgo, Cancer, Pisces
Melon	2nd	Cancer, Scorpio, Pisces
Moon vine	1st or 2nd	Virgo

Plant	Quarter	Sign
Morning glory	1st or 2nd	Cancer, Scorpio, Pisces, Virgo
Oak tree	2nd or 3rd	Taurus, Virgo, Cancer, Pisces
Oats	1st or 2nd	Cancer, Scorpio, Pisces, Libra
Okra	1st or 2nd	Cancer, Scorpio, Pisces, Libra
Onion seed	2nd	Cancer, Scorpio, Sagittarius
Onion set	3rd or 4th	Cancer, Pisces, Taurus, Libra
Pansies	1st or 2nd	Cancer, Scorpio, Pisces
Parsley	1st	Cancer, Scorpio, Pisces, Libra
Parsnip	3rd	Cancer, Scorpio, Taurus, Capricorn
Peach tree	2nd or 3rd	Cancer, Taurus, Virgo, Libra
Peanuts	3rd	Cancer, Scorpio, Pisces
Pear tree	2nd or 3rd	Cancer, Scorpio, Pisces, Libra
Peas	2nd	Cancer, Scorpio, Pisces, Libra
Peony	1st or 2nd	Virgo
Peppers	2nd	Cancer, Scorpio, Pisces
Perennials	3rd	
Petunia	1st or 2nd	Libra, Virgo
Plum tree	2nd or 3rd	Cancer, Pisces, Taurus, Virgo
Poppies	1st or 2nd	Virgo
Portulaca	1st or 2nd	Virgo
Potatoes	3rd	Cancer, Scorpio, Libra, Taurus, Capricorn
Privet	1st or 2nd	Taurus, Libra
Pumpkin	2nd	Cancer, Scorpio, Pisces, Libra
Quince	1st or 2nd	Capricorn
Radishes	3rd	Cancer, Scorpio, Pisces, Libra, Capricorn
Rhubarb	3rd	Cancer, Pisces
Rice	1st or 2nd	Scorpio
Roses	1st or 2nd	Cancer, Virgo
Rutabaga	3rd	Cancer, Scorpio, Pisces, Taurus
Saffron	1st or 2nd	Cancer, Scorpio, Pisces
Sage	3rd	Cancer, Scorpio, Pisces

Plant	Quarter	Sign
Salsify	1st	Cancer, Scorpio, Pisces
Shallot	2nd	Scorpio
Spinach	1st	Cancer, Scorpio, Pisces
Squash	2nd	Cancer, Scorpio, Pisces, Libra
Strawberries	3rd	Cancer, Scorpio, Pisces
String beans	1st or 2nd	Taurus
Sunflowers	1st or 2nd	Libra, Cancer
Sweet peas	1st or 2nd	Any
Tomatoes	2nd	Cancer, Scorpio, Pisces, Capricorn
Trees, shade	3rd	Taurus, Capricorn
Trees, ornamental	2nd	Libra, Taurus
Trumpet vine	1st or 2nd	Cancer, Scorpio, Pisces
Tubers for seed	3rd	Cancer, Scorpio, Pisces, Libra
Tulips	1st or 2nd	Libra, Virgo
Turnips	3rd	Cancer, Scorpio, Pisces, Taurus, Capricorn, Libra
Valerian	1st or 2nd	Virgo, Gemini
Watermelon	1st or 2nd	Cancer, Scorpio, Pisces, Libra
Wheat	1st or 2nd	Cancer, Scorpio, Pisces, Libra

Companion Planting Guide

Plant	Companions	Hindered by
Asparagus	Tomatoes, parsley, basil	None known
Beans	Tomatoes, carrots, cucumbers, garlic, cabbage, beets, corn	Onions, gladiolas
Beets	Onions, cabbage, lettuce, mint, catnip	Pole beans
Broccoli	Beans, celery, potatoes, onions	Tomatoes
Cabbage	Peppermint, sage, thyme, tomatoes	Strawberries, grapes
Carrots	Peas, lettuce, chives, radishes, leeks, onions, sage	Dill, anise
Citrus trees	Guava, live oak, rubber trees, peppers	None known
Corn	Potatoes, beans, peas, melon, squash, pumpkin, sunflowers, soybeans	Quack grass, wheat, straw, mulch
Cucumbers	Beans, cabbage, radishes, sunflowers, lettuce, broccoli, squash	Aromatic herbs
Eggplant	Green beans, lettuce, kale	None known
Grapes	Peas, beans, blackberries	Cabbage, radishes
Melons	Corn, peas	Potatoes, gourds
Onions, leeks	Beets, chamomile, carrots, lettuce	Peas, beans, sage
Parsnip	Peas	None known
Peas	Radishes, carrots, corn, cucumbers, beans, tomatoes, spinach, turnips	Onion, garlic
Potatoes	Beans, corn, peas, cabbage, hemp, cucumbers, eggplant, catnip	Raspberries, pumpkins, tomatoes, sunflowers
Radishes	Peas, lettuce, nasturtiums, cucumbers	Hyssop
Spinach	Strawberries	None known
Squash/Pumpkin	Nasturtiums, corn, mint, catnip	Potatoes
Tomatoes	Asparagus, parsley, chives, onions, carrots, marigolds, nasturtiums, dill	Black walnut roots, fennel, potatoes
Turnips	Peas, beans, brussels sprouts	Potatoes

Plant	Companions	Uses
Anise	Coriander	Flavor candy, pastry, cheeses, cookies
Basil	Tomatoes	Dislikes rue; repels flies and mosquitoes
Borage	Tomatoes, squash	Use in teas
Buttercup	Clover	Hinders delphinium, peonies, monkshood, columbine
Catnip		Repels flea beetles
Chamomile	Peppermint, wheat, onions, cabbage	Roman chamomile may control damping-off disease; use in herbal sprays
Chervil	Radishes	Good in soups and other dishes
Chives	Carrots	Use in spray to deter black spot on roses
Coriander	Plant anywhere	Hinders seed formation in fennel
Cosmos		Repels corn earworms
Dill	Cabbage	Hinders carrots and tomatoes
Fennel	Plant in borders	Disliked by all garden plants
Horseradish		Repels potato bugs
Horsetail		Makes fungicide spray
Hyssop		Attracts cabbage flies; harmful to radishes
Lavender	Plant anywhere	Use in spray to control insects on cotton, repels clothes moths
Lovage		Lures horn worms away from tomatoes
Marigolds		Pest repellent; use against Mexican bean beetles and nematodes
Mint	Cabbage, tomatoes	Repels ants, flea beetles, cabbage worm butterflies
Morning glory	Corn	Helps melon germination
Nasturtium	Cabbage, cucumbers	Deters aphids, squash bugs, pumpkin beetles
Okra	Eggplant	Attracts leafhopper (lure insects from other plants)
Parsley	Tomatoes, asparagus	Freeze chopped-up leaves to flavor foods
Purslane		Good ground cover
Rosemary		Repels cabbage moths, bean beetles, carrot flies
Savory		Plant with onions for added sweetness
Tansy		Deters Japanese beetles, striped cucumber beetles, squash bugs
Thyme		Repels cabbage worms
Yarrow		Increases essential oils of neighbors

Moon Void-of-Course

By Kim Rogers-Gallagher

The Moon circles the Earth in about twenty-eight days, moving through each zodiac sign in two-and-a-half days. As she passes through the thirty degrees of each sign, she "visits" with the planets in numerical order, forming aspects with them. Because she moves one degree in just two to two-and-a-half hours, her influence on each planet lasts only a few hours. She eventually reaches the planet that's in the highest degree of any sign and forms what will be her final aspect before leaving the sign. From this point until she enters the next sign, she is referred to as void-of-course.

Think of it this way: the Moon is the emotional "tone" of the day, carrying feelings with her particular to the sign she's "wearing" at the moment. After she has contacted each of the planets, she symbolically "rests" before changing her costume, so her instinct is temporarily on hold. It's during this time that many people feel "fuzzy" or "vague." Plans or decisions made now often do not pan out. Without the instinctual "knowing" the Moon provides as she touches each planet, we tend to be unrealistic or exercise poor judgment. The traditional definition of the void Moon is that "nothing will come of this." Actions initiated under a void Moon are often wasted, irrelevant, or incorrect—usually because information is hidden, missing, or has been overlooked.

Although it's not a good time to initiate plans, routine tasks seem to go along just fine. This period is ideal for reflection. On the lighter side, remember there are good uses for the void Moon. It is the period when the universe seems to be most open to loopholes. It's a great time to make plans you don't want to fulfill or schedule things you don't want to do. See the table on pages 76–81 for a schedule of the Moon's void-of-course times.

Last Aspect   Moon Enters New Sign

		January		
1	7:19 am	1	Gemini	12:09 pm
3	6:55 am	3	Cancer	8:08 pm
4	11:53 pm	6	Leo	6:03 am
8	12:05 pm	8	Virgo	5:58 pm
10	10:46 am	11	Libra	6:57 am
13	4:46 am	13	Scorpio	6:44 pm
15	6:52 pm	16	Sagittarius	3:01 am
17	2:25 pm	18	Capricorn	7:04 am
19	5:51 am	20	Aquarius	7:59 am
21	8:45 pm	22	Pisces	7:48 am
23	6:13 am	24	Aries	8:31 am
26	9:23 am	26	Taurus	11:37 am
27	9:18 pm	28	Gemini	5:36 pm
30	4:24 am	31	Cancer	2:09 am
		February		
1	8:37 am	2	Leo	12:41 pm
4	12:31 am	5	Virgo	12:46 am
6	5:09 pm	7	Libra	1:44 pm
9	6:58 am	10	Scorpio	2:05 am
12	12:32 am	12	Sagittarius	11:46 am
14	10:15 am	14	Capricorn	5:24 pm
16	3:17 pm	16	Aquarius	7:13 pm
18	6:47 pm	18	Pisces	6:47 pm
19	6:02 pm	20	Aries	6:13 pm
21	7:36 pm	22	Taurus	7:28 pm
23	9:57 pm	24	Gemini	11:54 pm
26	3:43 am	27	Cancer	7:50 am
28	12:53 pm	3/1	Leo	6:34 pm

Last Aspect   Moon Enters New Sign

			March		
3	3:48 am	4		Virgo	6:58 am
5	1:36 pm	6		Libra	7:52 pm
8	9:24 pm	9		Scorpio	9:10 am
11	3:46 pm	11		Sagittarius	7:30 pm
13	7:11 pm	14		Capricorn	2:40 am
16	4:02 am	16		Aquarius	6:14 am
17	2:18 pm	18		Pisces	6:58 am
20	5:36 am	20		Aries	6:28 am
21	6:51 pm	22		Taurus	6:40 am
23	10:25 am	24		Gemini	9:23 am
26	8:35 am	26		Cancer	3:45 pm
28	9:58 pm	29		Leo	1:48 am
30	9:57 am	31		Virgo	2:12 pm
			April		
2	5:01 am	3		Libra	3:07 am
4	11:59 am	5		Scorpio	3:04 pm
7	4:42 pm	8		Sagittarius	1:08 am
9	1:42 pm	10		Capricorn	8:47 am
12	4:15 am	12		Aquarius	1:44 pm
14	3:45 pm	14		Pisces	4:12 pm
15	5:37 pm	16		Aries	5:00 pm
18	2:57 pm	18		Taurus	5:31 pm
19	7:07 pm	20		Gemini	7:28 pm
22	1:38 am	23		Cancer	12:25 am
24	1:04 pm	25		Leo	9:13 am
27	10:12 am	27		Virgo	9:07 pm
30	8:23 am	30		Libra	10:03 am

Last Aspect   **Moon Enters New Sign**

			May		
2	10:03 am	2	Scorpio	9:47 pm
4	9:49 pm	5	Sagittarius	7:13 am
7	1:51 pm	7	Capricorn	2:16 pm
9	4:35 pm	9	Aquarius	7:22 pm
11	6:36 am	11	Pisces	10:53 pm
13	12:55 pm	14	Aries	1:13 am
15	8:04 am	16	Taurus	3:02 am
18	12:13 am	18	Gemini	5:27 am
19	1:57 pm	20	Cancer	9:56 am
21	8:36 pm	22	Leo	5:42 pm
24	6:50 am	25	Virgo	4:52 am
26	10:21 pm	27	Libra	5:42 pm
29	4:20 pm	30	Scorpio	5:34 am
			June		
1	7:01 am	1	Sagittarius	2:39 pm
3	1:59 am	3	Capricorn	8:50 pm
5	6:54 am	6	Aquarius	1:02 am
7	10:30 am	8	Pisces	4:16 am
9	2:08 pm	10	Aries	7:14 am
11	7:43 pm	12	Taurus	10:16 am
13	6:06 pm	14	Gemini	1:51 pm
16	10:05 am	16	Cancer	6:51 pm
19	1:52 am	19	Leo	2:23 am
21	12:09 pm	21	Virgo	12:59 pm
24	1:12 am	24	Libra	1:41 am
25	7:22 pm	26	Scorpio	1:57 pm
28	9:50 pm	28	Sagittarius	11:21 pm
30	2:18 pm	7/1	Capricorn	5:11 am

Last Aspect   Moon Enters New Sign

		July			
3	6:38 am	3	Aquarius	8:21 am
5	8:32 am	5	Pisces	10:23 am
7	10:36 am	7	Aries	12:38 pm
9	9:47 am	9	Taurus	3:49 pm
11	5:52 pm	11	Gemini	8:16 pm
13	11:31 pm	14	Cancer	2:14 am
16	7:24 am	16	Leo	10:15 am
18	5:41 pm	18	Virgo	8:47 pm
21	6:07 am	21	Libra	9:23 am
23	2:12 pm	23	Scorpio	10:07 pm
26	5:14 am	26	Sagittarius	8:24 am
28	9:36 am	28	Capricorn	2:47 pm
30	2:50 pm	30	Aquarius	5:40 pm
		August			
1	6:02 pm	1	Pisces	6:36 pm
3	4:35 pm	3	Aries	7:24 pm
5	7:29 pm	5	Taurus	9:29 pm
8	12:46 am	8	Gemini	1:40 am
10	7:45 am	10	Cancer	8:08 am
12	1:44 pm	12	Leo	4:52 pm
15	12:36 am	15	Virgo	3:46 am
17	1:16 pm	17	Libra	4:23 pm
19	10:56 pm	20	Scorpio	5:24 am
22	3:31 pm	22	Sagittarius	4:41 pm
24	6:04 pm	25	Capricorn	12:22 am
27	3:20 am	27	Aquarius	4:03 am
29	3:03 am	29	Pisces	4:51 am
31	2:53 am	31	Aries	4:33 am

Last Aspect   Moon Enters New Sign

		September			
1	12:37 pm	2		Taurus	5:02 am
4	6:20 am	4		Gemini	7:48 am
5	7:04 pm	6		Cancer	1:40 pm
8	9:28 pm	8		Leo	10:36 pm
11	9:03 am	11		Virgo	9:56 am
13	10:08 pm	13		Libra	10:41 pm
16	12:22 am	16		Scorpio	11:43 am
18	3:49 pm	18		Sagittarius	11:32 pm
21	4:59 am	21		Capricorn	8:33 am
22	7:13 pm	23		Aquarius	1:51 pm
25	12:02 am	25		Pisces	3:43 pm
26	12:32 pm	27		Aries	3:29 pm
29	3:45 am	29		Taurus	2:57 pm
		October			
1	6:44 am	1		Gemini	4:03 pm
3	1:18 pm	3		Cancer	8:22 pm
5	7:04 am	6		Leo	4:31 am
7	5:10 pm	8		Virgo	3:50 pm
9	6:12 pm	11		Libra	4:45 am
12	8:06 pm	13		Scorpio	5:38 pm
14	8:58 pm	16		Sagittarius	5:18 am
18	4:48 am	18		Capricorn	2:52 pm
20	4:31 pm	20		Aquarius	9:38 pm
23	12:22 am	23		Pisces	1:18 am
24	7:18 am	25		Aries	2:22 am
26	8:25 am	27		Taurus	2:07 am
28	11:20 am	29		Gemini	2:24 am
30	10:52 pm	31		Cancer	5:09 am

Last Aspect		**Moon Enters New Sign**		
		November		
1	10:35 pm	2	Leo	10:48 am
3	8:46 pm	4	Virgo	9:22 pm
7	7:47 am	7	Libra	10:14 am
8	9:42 pm	9	Scorpio	11:02 pm
12	9:54 am	12	Sagittarius	10:14 am
13	10:19 pm	14	Capricorn	7:21 pm
16	3:53 pm	17	Aquarius	2:24 am
19	3:19 am	19	Pisces	7:21 am
21	8:23 am	21	Aries	10:12 am
22	2:16 pm	23	Taurus	11:26 am
24	8:26 pm	25	Gemini	12:15 pm
26	10:35 pm	27	Cancer	2:27 pm
29	7:46 am	29	Leo	7:47 pm
		December		
1	10:09 pm	2	Virgo	5:09 am
3	11:59 pm	4	Libra	5:34 pm
6	9:03 pm	7	Scorpio	6:26 am
9	1:39 am	9	Sagittarius	5:25 pm
11	11:06 am	12	Capricorn	1:46 am
13	6:07 pm	14	Aquarius	7:59 am
16	2:17 am	16	Pisces	12:45 pm
18	10:14 am	18	Aries	4:26 pm
20	5:01 pm	20	Taurus	7:13 pm
22	9:26 am	22	Gemini	9:31 pm
24	3:04 pm	25	Cancer	12:27 am
26	10:36 pm	27	Leo	5:31 am
29	12:38 pm	29	Virgo	1:58 pm

2014 © kotenko Image from BigStockPhoto.com

The Moon's Rhythm

The Moon journeys around Earth in an elliptical orbit that takes about 27.33 days, which is known as a sidereal month (period of revolution of one body about another). She can move up to 15 degrees or as few as 11 degrees in a day, with the fastest motion occurring when the Moon is at perigee (closest approach to Earth). The Moon is never retrograde, but when her motion is slow, the effect is similar to a retrograde period.

Astrologers have observed that people born on a day when the Moon is fast will process information differently from those who are born when the Moon is slow in motion. People born when the Moon is fast process information quickly and tend to react quickly, while those born during a slow Moon will be more deliberate.

The time from New Moon to New Moon is called the synodic month (involving a conjunction), and the average time span between this Sun-Moon alignment is 29.53 days. Since 29.53

won't divide into 365 evenly, we can have a month with two Full Moons or two New Moons.

Moon Aspects

The aspects the Moon will make during the times you are considering are also important. A trine or sextile, and sometimes a conjunction, are considered favorable aspects. A trine or sextile between the Sun and Moon is an excellent foundation for success. Whether or not a conjunction is considered favorable depends upon the planet the Moon is making a conjunction to. If it's joining the Sun, Venus, Mercury, Jupiter, or even Saturn, the aspect is favorable. If the Moon joins Pluto or Mars, however, that would not be considered favorable. There may be exceptions, but it would depend on what you are electing to do. For example, a trine to Pluto might hasten the end of a relationship you want to be free of.

It is important to avoid times when the Moon makes an aspect to or is conjoining any retrograde planet, unless, of course, you want the thing started to end in failure.

After the Moon has completed an aspect to a planet, that planetary energy has passed. For example, if the Moon squares Saturn at 10:00 am, you can disregard Saturn's influence on your activity if it will occur after that time. You should always look ahead at aspects the Moon will make on the day in question, though, because if the Moon opposes Mars at 11:30 pm on that day, you can expect events that stretch into the evening to be affected by the Moon-Mars aspect. A testy conversation might lead to an argument, or more.

Moon Signs

Much agricultural work is ruled by earth signs—Virgo, Capricorn, and Taurus; and the air signs—Gemini, Aquarius, and Libra—rule flying and intellectual pursuits.

Each planet has one or two signs in which its characteristics are enhanced or "dignified," and the planet is said to "rule" that sign. The Sun rules Leo and the Moon rules Cancer, for example. The ruling planet for each sign is listed below. These should not be considered complete lists. We recommend that you purchase a book of planetary rulerships for more complete information.

Aries Moon

The energy of an Aries Moon is masculine, dry, barren, and fiery. Aries provides great start-up energy, but things started at this time may be the result of impulsive action that lacks research or necessary support. Aries lacks staying power.

Use this assertive, outgoing Moon sign to initiate change, but have a plan in place for someone to pick up the reins when you're impatient to move on to the next thing. Work that requires skillful, but not necessarily patient, use of tools—hammering, cutting down trees, etc.—is appropriate in Aries. Expect things to occur rapidly but to also quickly pass. If you are prone to injury or accidents, exercise caution and good judgment in Aries-related activities.

RULER: Mars

IMPULSE: Action

RULES: Head and face

Taurus Moon

A Taurus Moon's energy is feminine, semi-fruitful, and earthy. The Moon is exalted—very strong—in Taurus. Taurus is known as the farmer's sign because of its associations with farmland and precipitation that is the typical day-long "soaker" variety. Taurus energy is good to incorporate into your plans when patience, practicality, and perseverance are needed. Be aware, though, that you may also experience stubbornness in this sign.

Things started in Taurus tend to be long lasting and to increase in value. This can be very supportive energy in a marriage election. On the downside, the fixed energy of this sign resists change or the letting go of even the most difficult situations. A divorce following a marriage that occurred during a Taurus Moon may be difficult and costly to end. Things begun now tend to become habitual and hard to alter. If you want to make changes in something you started, it would be better to wait for Gemini. This is a good time to get a loan, but expect the people in charge of money to be cautious and slow to make decisions.

RULER: Venus

IMPULSE: Stability

RULES: Neck, throat, and voice

Gemini Moon

A Gemini Moon's energy is masculine, dry, barren, and airy. People are more changeable than usual and may prefer to follow intellectual pursuits and play mental games rather than apply themselves to practical concerns.

This sign is not favored for agricultural matters, but it is an excellent time to prepare for activities, to run errands, and write letters. Plan to use a Gemini Moon to exchange ideas, meet people, go on vacations that include walking or biking, or be in situations that require versatility and quick thinking on your feet.

RULER: Mercury

IMPULSE: Versatility

RULES: Shoulders, hands, arms, lungs, and nervous system

Cancer Moon

A Cancer Moon's energy is feminine, fruitful, moist, and very strong. Use this sign when you want to grow things—flowers, fruits, vegetables, commodities, stocks, or collections—for example. This sensitive sign stimulates rapport between people. Considered the most fertile of the signs, it is often associated with mothering. You can use this moontime to build personal friendships that support mutual growth.

Cancer is associated with emotions and feelings. Prominent Cancer energy promotes growth, but it can also turn people pouty and prone to withdrawing into their shells.

RULER: The Moon

IMPULSE: Tenacity

RULES: Chest area, breasts, and stomach

Leo Moon

A Leo Moon's energy is masculine, hot, dry, fiery, and barren. Use it whenever you need to put on a show, make a presentation, or entertain colleagues or guests. This is a proud yet playful energy that exudes self-confidence and is often associated with romance.

This is an excellent time for fund-raisers and ceremonies or to be straightforward, frank, and honest about something. It is advisable not to put yourself in a position of needing public approval or where you might have to cope with underhandedness, as trouble in these areas can bring out the worst Leo traits. There is a tendency in this sign to become arrogant or self-centered.

RULER: The Sun

IMPULSE: I am

RULES: Heart and upper back

Virgo Moon

A Virgo Moon is feminine, dry, barren, earthy energy. It is favorable for anything that needs painstaking attention—especially those things where exactness rather than innovation is preferred.

Use this sign for activities when you must analyze information or when you must determine the value of something. Virgo is the sign of bargain hunting. It's friendly toward agricultural matters with an emphasis on animals and harvesting vegetables. It is an excellent time to care for animals, especially training them and veterinary work.

This sign is most beneficial when decisions have already been made and now need to be carried out. The inclination here is to see details rather than the bigger picture.

There is a tendency in this sign to overdo. Precautions should be taken to avoid becoming too dull from all work and no play. Build a little relaxation and pleasure into your routine from the beginning.

RULER: Mercury

IMPULSE: Discriminating

RULES: Abdomen and intestines

Libra Moon

A Libra Moon's energy is masculine, semi-fruitful, and airy. This energy will benefit any attempt to bring beauty to a place or thing. Libra is considered good energy for starting things of an intellectual nature. Libra is the sign of partnership and unions, which makes it an excellent time to form partnerships of any kind, to make agreements, and to negotiate. Even though this sign is good for initiating things, it is crucial to work with a partner who will provide incentive and encouragement, however. A Libra Moon accentuates teamwork (particularly teams of two) and artistic work (especially work that involves color). Make use of this sign when you are decorating your home or shopping for better-quality clothing.

RULER: Venus

IMPULSE: Balance

RULES: Lower back, kidneys, and buttocks

Scorpio Moon

The Scorpio Moon is feminine, fruitful, cold, and moist. It is useful when intensity (that sometimes borders on obsession) is needed. Scorpio is considered a very psychic sign. Use this Moon sign when you must back up something you strongly believe in, such as union or employer relations. There is strong group loyalty here, but a Scorpio Moon is also a good time to end connections thoroughly. This is also a good time to conduct research.

The desire nature is so strong here that there is a tendency to manipulate situations to get what one wants or to not see one's responsibility in an act.

RULER: Pluto, Mars (traditional)

IMPULSE: Transformation

RULES: Reproductive organs, genitals, groin, and pelvis

Sagittarius Moon

The Moon's energy is masculine, dry, barren, and fiery in Sagittarius, encouraging flights of imagination and confidence in the flow of life. Sagittarius is the most philosophical sign. Candor and honesty are enhanced when the Moon is here. This is an excellent time to "get things off your chest" and to deal with institutions of higher learning, publishing companies, and the law. It's also a good time for sport and adventure.

Sagittarians are the crusaders of this world. This is a good time to tackle things that need improvement, but don't try to be the diplomat while influenced by this energy. Opinions can run strong, and the tendency to proselytize is increased.

RULER: Jupiter

IMPULSE: Expansion

RULES: Thighs and hips

Capricorn Moon

In Capricorn the Moon's energy is feminine, semi-fruitful, and earthy. Because Cancer and Capricorn are polar opposites, the Moon's energy is thought to be weakened here. This energy encourages the need for structure, discipline, and organization. This is a good time to set goals and plan for the future, tend to family business, and to take care of details requiring patience or a businesslike manner. Institutional activities are favored. This sign should be avoided if you're seeking favors, as those in authority can be insensitive under this influence.

RULER: Saturn

IMPULSE: Ambitious

RULES: Bones, skin, and knees

Aquarius Moon

An Aquarius Moon's energy is masculine, barren, dry, and airy. Activities that are unique, individualistic, concerned with humanitarian issues, society as a whole, and making improvements are favored under this Moon. It is this quality of making improvements that has caused this sign to be associated with inventors and new inventions.

An Aquarius Moon promotes the gathering of social groups for friendly exchanges. People tend to react and speak from an intellectual rather than emotional viewpoint when the Moon is in this sign.

RULER: Uranus and Saturn

IMPULSE: Reformer

RULES: Calves and ankles

Pisces Moon

A Pisces Moon is feminine, fruitful, cool, and moist. This is an excellent time to retreat, meditate, sleep, pray, or make that dreamed-of escape into a fantasy vacation. However, things are not always what they seem to be with the Moon in Pisces. Personal boundaries tend to be fuzzy, and you may not be seeing things clearly. People tend to be idealistic under this sign, which can prevent them from seeing reality.

There is a live-and-let-live philosophy attached to this sign, which in the idealistic world may work well enough, but chaos is frequently the result. That's why this sign is also associated with alcohol and drug abuse, drug trafficking, and counterfeiting. On the lighter side, many musicians and artists are ruled by Pisces. It's only when they move too far away from reality that the dark side of substance abuse, suicide, or crime takes away life.

RULER: Jupiter and Neptune

IMPULSE: Empathetic

RULES: Feet

More About Zodiac Signs

Element (Triplicity)

Each of the zodiac signs is classified as belonging to an element; these are the four basic elements:

Fire Signs

Aries, Sagittarius, and Leo are action-oriented, outgoing, energetic, and spontaneous.

Earth Signs

Taurus, Capricorn, and Virgo are stable, conservative, practical, and oriented to the physical and material realm.

Air Signs

Gemini, Aquarius, and Libra are sociable and critical, and they tend to represent intellectual responses rather than feelings.

Water Signs

Cancer, Scorpio, and Pisces are emotional, receptive, intuitive, and can be very sensitive.

Quality (Quadruplicity)

Each zodiac sign is further classified as being cardinal, mutable, or fixed. There are four signs in each quadruplicity, one sign from each element.

Cardinal Signs

Aries, Cancer, Libra, and Capricorn represent beginnings and newly initiated action. They initiate each new season in the cycle of the year.

Fixed Signs

Taurus, Leo, Scorpio, and Aquarius want to maintain the status quo through stubbornness and persistence; they represent that "between" time. For example, Leo is the month when summer really feels like summer.

Mutable Signs

Pisces, Gemini, Virgo, and Sagittarius adapt to change and tolerate situations. They represent the last month of each season, when things are changing in preparation for the coming season.

Nature and Fertility

In addition to a sign's element and quality, each sign is further classified as either fruitful, semi-fruitful, or barren. This classification is the most important for readers who use the gardening information in the *Moon Sign Book* because the timing of most events depends on the fertility of the sign occupied by the Moon. The water signs of Cancer, Scorpio, and Pisces are the most fruitful. The semi-fruitful signs are the earth signs Taurus and Capricorn, and the air sign Libra. The barren signs correspond to fire-signs Aries, Leo, and Sagittarius; air-signs Gemini and Aquarius; and earth-sign Virgo.

Good Timing

By Sharon Leah

Electional astrology is the art of electing times to begin any undertaking. Say, for example, you want to start a business. That business will experience ups and downs, as well as reach its potential, according to the promise held in the universe at the time the business was started—its birth time. The horoscope (birth chart) set for the date, time, and place that a business starts would indicate the outcome—its potential to succeed.

So, you might ask yourself the question: If the horoscope for a business start can show success or failure, why not begin at a time that is more favorable to the venture? Well, you can.

While no time is perfect, there are better times and better days to undertake specific activities. There are thousands of examples that prove electional astrology is not only practical, but that it can make a difference in our lives. There are rules for electing times to begin various activities—even shopping. You'll find detailed instructions about how to make elections beginning on page 107.

Personalizing Elections

The election rules in this almanac are based upon the planetary positions at the time for which the election is made. They do not depend on any type of birth chart. However, a birth chart based upon the time, date, and birthplace of an event has advantages. No election is effective for every person. For example, you may leave home to begin a trip at the same time as a friend, but each of you will have a different experience according to whether or not your birth chart favors the trip.

Not all elections require a birth chart, but the timing of very important events—business starts, marriages, etc.—would benefit from the additional accuracy a birth chart provides. To order a birth chart for yourself or a planned event, visit our Web site at www .llewellyn.com.

Some Things to Consider

You've probably experienced good timing in your life. Maybe you were at the right place at the right time to meet a friend whom you hadn't seen in years. Frequently, when something like that happens, it is the result of following an intuitive impulse—that "gut instinct." Consider for a moment that you were actually responding to planetary energies. Electional astrology is a tool that can help you to align with energies, present and future, that are available to us through planetary placements.

Significators

Decide upon the important significators (planet, sign, and house ruling the matter) for which the election is being made. The Moon is the most important significator in any election, so the Moon should always be fortified (strong by sign and making favorable aspects to other planets). The Moon's aspects to other planets are more important than the sign the Moon is in.

Other important considerations are the significators of the Ascendant and Midheaven—the house ruling the election matter and the ruler of the sign on that house cusp. Finally, any planet or sign that has a general rulership over the matter in question should be taken into consideration.

Nature and Fertility

Determine the general nature of the sign that is appropriate for your election. For example, much agricultural work is ruled by the earth signs of Virgo, Capricorn, and Taurus; while the air signs—Gemini, Aquarius, and Libra—rule intellectual pursuits.

One Final Comment

Use common sense. If you must do something, like plant your garden or take an airplane trip on a day that doesn't have the best aspects, proceed anyway, but try to minimize problems. For example, leave early for the airport to avoid being left behind due to delays in the security lanes. When you have no other choice, do the best that you can under the circumstances at the time.

If you want to personalize your elections, please turn to page 107 for more information. If you want a quick and easy answer, you can refer to Llewellyn's Astro Almanac on the following pages.

Llewellyn's Astro Almanac

The Astro Almanac tables, beginning on the next page, can help you find the dates best suited to particular activities. The dates provided are determined from the Moon's sign, phase, and aspects to other planets. Please note that the Astro Almanac does not take personal factors, such as your Sun and Moon sign, into account. The dates are general, and they will apply for everyone. Some activities will not have ideal dates during a particular month.

Activity	January
Animals (Neuter or spay)	17, 18, 19
Animals (Sell or buy)	1, 3, 25, 30, 31
Automobile (Buy)	2, 29
Brewing	5, 14, 15
Build (Start foundation)	20
Business (Conducting for self and others)	10, 15, 24, 29
Business (Start new)	27
Can Fruits and Vegetables	5, 14, 15
Can Preserves	5, 14, 15
Concrete (Pour)	7, 8
Construction (Begin new)	3, 10, 13, 17, 24, 25, 29, 30
Consultants (Begin work with)	1, 3, 8, 12, 13, 17, 21, 25, 29, 30
Contracts (Bid on)	1, 3, 21, 25, 29, 30
Cultivate	no ideal dates
Decorating	1, 2, 3, 20, 21, 28, 29, 30
Demolition	6, 7, 16, 17
Electronics (Buy)	2, 12, 21, 29
Entertain Guests	12, 31
Floor Covering (Laying new)	6–13
Habits (Break)	18, 19
Hair (Cut to increase growth)	1, 2, 23, 26–30
Hair (Cut to decrease growth)	6, 16–19
Harvest (Grain for storage)	6, 7, 8
Harvest (Root crops)	6, 7, 8, 16, 17
Investments (New)	10, 29
Loan (Ask for)	1, 26, 27, 28
Massage (Relaxing)	1, 12, 21, 31
Mow Lawn (Decrease growth)	5–19
Mow Lawn (Increase growth)	1, 2, 3, 21–31
Mushrooms (Pick)	3, 4, 5
Negotiate (Business for the elderly)	6, 11, 20, 24
Prune for Better Fruit	13–17
Prune to Promote Healing	18, 19
Wean Children	16–21
Wood Floors (Installing)	18, 19
Write Letters or Contracts	2, 7, 17, 21, 29

Activity	February
Animals (Neuter or spay)	12, 13, 15, 16
Animals (Sell or buy)	21, 26
Automobile (Buy)	25, 26
Brewing	10, 11
Build (Start foundation)	no ideal dates
Business (Conducting for self and others)	9, 14, 23, 28
Business (Start new)	23
Can Fruits and Vegetables	10, 11
Can Preserves	10, 11
Concrete (Pour)	17
Construction (Begin new)	9, 13, 14, 21, 23, 26, 28
Consultants (Begin work with)	4, 7, 9, 12, 13, 17, 21, 25, 26
Contracts (Bid on)	21, 25, 26
Cultivate	17
Decorating	18, 25, 26, 27
Demolition	3, 4, 12, 13
Electronics (Buy)	7, 17, 25, 26
Entertain Guests	25
Floor Covering (Laying new)	4–9, 17
Habits (Break)	15, 16
Hair (Cut to increase growth)	2, 19, 22–26
Hair (Cut to decrease growth)	12–15
Harvest (Grain for storage)	4
Harvest (Root crops)	4, 12, 13, 14, 17
Investments (New)	9, 28
Loan (Ask for)	2, 3, 22, 23, 24
Massage (Relaxing)	no ideal dates
Mow Lawn (Decrease growth)	4–17
Mow Lawn (Increase growth)	1, 2, 19–28
Mushrooms (Pick)	2, 3, 4
Negotiate (Business for the elderly)	2, 7
Prune for Better Fruit	10–13
Prune to Promote Healing	15, 16
Wean Children	13–18
Wood Floors (Installing)	14, 15, 16
Write Letters or Contracts	3, 13, 17, 26

Activity	March
Animals (Neuter or spay)	12, 13, 14, 16, 18, 19
Animals (Sell or buy)	2, 25
Automobile (Buy)	14, 25
Brewing	10, 11, 19
Build (Start foundation)	no ideal dates
Business (Conducting for self and others)	11, 15, 24, 29
Business (Start new)	23
Can Fruits and Vegetables	10, 11, 19
Can Preserves	10, 11
Concrete (Pour)	17
Construction (Begin new)	8, 12, 15, 21, 24, 25, 29
Consultants (Begin work with)	2, 8, 12, 14, 18, 21, 23, 25, 28, 30
Contracts (Bid on)	2, 21, 23, 25, 28, 30
Cultivate	12, 13, 16, 17
Decorating	24, 25, 26
Demolition	11–14
Electronics (Buy)	8, 17, 25
Entertain Guests	22, 27
Floor Covering (Laying new)	6, 7, 8, 16, 17
Habits (Break)	14, 16
Hair (Cut to increase growth)	1, 22–25
Hair (Cut to decrease growth)	11–15, 19
Harvest (Grain for storage)	11, 12, 13
Harvest (Root crops)	11, 12, 13, 16, 17
Investments (New)	11, 29
Loan (Ask for)	1–4, 22, 23, 24, 29, 30, 31
Massage (Relaxing)	2, 22, 27
Mow Lawn (Decrease growth)	6–19
Mow Lawn (Increase growth)	1–4, 21–31
Mushrooms (Pick)	4, 5, 6
Negotiate (Business for the elderly)	16, 20, 29
Prune for Better Fruit	9–13
Prune to Promote Healing	14, 15, 16
Wean Children	12–17
Wood Floors (Installing)	14, 15, 16
Write Letters or Contracts	2, 12, 17, 18, 30

Activity	April
Animals (Neuter or spay)	8–12, 14, 15, 16
Animals (Sell or buy)	2, 21
Automobile (Buy)	22, 30
Brewing	6, 15, 16
Build (Start foundation)	25
Business (Conducting for self and others)	9, 14, 23, 28
Business (Start new)	19
Can Fruits and Vegetables	6, 15, 16
Can Preserves	6
Concrete (Pour)	13, 14
Construction (Begin new)	4, 9, 14, 17, 21, 23, 28
Consultants (Begin work with)	4, 9, 14, 17, 19, 21, 24, 26, 30
Contracts (Bid on)	19, 21, 24, 26, 30
Cultivate	8, 9, 13, 14, 17
Decorating	3, 4, 20, 21, 22, 30
Demolition	8, 9, 16, 17
Electronics (Buy)	13, 14, 22
Entertain Guests	21
Floor Covering (Laying new)	5, 12, 13
Habits (Break)	12, 14, 16, 17
Hair (Cut to increase growth)	19, 20, 21, 22, 25
Hair (Cut to decrease growth)	8–11, 15, 18
Harvest (Grain for storage)	8, 9, 10
Harvest (Root crops)	8, 9, 12, 13, 14, 16, 17
Investments (New)	9, 28
Loan (Ask for)	19, 20, 25, 26, 27
Massage (Relaxing)	12, 26
Mow Lawn (Decrease growth)	5–17
Mow Lawn (Increase growth)	1–3, 19–30
Mushrooms (Pick)	3, 4, 5
Negotiate (Business for the elderly)	3, 12, 16, 25, 30
Prune for Better Fruit	5–9
Prune to Promote Healing	10, 11, 12
Wean Children	8–14
Wood Floors (Installing)	10, 11, 12
Write Letters or Contracts	9, 13, 19, 22, 26

Activity	May
Animals (Neuter or spay)	5–9, 12
Animals (Sell or buy)	1, 2, 19, 29
Automobile (Buy)	19
Brewing	4, 12
Build (Start foundation)	no ideal dates
Business (Conducting for self and others)	8, 13, 22, 28
Business (Start new)	no ideal dates
Can Fruits and Vegetables	4, 12
Can Preserves	4, 16, 17
Concrete (Pour)	10, 11, 16
Construction (Begin new)	1, 6, 8, 15, 19, 22, 28, 29
Consultants (Begin work with)	1, 6, 10, 14, 15, 19, 23, 24, 28, 29
Contracts (Bid on)	1, 19, 23, 24, 28, 29
Cultivate	6, 7, 11, 14, 15
Decorating	1, 2, 18, 19, 27–30
Demolition	5, 6, 14, 15
Electronics (Buy)	10, 11, 19, 28
Entertain Guests	2, 16, 21
Floor Covering (Laying new)	9, 10, 16, 17
Habits (Break)	14, 15
Hair (Cut to increase growth)	18, 19, 22
Hair (Cut to decrease growth)	5–8, 12, 13, 14, 16, 17
Harvest (Grain for storage)	5, 6, 7, 9, 10
Harvest (Root crops)	5, 6, 7, 9, 10, 11, 14, 15
Investments (New)	8, 28
Loan (Ask for)	18, 22, 23, 24
Massage (Relaxing)	2, 16, 21
Mow Lawn (Decrease growth)	4–16
Mow Lawn (Increase growth)	1, 2, 19–31
Mushrooms (Pick)	2, 3, 4
Negotiate (Business for the elderly)	9, 22, 27
Prune for Better Fruit	3–7
Prune to Promote Healing	8, 9
Wean Children	5–11
Wood Floors (Installing)	7, 8, 9
Write Letters or Contracts	6, 11, 19, 24

Activity	June
Animals (Neuter or spay)	3, 4, 5, 8
Animals (Sell or buy)	1, 25, 30
Automobile (Buy)	14, 16, 24
Brewing	9
Build (Start foundation)	19
Business (Conducting for self and others)	7, 11, 21, 27
Business (Start new)	24
Can Fruits and Vegetables	9
Can Preserves	13
Concrete (Pour)	6, 7, 13
Construction (Begin new)	2, 7, 11, 15, 21, 25, 30
Consultants (Begin work with)	2, 6, 10, 11, 14, 15, 19, 20, 25, 30
Contracts (Bid on)	19, 20, 25, 30
Cultivate	3, 11, 15
Decorating	16, 24, 25, 26
Demolition	2, 10, 11
Electronics (Buy)	6, 7, 14, 16, 25
Entertain Guests	15, 20, 25
Floor Covering (Laying new)	6, 7, 12–16
Habits (Break)	10, 11, 14, 15
Hair (Cut to increase growth)	1, 2, 29, 30
Hair (Cut to decrease growth)	3, 4, 5, 9, 12–15
Harvest (Grain for storage)	3, 6, 7
Harvest (Root crops)	2, 3, 6, 7, 10, 11, 14, 15
Investments (New)	7, 27
Loan (Ask for)	19, 20, 21
Massage (Relaxing)	20, 25
Mow Lawn (Decrease growth)	3–15
Mow Lawn (Increase growth)	1, 17–30
Mushrooms (Pick)	1, 2, 3, 30
Negotiate (Business for the elderly)	no ideal dates
Prune for Better Fruit	2, 3
Prune to Promote Healing	4, 5
Wean Children	2–7, 29, 30
Wood Floors (Installing)	4, 5
Write Letters or Contracts	3, 7, 14, 16, 20, 30

Activity	July
Animals (Neuter or spay)	2, 5, 6, 7
Animals (Sell or buy)	28
Automobile (Buy)	3, 13, 20, 21, 30
Brewing	6, 7, 14
Build (Start foundation)	16
Business (Conducting for self and others)	6, 11, 21, 26
Business (Start new)	21, 30
Can Fruits and Vegetables	6, 14, 15
Can Preserves	10, 11, 14, 15
Concrete (Pour)	4, 10, 11
Construction (Begin new)	9, 11, 13, 21, 23, 26, 28
Consultants (Begin work with)	5, 9, 13, 15, 18, 20, 23, 26, 28
Contracts (Bid on)	18, 20, 23, 26, 28
Cultivate	9, 12, 13
Decorating	21, 22, 23, 30
Demolition	7, 8
Electronics (Buy)	4, 5, 13
Entertain Guests	13, 18
Floor Covering (Laying new)	3, 4, 9–13
Habits (Break)	9, 12, 13
Hair (Cut to increase growth)	1, 16, 26, 27, 28, 29
Hair (Cut to decrease growth)	2, 6, 9–13
Harvest (Grain for storage)	3, 4, 7, 8
Harvest (Root crops)	3, 4, 7, 8, 9, 12, 13, 31
Investments (New)	6, 26
Loan (Ask for)	16, 17, 18
Massage (Relaxing)	no ideal dates
Mow Lawn (Decrease growth)	2–14
Mow Lawn (Increase growth)	16–30
Mushrooms (Pick)	1, 2, 30, 31
Negotiate (Business for the elderly)	7, 30
Prune for Better Fruit	no ideal dates
Prune to Promote Healing	1, 2, 3
Wean Children	1–5, 27–31
Wood Floors (Installing)	1, 2, 3
Write Letters or Contracts	4, 13, 27

Activity	August
Animals (Neuter or spay)	2, 3, 30
Animals (Sell or buy)	19, 24, 25
Automobile (Buy)	9, 16, 17, 27
Brewing	2, 3, 11, 12, 30
Build (Start foundation)	22
Business (Conducting for self and others)	4, 9, 19, 25
Business (Start new)	17, 25, 27
Can Fruits and Vegetables	2, 3, 11, 12, 30
Can Preserves	6, 11, 12
Concrete (Pour)	1, 6, 13
Construction (Begin new)	4, 5, 9, 10, 19, 25
Consultants (Begin work with)	5, 10, 15, 16, 20, 22, 25, 27
Contracts (Bid on)	15, 16, 20, 22, 25, 27
Cultivate	8, 9, 13
Decorating	18, 19, 27, 28, 29
Demolition	4, 12, 13, 14, 31
Electronics (Buy)	1, 9, 28
Entertain Guests	10, 14, 19
Floor Covering (Laying new)	1, 6–9, 12, 13, 14
Habits (Break)	9, 10, 12, 13
Hair (Cut to increase growth)	22–26
Hair (Cut to decrease growth)	2, 5–9, 12, 30
Harvest (Grain for storage)	1, 3, 4, 5, 31
Harvest (Root crops)	1, 4, 5, 8, 9, 12, 13, 31
Investments (New)	4, 25
Loan (Ask for)	14, 15
Massage (Relaxing)	14, 19
Mow Lawn (Decrease growth)	1–13, 30, 31
Mow Lawn (Increase growth)	15–28
Mushrooms (Pick)	1, 28, 29, 30
Negotiate (Business for the elderly)	3, 12, 17
Prune for Better Fruit	no ideal dates
Prune to Promote Healing	no ideal dates
Wean Children	1, 23–29
Wood Floors (Installing)	no ideal dates
Write Letters or Contracts	1, 9, 14, 16, 28

Activity	September
Animals (Neuter or spay)	no ideal dates
Animals (Sell or buy)	15, 17, 20, 22
Automobile (Buy)	5, 13
Brewing	7, 8
Build (Start foundation)	18
Business (Conducting for self and others)	2, 7, 18, 23
Business (Start new)	13, 22
Can Fruits and Vegetables	7, 8
Can Preserves	3, 7, 8, 30
Concrete (Pour)	3, 9, 10, 30
Construction (Begin new)	2, 7, 22, 23, 30
Consultants (Begin work with)	2, 5, 7, 10, 11, 15, 17, 20, 22, 24, 30
Contracts (Bid on)	15, 17, 20, 22, 24
Cultivate	5, 6, 9–12
Decorating	14, 15, 16, 23, 24, 25
Demolition	1, 9, 10, 27, 28
Electronics (Buy)	5, 15, 24
Entertain Guests	5, 10, 15
Floor Covering (Laying new)	2–6, 9–13, 29, 30
Habits (Break)	6, 9, 10, 11
Hair (Cut to increase growth)	18–22, 26
Hair (Cut to decrease growth)	2–5, 8, 29, 30
Harvest (Grain for storage)	1, 4, 28
Harvest (Root crops)	1, 4, 5, 6, 9, 10, 28, 29
Investments (New)	2, 23
Loan (Ask for)	no ideal dates
Massage (Relaxing)	10, 15
Mow Lawn (Decrease growth)	1–11, 28–30
Mow Lawn (Increase growth)	14–26
Mushrooms (Pick)	26, 27, 28
Negotiate (Business for the elderly)	8, 13, 23, 27
Prune for Better Fruit	no ideal dates
Prune to Promote Healing	no ideal dates
Wean Children	19–25
Wood Floors (Installing)	no ideal dates
Write Letters or Contracts	5, 10, 15, 20, 24

Activity	October
Animals (Neuter or spay)	no ideal dates
Animals (Sell or buy)	14, 19
Automobile (Buy)	2, 3, 30
Brewing	4, 5
Build (Start foundation)	no ideal dates
Business (Conducting for self and others)	2, 7, 18, 23, 31
Business (Start new)	19
Can Fruits and Vegetables	4, 5
Can Preserves	1, 4, 5
Concrete (Pour)	1, 7, 8
Construction (Begin new)	2, 4, 7, 18, 19, 23, 28, 31
Consultants (Begin work with)	2, 4, 6, 9, 11, 14, 16, 19, 21, 28, 30
Contracts (Bid on)	14, 16, 19, 21
Cultivate	6–10
Decorating	12, 13, 20–23
Demolition	6, 7
Electronics (Buy)	2, 3, 11, 21, 22, 30
Entertain Guests	3, 8, 28
Floor Covering (Laying new)	1, 2, 6–12, 28, 29, 30
Habits (Break)	6, 7, 8
Hair (Cut to increase growth)	16–19, 23, 24, 25
Hair (Cut to decrease growth)	1, 2, 6, 28, 29, 30
Harvest (Grain for storage)	1, 2, 3, 29, 30
Harvest (Root crops)	1, 2, 3, 6, 7, 8, 29, 30
Investments (New)	2, 23, 31
Loan (Ask for)	no ideal dates
Massage (Relaxing)	28
Mow Lawn (Decrease growth)	1–11, 28–31
Mow Lawn (Increase growth)	13–26
Mushrooms (Pick)	26, 27, 28
Negotiate (Business for the elderly)	11
Prune for Better Fruit	no ideal dates
Prune to Promote Healing	no ideal dates
Wean Children	16–23
Wood Floors (Installing)	no ideal dates
Write Letters or Contracts	3, 7, 11, 17, 22, 30

Activity	November
Animals (Neuter or spay)	no ideal dates
Animals (Sell or buy)	12, 16, 17, 24
Automobile (Buy)	5, 16, 26
Brewing	10, 28, 29
Build (Start foundation)	17
Business (Conducting for self and others)	6, 16, 21, 30
Business (Start new)	16, 24
Can Fruits and Vegetables	10, 11, 28, 29
Can Preserves	10, 11, 28, 29
Concrete (Pour)	3, 4, 30
Construction (Begin new)	1, 6, 16, 24, 29, 30
Consultants (Begin work with)	1, 5, 6, 11, 16, 21, 24, 29
Contracts (Bid on)	13, 16, 21, 24
Cultivate	3–6
Decorating	17, 18, 19
Demolition	2, 3, 29, 30
Electronics (Buy)	18, 26
Entertain Guests	1, 7, 26
Floor Covering (Laying new)	2–9, 26, 27, 29, 30
Habits (Break)	4
Hair (Cut to increase growth)	12–16, 20, 23, 24, 25
Hair (Cut to decrease growth)	2, 26, 29
Harvest (Grain for storage)	2, 26, 29, 30
Harvest (Root crops)	2, 3, 4, 26, 27, 29, 30
Investments (New)	21, 30
Loan (Ask for)	23, 24, 25
Massage (Relaxing)	1, 17
Mow Lawn (Decrease growth)	2–10, 26–30
Mow Lawn (Increase growth)	12–24
Mushrooms (Pick)	24, 25, 26
Negotiate (Business for the elderly)	2, 7, 17, 21, 30
Prune for Better Fruit	10, 11
Prune to Promote Healing	no ideal dates
Wean Children	13–19
Wood Floors (Installing)	no ideal dates
Write Letters or Contracts	3, 11, 13, 18, 26

Activity	December
Animals (Neuter or spay)	9, 10
Animals (Sell or buy)	12, 17, 22
Automobile (Buy)	12, 24
Brewing	8, 9, 26
Build (Start foundation)	15
Business (Conducting for self and others)	5, 16, 20, 30
Business (Start new)	13, 22
Can Fruits and Vegetables	8, 9, 26
Can Preserves	8, 9, 26
Concrete (Pour)	1, 28
Construction (Begin new)	5, 13, 16, 20, 22, 26, 30
Consultants (Begin work with)	1, 3, 6, 9, 12, 13, 17, 22, 26, 31
Contracts (Bid on)	12, 13, 17, 22
Cultivate	3, 4
Decorating	14, 15, 16, 22, 23, 24
Demolition	1, 9, 10, 11, 27, 28
Electronics (Buy)	6, 15, 24
Entertain Guests	1
Floor Covering (Laying new)	1–6, 27–31
Habits (Break)	no ideal dates
Hair (Cut to increase growth)	11, 12, 13, 17, 20–24
Hair (Cut to decrease growth)	9, 10, 27
Harvest (Grain for storage)	1, 2, 27, 28, 29
Harvest (Root crops)	1, 9, 10, 27, 28, 29
Investments (New)	20, 30
Loan (Ask for)	20, 21, 22
Massage (Relaxing)	1, 26
Mow Lawn (Decrease growth)	1–10, 26–31
Mow Lawn (Increase growth)	12–24
Mushrooms (Pick)	24, 25, 26
Negotiate (Business for the elderly)	5, 19
Prune for Better Fruit	7–10
Prune to Promote Healing	no ideal dates
Wean Children	10–16
Wood Floors (Installing)	no ideal dates
Write Letters or Contracts	1, 11, 12, 15, 24, 28

Choose the Best Time for Your Activities

When rules for elections refer to "favorable" and "unfavorable" aspects to your Sun or other planets, please refer to the Favorable and Unfavorable Days Tables and Lunar Aspectarian for more information. You'll find instructions beginning on page 129 and the tables beginning on page 136.

The material in this section came from several sources including: *The New A to Z Horoscope Maker and Delineator* by Llewellyn George (Llewellyn, 1999), *Moon Sign Book* (Llewellyn, 1945), and *Electional Astrology* by Vivian Robson (Slingshot Publishing, 2000). Robson's book was originally published in 1937.

Advertise (Internet)

The Moon should be conjunct, sextile, or trine Mercury or Uranus and in the sign of Gemini, Capricorn, or Aquarius.

Advertise (Print)

Write ads on a day favorable to your Sun. The Moon should be conjunct, sextile, or trine Mercury or Venus. Avoid hard aspects to Mars and Saturn. Ad campaigns produce the best results when the Moon is well aspected in Gemini (to enhance communication) or Capricorn (to build business).

Animals

Take home new pets when the day is favorable to your Sun, or when the Moon is trine, sextile, or conjunct Mercury, Venus, or Jupiter, or in the sign of Virgo or Pisces. However, avoid days when the Moon is either square or opposing the Sun, Mars, Saturn, Uranus, Neptune, or Pluto. When selecting a pet, have the Moon well aspected by the planet that rules the animal. Cats are ruled by the Sun, dogs by Mercury, birds by Venus, horses by Jupiter, and fish by Neptune. Buy large animals when the Moon is in Sagittarius or Pisces and making favorable aspects to Jupiter or Mercury. Buy animals smaller than sheep when the Moon is in Virgo with favorable aspects to Mercury or Venus.

Animals (Breed)

Animals are easiest to handle when the Moon is in Taurus, Cancer, Libra, or Pisces, but try to avoid the Full Moon. To encourage healthy births, animals should be mated so births occur when the Moon is increasing in Taurus, Cancer, Pisces, or Libra. Those born during a semi-fruitful sign (Taurus and Capricorn) will produce leaner meat. Libra yields beautiful animals for showing and racing.

Animals (Declaw)

Declaw cats for medical purposes in the dark of the Moon. Avoid the week before and after the Full Moon and the sign of Pisces.

Animals (Neuter or spay)

Have livestock and pets neutered or spayed when the Moon is in Sagittarius, Capricorn, or Pisces, after it has passed through Scorpio, the sign that rules reproductive organs. Avoid the week before and after the Full Moon.

Animals (Sell or buy)

In either buying or selling, it is important to keep the Moon and Mercury free from any aspect to Mars. Aspects to Mars will create discord and increase the likelihood of wrangling over price and quality. The Moon should be passing from the first quarter to full and sextile or trine Venus or Jupiter. When buying racehorses, let the Moon be in an air sign. The Moon should be in air signs when you buy birds. If the birds are to be pets, let the Moon be in good aspect to Venus.

Animals (Train)

Train pets when the Moon is in Virgo or trine to Mercury.

Animals (Train dogs to hunt)

Let the Moon be in Aries in conjunction with Mars, which makes them courageous and quick to learn. But let Jupiter also be in aspect to preserve them from danger in hunting.

Automobiles

When buying an automobile, select a time when the Moon is conjunct, sextile, or trine to Mercury, Saturn, or Uranus and in the sign of Gemini or Capricorn. Avoid times when Mercury is in retrograde motion.

Baking Cakes

Your cakes will have a lighter texture if you see that the Moon is in Gemini, Libra, or Aquarius and in good aspect to Venus or Mercury. If you are decorating a cake or confections are being made, have the Moon placed in Libra.

Beauty Treatments (Massage, etc.)

See that the Moon is in Taurus, Cancer, Leo, Libra, or Aquarius and in favorable aspect to Venus. In the case of plastic surgery, aspects to Mars should be avoided, and the Moon should not be in the sign ruling the part to be operated on.

Borrow (Money or goods)

See that the Moon is not placed between 15 degrees Libra and 15 degrees Scorpio. Let the Moon be waning and in Leo, Scorpio (16 to 30 degrees), Sagittarius, or Pisces. Venus should be in good aspect to the Moon, and the Moon should not be square, opposing, or conjunct either Saturn or Mars.

Brewing

Start brewing during the third or fourth quarter, when the Moon is in Cancer, Scorpio, or Pisces.

Build (Start foundation)

Turning the first sod for the foundation marks the beginning of the building. For best results, excavate the site when the Moon is in the first quarter of a fixed sign and making favorable aspects to Saturn.

Business (Start new)

When starting a business, have the Moon be in Taurus, Virgo, or Capricorn and increasing. The Moon should be sextile or trine Jupiter or Saturn, but avoid oppositions or squares. The planet ruling the business should be well aspected, too.

Buy Goods

Buy during the third quarter, when the Moon is in Taurus for quality or in a mutable sign (Gemini, Sagittarius, Virgo, or Pisces) for savings. Good aspects to Venus or the Sun are desirable. If you are buying for yourself, it is good if the day is favorable for your Sun sign. You may also apply rules for buying specific items.

Canning

Can fruits and vegetables when the Moon is in either the third or fourth quarter and in the water sign Cancer or Pisces. Preserves and jellies use the same quarters and the signs Cancer, Pisces, or Taurus.

Clothing

Buy clothing on a day that is favorable for your Sun sign and when Venus or Mercury is well aspected. Avoid aspects to Mars and Saturn. Buy your clothing when the Moon is in Taurus if you want to remain satisfied. Do not buy clothing or jewelry when the Moon is in Scorpio or Aries. See that the Moon is sextile or trine the Sun during the first or second quarters.

Collections

Try to make collections on days when your natal Sun is well aspected. Avoid days when the Moon is opposing or square Mars or Saturn. If possible, the Moon should be in a cardinal sign (Aries, Cancer, Libra, or Capricorn). It is more difficult to collect when the Moon is in Taurus or Scorpio.

Concrete

Pour concrete when the Moon is in the third quarter of the fixed sign Taurus, Leo, or Aquarius.

Construction (Begin new)

The Moon should be sextile or trine Jupiter. According to Hermes, no building should be begun when the Moon is in Scorpio or Pisces. The best time to begin building is when the Moon is in Aquarius.

Consultants (Work with)

The Moon should be conjunct, sextile, or trine Mercury or Jupiter.

Contracts (Bid on)

The Moon should be in Gemini or Capricorn and either the Moon or Mercury should be conjunct, sextile, or trine Jupiter.

Copyrights/Patents

The Moon should be conjunct, trine, or sextile either Mercury or Jupiter.

Coronations and Installations

Let the Moon be in Leo and in favorable aspect to Venus, Jupiter, or Mercury. The Moon should be applying to these planets.

Cultivate

Cultivate when the Moon is in a barren sign and waning, ideally the fourth quarter in Aries, Gemini, Leo, Virgo, or Aquarius. The third quarter in the sign of Sagittarius will also work.

Cut Timber

Timber cut during the waning Moon does not become worm-eaten; it will season well and not warp, decay, or snap during burning. Cut when the Moon is in Taurus, Gemini, Virgo, or Capricorn—especially in August. Avoid the water signs. Look for favorable aspects to Mars.

Decorating or Home Repairs

Have the Moon waxing and in the sign of Libra, Gemini, or Aquarius. Avoid squares or oppositions to either Mars or Saturn. Venus in good aspect to Mars or Saturn is beneficial.

Demolition

Let the waning Moon be in Leo, Sagittarius, or Aries.

Dental and Dentists

Visit the dentist when the Moon is in Virgo, or pick a day marked favorable for your Sun sign. Mars should be marked

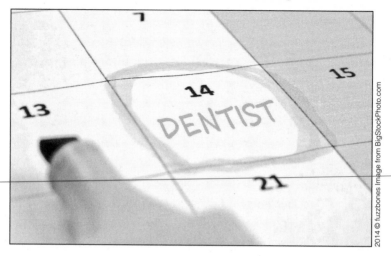

sextile, conjunct, or trine; avoid squares or oppositions to Saturn, Uranus, or Jupiter.

Teeth are best removed when the Moon is in Gemini, Virgo, Sagittarius, or Pisces and during the first or second quarter. Avoid the Full Moon! The day should be favorable for your lunar cycle, and Mars and Saturn should be marked conjunct, trine, or sextile. Fillings should be done in the third or fourth quarters in the sign of Taurus, Leo, Scorpio, or Pisces. The same applies for dentures.

Dressmaking

William Lilly wrote in 1676: "Make no new clothes, or first put them on when the Moon is in Scorpio or afflicted by Mars, for they will be apt to be torn and quickly worn out." Design, repair, and sew clothes in the first and second quarters of Taurus, Leo, or Libra on a day marked favorable for your Sun sign. Venus, Jupiter, and Mercury should be favorably aspected, but avoid hard aspects to Mars or Saturn.

Egg-setting (see p. 161)

Eggs should be set so chicks will hatch during fruitful signs. To set eggs, subtract the number of days given for incubation or gestation from the fruitful dates. Chickens incubate in twenty-one days, turkeys and geese in twenty-eight days.

A freshly laid egg loses quality rapidly if it is not handled properly. Use plenty of clean litter in the nests to reduce the number of dirty or cracked eggs. Gather eggs daily in mild weather and at least two times daily in hot or cold weather. The eggs should be placed in a cooler immediately after gathering and stored at 50 to 55° F. Do not store eggs with foods or products that give off pungent odors since eggs may absorb the odors.

Eggs saved for hatching purposes should not be washed. Only clean and slightly soiled eggs should be saved for hatching. Dirty eggs should not be incubated. Eggs should be stored in a cool place with the large ends up. It is not advisable to store the eggs longer than one week before setting them in an incubator.

Electricity and Gas (Install)

The Moon should be in a fire sign, and there should be no squares, oppositions, or conjunctions with Uranus (ruler of electricity), Neptune (ruler of gas), Saturn, or Mars. Hard aspects to Mars can cause fires.

Electronics (Buying)

Choose a day when the Moon is in an air sign (Gemini, Libra, Aquarius) and well aspected by Mercury and/or Uranus when buying electronics.

Electronics (Repair)

The Moon should be sextile or trine Mars or Uranus and in a fixed sign (Taurus, Leo, Scorpio, Aquarius).

Entertain Friends

Let the Moon be in Leo or Libra and making good aspects to Venus. Avoid squares or oppositions to either Mars or Saturn by the Moon or Venus.

Eyes and Eyeglasses

Have your eyes tested and glasses fitted on a day marked favorable for your Sun sign, and on a day that falls during your favorable lunar cycle. Mars should not be in aspect with the Moon. The same applies for any treatment of the eyes, which should also be started during the Moon's first or second quarter.

Fence Posts

Set posts when the Moon is in the third or fourth quarter of the fixed sign Taurus or Leo.

Fertilize and Compost

Fertilize when the Moon is in a fruitful sign (Cancer, Scorpio, Pisces). Organic fertilizers are best when the Moon is waning. Use chemical fertilizers when the Moon is waxing. Start compost when the Moon is in the fourth quarter in a water sign.

Find Hidden Treasure

Let the Moon be in good aspect to Jupiter or Venus. If you erect a horoscope for this election, place the Moon in the Fourth House.

Find Lost Articles

Search for lost articles during the first quarter and when your Sun sign is marked favorable. Also check to see that the planet ruling the lost item is trine, sextile, or conjunct the Moon. The Moon rules household utensils; Mercury rules letters and books; and Venus rules clothing, jewelry, and money.

Fishing

During the summer months, the best time of the day to fish is from sunrise to three hours after and from two hours before sunset until one hour after. Fish do not bite in cooler months until the air is warm, from noon to 3 pm. Warm, cloudy days are good. The most favorable winds are from the south and southwest. Easterly winds are unfavorable. The best days of the month for fishing are when the Moon changes quarters, especially if the change occurs on a day when the Moon is in a water sign (Cancer, Scorpio, Pisces). The best period in any month is the day after the Full Moon.

Friendship

The need for friendship is greater when the Moon is in Aquarius or when Uranus aspects the Moon. Friendship prospers when Venus or Uranus is trine, sextile, or conjunct the Moon. The Moon in Gemini facilitates the chance meeting of acquaintances and friends.

Grafting or Budding

Grafting is the process of introducing new varieties of fruit on less desirable trees. For this process you should use the increasing phase of the Moon in fruitful signs such as Cancer, Scorpio, or Pisces. Capricorn may be used, too. Cut your grafts while trees are dormant, from December to March. Keep them in a cool, dark place, not too dry or too damp. Do the grafting before the sap starts to flow and while the Moon is waxing, preferably while it is in Cancer, Scorpio, or Pisces. The type of plant should determine both cutting and planting times.

Habit (Breaking)

To end an undesirable habit, and this applies to ending everything from a bad relationship to smoking, start on a day when the Moon is in the fourth quarter and in the barren sign of Gemini, Leo, or

Aquarius. Aries, Virgo, and Capricorn may be suitable as well, depending on the habit you want to be rid of. Make sure that your lunar cycle is favorable. Avoid lunar aspects to Mars or Jupiter. However, favorable aspects to Pluto are helpful.

Haircuts

Cut hair when the Moon is in Gemini, Sagittarius, Pisces, Taurus, or Capricorn, but not in Virgo. Look for favorable aspects to Venus. For faster growth, cut hair when the Moon is increasing in Cancer or Pisces. To make hair grow thicker, cut when the Moon is full in the signs of Taurus, Cancer, or Leo. If you want your hair to grow more slowly, have the Moon be decreasing in Aries, Gemini, or Virgo, and have the Moon square or opposing Saturn.

Permanents, straightening, and hair coloring will take well if the Moon is in Taurus or Leo and trine or sextile Venus. Avoid hair treatments if Mars is marked as square or in opposition, especially if heat is to be used. For permanents, a trine to Jupiter is helpful. The Moon also should be in the first quarter. Check the lunar cycle for a favorable day in relation to your Sun sign.

Harvest Crops

Harvest root crops when the Moon is in a dry sign (Aries, Leo, Sagittarius, Gemini, Aquarius) and waning. Harvest grain for storage just after the Full Moon, avoiding Cancer, Scorpio, or Pisces. Harvest in the third and fourth quarters in dry signs. Dry crops in the third quarter in fire signs.

Health

A diagnosis is more likely to be successful when the Moon is in Aries, Cancer, Libra, or Capricorn and less so when in Gemini, Sagittarius, Pisces, or Virgo. Begin a recuperation program or enter a hospital when the Moon is in a cardinal or fixed sign and the day is favorable to your Sun sign. For surgery, see "Surgical Procedures." Buy medicines when the Moon is in Virgo or Scorpio.

Home (Buy new)

If you desire a permanent home, buy when the New Moon is in a fixed sign—Taurus or Leo, for example. Each sign will affect your decision in a different way. A house bought when the Moon is in Taurus is likely to be more practical and have a country look—right down to the split-rail fence. A house purchased when the Moon is in Leo will more likely be a real showplace.

If you're buying for speculation and a quick turnover, be certain that the Moon is in a cardinal sign (Aries, Cancer, Libra, Capricorn). Avoid buying when the Moon is in a fixed sign (Leo, Scorpio, Aquarius, Taurus).

Home (Make repairs)

In all repairs, avoid squares, oppositions, or conjunctions to the planet ruling the place or thing to be repaired. For example, bathrooms are ruled by Scorpio and Cancer. You would not want to start a project in those rooms when the Moon or Pluto is receiving hard aspects. The front entrance, hall, dining room, and porch are ruled by the Sun. So you would want to avoid times when Saturn or Mars are square, opposing, or conjunct the Sun. Also, let the Moon be waxing.

Home (Sell)

Make a strong effort to list your property for sale when the Sun is marked favorable in your sign and in good aspect to Jupiter. Avoid adverse aspects to as many planets as possible.

Home Furnishings (Buy new)

Saturn days (Saturday) are good for buying, and Jupiter days (Thursday) are good for selling. Items bought on days when Saturn is well aspected tend to wear longer and purchases tend to be more conservative.

Job (Start new)

Jupiter and Venus should be sextile, trine, or conjunct the Moon. A day when your Sun is receiving favorable aspects is preferred.

Legal Matters

Good Moon-Jupiter aspects improve the outcome in legal decisions. To gain damages through a lawsuit, begin the process during the increasing Moon. To avoid paying damages, a court date during the decreasing Moon is desirable. Good Moon-Sun aspects strengthen your chance of success. A well-aspected Moon in Cancer or Leo, making good aspects to the Sun, brings the best results in custody cases. In divorce cases, a favorable Moon-Venus aspect is best.

Loan (Ask for)

A first and second quarter phase favors the lender, the third and fourth quarters favor the borrower. Good aspects of Jupiter and

Venus to the Moon are favorable to both, as is having the Moon in Leo or Taurus.

Machinery, Appliances, or Tools (Buy)

Tools, machinery, and other implements should be bought on days when your lunar cycle is favorable and when Mars and Uranus are trine, sextile, or conjunct the Moon. Any quarter of the Moon is suitable. When buying gas or electrical appliances, the Moon should be in Aquarius.

Make a Will

Let the Moon be in a fixed sign (Taurus, Leo, Scorpio, or Aquarius) to ensure permanence. If the Moon is in a cardinal sign (Aries, Cancer, Libra, or Capricorn), the will could be altered. Let the Moon be waxing—increasing in light—and in good aspect to Saturn, Venus, or Mercury. In case the will is made in an emergency during illness and the Moon is slow in motion, void-of-course, combust, or under the Sun's beams, the testator will die and the will remain unaltered. There is some danger that it will be lost or stolen, however.

Marriage

The best time for marriage to take place is when the Moon is increasing, but not yet full. Good signs for the Moon to be in are Taurus, Cancer, Leo, or Libra.

The Moon in Taurus produces the most steadfast marriages, but if the partners later want to separate, they may have a difficult time. Make sure that the Moon is well aspected, especially to Venus or Jupiter. Avoid aspects to Mars, Uranus, or Pluto and the signs Aries, Gemini, Virgo, Scorpio, or Aquarius.

The values of the signs are as follows:

- Aries is not favored for marriage
- Taurus from 0 to 19 degrees is good, the remaining degrees are less favorable

- Cancer is unfavorable unless you are marrying a widow
- Leo is favored, but it may cause one party to deceive the other as to his or her money or possessions
- Virgo is not favored except when marrying a widow
- Libra is good for engagements but not for marriage
- Scorpio from 0 to 15 degrees is good, but the last 15 degrees are entirely unfortunate. The woman may be fickle, envious, and quarrelsome
- Sagittarius is neutral
- Capricorn, from 0 to 10 degrees, is difficult for marriage; however, the remaining degrees are favorable, especially when marrying a widow
- Aquarius is not favored
- Pisces is favored, although marriage under this sign can incline a woman to chatter a lot

These effects are strongest when the Moon is in the sign. If the Moon and Venus are in a cardinal sign, happiness between the couple may not continue long.

On no account should the Moon apply to Saturn or Mars, even by good aspect.

Medical Treatment for the Eyes

Let the Moon be increasing in light and motion and making favorable aspects to Venus or Jupiter and be unaspected by Mars. Keep the Moon out of Taurus, Capricorn, or Virgo. If an aspect between the Moon and Mars is unavoidable, let it be separating.

Medical Treatment for the Head

If possible, have Mars and Saturn free of hard aspects. Let the Moon be in Aries or Taurus, decreasing in light, in conjunction or aspect with Venus or Jupiter and free of hard aspects. The Sun should not be in any aspect to the Moon.

Medical Treatment for the Nose

Let the Moon be in Cancer, Leo, or Virgo and not aspecting Mars or Saturn and also not in conjunction with a retrograde or weak planet.

Mining

Saturn rules mining. Begin work when Saturn is marked conjunct, trine, or sextile. Mine for gold when the Sun is marked conjunct, trine, or sextile. Mercury rules quicksilver, Venus rules copper, Jupiter rules tin, Saturn rules lead and coal, Uranus rules radioactive elements, Neptune rules oil, the Moon rules water. Mine for these items when the ruling planet is marked conjunct, trine, or sextile.

Move to New Home

If you have a choice, and sometimes you don't, make sure that Mars is not aspecting the Moon. Move on a day favorable to your Sun sign or when the Moon is conjunct, sextile, or trine the Sun.

Mow Lawn

Mow in the first and second quarters (waxing phase) to increase growth and lushness, and in the third and fourth quarters (waning phase) to decrease growth.

Negotiate

When you are choosing a time to negotiate, consider what the meeting is about and what you want to have happen. If it is agreement or compromise between two parties that you desire, have the Moon be in the sign of Libra. When you are making contracts, it is best to have the Moon in the same element. For example, if your concern is communication, then elect a time when the Moon is in an air sign. If, on the other hand, your concern is about possessions, an earth sign would be more appropriate.

Fixed signs are unfavorable, with the exception of Leo; so are cardinal signs, except for Capricorn. If you are negotiating the end of something, use the rules that apply to ending habits.

Occupational Training

When you begin training, see that your lunar cycle is favorable that day and that the planet ruling your occupation is marked conjunct or trine.

Paint

Paint buildings during the waning Libra or Aquarius Moon. If the weather is hot, paint when the Moon is in Taurus. If the weather is cold, paint when the Moon is in Leo. Schedule the painting to start in the fourth quarter as the wood is drier and paint will penetrate wood better. Avoid painting around the New Moon, though, as the wood is likely to be damp, making the paint subject to scalding when hot weather hits it. If the temperature is below 70° F, it is not advisable to paint while the Moon is in Cancer, Scorpio, or Pisces as the paint is apt to creep, check, or run.

Party (Host or attend)

A party timed so the Moon is in Gemini, Leo, Libra, or Sagittarius, with good aspects to Venus and Jupiter, will be fun and well attended. There should be no aspects between the Moon and Mars or Saturn.

Pawn

Do not pawn any article when Jupiter is receiving a square or opposition from Saturn or Mars or when Jupiter is within 17 degrees of the Sun, for you will have little chance to redeem the items.

Pick Mushrooms

Mushrooms, one of the most promising traditional medicines in the world, should be gathered at the Full Moon.

Plant

Root crops, like carrots and potatoes, are best if planted in the sign Taurus or Capricorn. Beans, peas, tomatoes, peppers, and other fruit-bearing plants are best if planted in a sign that supports seed growth. Leaf plants, like lettuce, broccoli, or cauliflower, are best planted when the Moon is in a water sign.

It is recommended that you transplant during a decreasing Moon, when forces are streaming into the lower part of the plant. This helps root growth.

Promotion (Ask for)

Choose a day favorable to your Sun sign. Mercury should be marked conjunct, trine, or sextile. Avoid days when Mars or Saturn is aspected.

Prune

Prune during the third and fourth quarter of a Scorpio Moon to retard growth and to promote better fruit. Prune when the Moon is in cardinal Capricorn to promote healing.

Reconcile with People

If the reconciliation is with a woman, let Venus be strong and well aspected. If elders or superiors are involved, see that Saturn is receiving good aspects; if the reconciliation is between young people or between an older and younger person, see that Mercury is well aspected.

Romance

There is less control of when a romance starts, but romances begun under an increasing Moon are more likely to be permanent or satisfying, while those begun during the decreasing Moon tend to transform the participants. The tone of the relationship can be guessed from the sign the Moon is in. Romances begun with the Moon in Aries may be impulsive. Those begun in Capricorn will

2014 © soupstock Image from BigStockPhoto.com

take greater effort to bring to a desirable conclusion, but they may be very rewarding. Good aspects between the Moon and Venus will have a positive influence on the relationship. Avoid unfavorable aspects to Mars, Uranus, and Pluto. A decreasing Moon, particularly the fourth quarter, facilitates ending a relationship and causes the least pain.

Roof a Building
Begin roofing a building during the third or fourth quarter, when the Moon is in Aries or Aquarius. Shingles laid during the New Moon have a tendency to curl at the edges.

Sauerkraut
The best-tasting sauerkraut is made just after the Full Moon in the fruitful signs of Cancer, Scorpio, or Pisces.

Select a Child's Sex
Count from the last day of menstruation to the first day of the next cycle and divide the interval between the two dates in half.

Pregnancy in the first half produces females, but copulation should take place with the Moon in a feminine sign. Pregnancy in the latter half, up to three days before the beginning of menstruation, produces males, but copulation should take place with the Moon in a masculine sign. The three-day period before the next period again produces females.

Sell or Canvass

Begin these activities during a day favorable to your Sun sign. Otherwise, sell on days when Jupiter, Mercury, or Mars is trine, sextile, or conjunct the Moon. Avoid days when Saturn is square or opposing the Moon, for that always hinders business and causes discord. If the Moon is passing from the first quarter to full, it is best to have the Moon swift in motion and in good aspect with Venus and/or Jupiter.

Sign Papers

Sign contracts or agreements when the Moon is increasing in a fruitful sign and on a day when the Moon is making favorable aspects to Mercury. Avoid days when Mars, Saturn, or Neptune are square or opposite the Moon.

Spray and Weed

Spray pests and weeds during the fourth quarter when the Moon is in the barren sign Leo or Aquarius and making favorable aspects to Pluto. Weed during a waning Moon in a barren sign.

Staff (Fire)

Have the Moon in the third or fourth quarter, but not full. The Moon should not be square any planets.

Staff (Hire)

The Moon should be in the first or second quarter, and preferably in the sign of Gemini or Virgo. The Moon should be conjunct, trine, or sextile Mercury or Jupiter.

Stocks (Buy)

The Moon should be in Taurus or Capricorn, and there should be a sextile or trine to Jupiter or Saturn.

Surgical Procedures

Blood flow, like ocean tides, appears to be related to Moon phases. To reduce hemorrhage after a surgery, schedule it within one week before or after a New Moon. Schedule surgery to occur during the increase of the Moon if possible, as wounds heal better and vitality is greater than during the decrease of the Moon. Avoid surgery within one week before or after the Full Moon. Select a date when the Moon is past the sign governing the part of the body involved in the operation. For example, abdominal operations should be done when the Moon is in Sagittarius, Capricorn, or Aquarius. The further removed the Moon sign is from the sign ruling the afflicted part of the body, the better.

For successful operations, avoid times when the Moon is applying to any aspect of Mars. (This tends to promote inflammation and complications.) See the Lunar Aspectarian on odd pages 137–159 to find days with negative Mars aspects and positive Venus and Jupiter aspects. Never operate with the Moon in the same sign as a person's Sun sign or Ascendant. Let the Moon be in a fixed sign and avoid square or opposing aspects. The Moon should not be void-of-course. Cosmetic surgery should be done in the increase of the Moon, when the Moon is not square or in opposition to Mars. Avoid days when the Moon is square or opposing Saturn or the Sun.

Travel (Air)

Start long trips when the Moon is making favorable aspects to the Sun. For enjoyment, aspects to Jupiter are preferable; for visiting, look for favorable aspects to Mercury. To prevent accidents, avoid squares or oppositions to Mars, Saturn, Uranus, or

Pluto. Choose a day when the Moon is in Sagittarius or Gemini and well aspected to Mercury, Jupiter, or Uranus. Avoid adverse aspects of Mars, Saturn, or Uranus.

Visit

On setting out to visit a person, let the Moon be in aspect with any retrograde planet, for this ensures that the person you're visiting will be at home. If you desire to stay a long time in a place, let the Moon be in good aspect to Saturn. If you desire to leave the place quickly, let the Moon be in a cardinal sign.

Wean Children

To wean a child successfully, do so when the Moon is in Sagittarius, Capricorn, Aquarius, or Pisces—signs that do not rule vital human organs. By observing this astrological rule, much trouble for parents and child may be avoided.

Weight (Reduce)

If you want to lose weight, the best time to get started is when the Moon is in the third or fourth quarter and in the barren sign of Virgo. Review the section on How to Use the Moon Tables and Lunar Aspectarian beginning on page 136 to help you select a date that is favorable to begin your weight-loss program.

Wine and Drink Other Than Beer

Start brewing when the Moon is in Pisces or Taurus. Sextiles or trines to Venus are favorable, but avoid aspects to Mars or Saturn.

Write

Write for pleasure or publication when the Moon is in Gemini. Mercury should be making favorable aspects to Uranus and Neptune.

How to Use the Moon Tables and Lunar Aspectarian

Timing activities is one of the most important things you can do to ensure success. In many Eastern countries, timing by the planets is so important that practically no event takes place without first setting up a chart for it. Weddings have occurred in the middle of the night because the influences were best then. You may not want to take it that far, but you can still make use of the influences of the Moon whenever possible. It's easy and it works!

Llewellyn's Moon Sign Book has information to help you plan just about any activity: weddings, fishing, making purchases, cutting your hair, traveling, and more. We provide the guidelines you need to pick the best day out of the several from which you have to choose. The Moon Tables are the *Moon Sign Book's* primary method for choosing dates. Following are instructions, examples, and directions on how to read the Moon Tables. More advanced information on using the tables containing the Lunar Aspectarian and favorable and unfavorable days (found on odd-numbered pages opposite the Moon Tables), Moon void-of-course and retrograde information to choose the dates best for you is also included.

The Five Basic Steps

Step 1: Directions for Choosing Dates

Look up the directions for choosing dates for the activity that you wish to begin, then go to step 2.

Step 2: Check the Moon Tables

You'll find two tables for each month of the year beginning on page 136. The Moon Tables (on the left-hand pages) include the day, date, and sign the Moon is in; the element and nature of the sign; the Moon's phase; and when it changes sign or phase. If there is a time listed after a date, that time is the time when the Moon moves into that zodiac sign. Until then, the Moon is considered to be in the sign for the previous day.

The abbreviation Full signifies Full Moon and New signifies New Moon. The times listed with dates indicate when the Moon changes sign. The times listed after the phase indicate when the Moon changes phase.

Turn to the month you would like to begin your activity. You will be using the Moon's sign and phase information most often when you begin choosing your own dates. Use the Time Zone Map on page 164 and the Time Zone Conversions table on page 165 to convert time to your own time zone.

When you find dates that meet the criteria for the correct Moon phase and sign for your activity, you may have completed the process. For certain simple activities, such as getting a haircut, the phase and sign information is all that is needed. If the directions for your activity include information on certain lunar aspects, however, you should consult the Lunar Aspectarian. An example of this would be if the directions told you not to perform a certain activity when the Moon is square (Q) Jupiter.

Step 3: Check the Lunar Aspectarian

On the pages opposite the Moon Tables you will find tables containing the Lunar Aspectarian and Favorable and Unfavorable Days. The Lunar Aspectarian gives the aspects (or angles) of the Moon to other planets. Some aspects are favorable, while others are not. To use the Lunar Aspectarian, find the planet that the directions list as favorable for your activity, and run down the column to the date desired. For example, you should avoid aspects to Mars if you are planning surgery. So you would look for Mars across the top and then run down that column looking for days where there are no aspects to Mars (as signified by empty boxes). If you want to find a *favorable* aspect (sextile (X) or trine (T)) to Mercury, run your finger down the column under Mercury until you find an X or T. *Adverse* aspects to planets are squares (Q) or oppositions (O). A conjunction (C) is sometimes beneficial, sometimes not, depending on the activity or planets involved.

Step 4: Favorable and Unfavorable Days

The tables listing favorable and unfavorable days are helpful when you want to choose your personal best dates because your Sun sign is taken into consideration. The twelve Sun signs are listed on the right side of the tables. Once you have determined which days meet your criteria for phase, sign, and aspects, you can determine whether or not those days are positive for you by checking the favorable and unfavorable days for your Sun sign.

To find out if a day is positive for you, find your Sun sign and then look down the column. If it is marked F, it is very favorable. The Moon is in the same sign as your Sun on a favorable day. If it is marked f, it is slightly favorable; U is very unfavorable; and u means slightly unfavorable. A day marked very unfavorable (U) indicates that the Moon is in the sign opposing your Sun.

Once you have selected good dates for the activity you are about to begin, you can go straight to "Using What You've Learned," beginning on the next page. To learn how to fine-tune your selections even further, read on.

Step 5: Void-of-Course Moon and Retrogrades

This last step is perhaps the most advanced portion of the procedure. It is generally considered poor timing to make decisions, sign important papers, or start special activities during a Moon void-of-course period or during a Mercury retrograde. Once you have chosen the best date for your activity based on steps one through four, you can check the Void-of-Course tables, beginning on page 76, to find out if any of the dates you have chosen have void periods.

The Moon is said to be void-of-course after it has made its last aspect to a planet within a particular sign, but before it has moved into the next sign. Put simply, the Moon is "resting" during the void-of-course period, so activities initiated at this time generally don't come to fruition. You will notice that there are many void periods during the year, and it is nearly impossible to avoid all of them. Some people choose to ignore these altogether and do not take them into consideration when planning activities.

Next, you can check the Retrograde Planets tables on page 160 to see what planets are retrograde during your chosen date(s).

A planet is said to be retrograde when it appears to move backward in the sky as viewed from the Earth. Generally, the farther a planet is away from the Sun, the longer it can stay retrograde. Some planets will retrograde for several months at a time. Avoiding retrogrades is not as important in lunar planning as avoiding the Moon void-of-course, with the exception of the planet Mercury.

Mercury rules thought and communication, so it is advisable not to sign important papers, initiate important business or legal work, or make crucial decisions during these times. As with the Moon void-of-course, it is difficult to avoid all planetary retrogrades when beginning events, and you may choose to ignore this step of the process. Following are some examples using some or all of the steps outlined above.

Using What You've Learned

Let's say it's a new year and you want to have your hair cut. It's thin and you would like it to look fuller, so you find the directions for hair care and you see that for thicker hair you should cut hair while the Moon is Full and in the sign of Taurus, Cancer, or Leo. You should avoid the Moon in Aries, Gemini, or Virgo. Look at the January Moon Table on page 136. You see that the Full Moon is on January 4 at 11:53 pm. The Moon is in Cancer that day and remains in Leo until January 8 at 5:58 pm, so January 4–8 meets both the phase and sign criteria.

Let's move on to a more difficult example using the sign and phase of the Moon. You want to buy a permanent home. After checking the instructions for purchasing a house: "Home (Buy new)" on page 118, you see that you should buy a home when the Moon is in Taurus, Cancer, or Leo. You need to get a loan, so you should also look under "Loan (Ask for)" on page 119. Here it says that the third and fourth quarters favor the borrower (you). You are going to buy the house in October, so go to page 154. The Moon is in the third quarter October 1–4. The Moon is in Cancer from 8:22 pm on October 3 until October 6 at 4:31 am. The best days for obtaining a loan would be October 3 or 4, while the Moon is in Cancer.

Just match up the best sign and phase (quarter) to come up with the best date. With all activities, be sure to check the favorable and unfavorable days for your Sun sign in the table adjoining the Lunar Aspectarian. If there is a choice between several dates, pick the one most favorable for you. Because buying a home is an important business decision, you may also wish to see if the Moon is void or if Mercury is retrograde during these dates.

Now let's look at an example that uses signs, phases, and aspects. Our example is starting new home construction. We will use the month of May. Look under "Build (Start foundation)" on page 110 and you'll see that the Moon should be in the first quarter of a fixed sign—Leo, Taurus, Aquarius, or Scorpio. You should select a time when the Moon is not making unfavorable aspects to Saturn. (Conjunctions are usually considered unfavorable if they are to Mars, Saturn, or Neptune.) Look in the May Moon Table. You will see that the Moon is in the first quarter May 18–25 and in Leo from 5:42 pm on May 22 until 4:52 am on May 25. Now, look to the May Lunar Aspectarian. We see that there is a favorable trine to Saturn on May 22 and a challenging square on May 25. Therefore, May 22 (evening), 23, or 24 would be the best date to start a foundation.

A Note About Time and Time Zones

All tables in the Moon Sign Book use Eastern Time. You must calculate the difference between your time zone and the Eastern Time Zone. Please refer to the Time Zone Conversions chart on page 165 for help with time conversions. The sign the Moon is in at midnight is the sign shown in the Aspectarian and Favorable and Unfavorable Days tables.

How Does the Time Matter?

Due to the three-hour time difference between the East and West Coasts of the United States, those of you living on the East Coast may be, for example, under the influence of a Virgo Moon, while those of you living on the West Coast will still have a Leo Moon influence.

We follow a commonly held belief among astrologers: whatever sign the Moon is in at the start of a day—12:00 am Eastern Time—is considered the dominant influence of the day. That sign is indicated in the Moon Tables. If the date you select for an activity shows the Moon changing signs, you can decide how important the sign change may be for your specific election and adjust your election date and time accordingly.

Use Common Sense

Some activities depend on outside factors. Obviously, you can't go out and plant when there is a foot of snow on the ground. You should adjust to the conditions at hand. If the weather was bad during the first quarter, when it was best to plant crops, do it during the second quarter while the Moon is in a fruitful sign. If the Moon is not in a fruitful sign during the first or second quarter, choose a day when it is in a semi-fruitful sign. The best advice is to choose either the sign or phase that is most favorable, when the two don't coincide.

To Summarize

First, look up the activity under the proper heading, then look for the information given in the tables. Choose the best date considering the number of positive factors in effect. If most of the dates are favorable, there is no problem choosing the one that will fit your schedule. However, if there aren't any really good dates, pick the ones with the least number of negative influences. Please keep in mind that the information found here applies in the broadest sense to the events you want to plan or are considering. To be the most effective, when you use electional astrology, you should also consider your own birth chart in relation to a chart drawn for the time or times you have under consideration. The best advice we can offer you is: read the entire introduction to each section.

January Moon Table

Date	Sign	Element	Nature	Phase
1 Thu 12:09 pm	Gemini	Air	Barren	2nd
2 Fri	Gemini	Air	Barren	2nd
3 Sat 8:08 pm	Cancer	Water	Fruitful	2nd
4 Sun	Cancer	Water	Fruitful	Full 11:53 pm
5 Mon	Cancer	Water	Fruitful	3rd
6 Tue 6:03 am	Leo	Fire	Barren	3rd
7 Wed	Leo	Fire	Barren	3rd
8 Thu 5:58 pm	Virgo	Earth	Barren	3rd
9 Fri	Virgo	Earth	Barren	3rd
10 Sat	Virgo	Earth	Barren	3rd
11 Sun 6:57 am	Libra	Air	Semi-fruitful	3rd
12 Mon	Libra	Air	Semi-fruitful	3rd
13 Tue 6:44 pm	Scorpio	Water	Fruitful	4th 4:46 am
14 Wed	Scorpio	Water	Fruitful	4th
15 Thu	Scorpio	Water	Fruitful	4th
16 Fri 3:01 am	Sagittarius	Fire	Barren	4th
17 Sat	Sagittarius	Fire	Barren	4th
18 Sun 7:04 am	Capricorn	Earth	Semi-fruitful	4th
19 Mon	Capricorn	Earth	Semi-fruitful	4th
20 Tue 7:59 am	Aquarius	Air	Barren	New 8:14 am
21 Wed	Aquarius	Air	Barren	1st
22 Thu 7:48 am	Pisces	Water	Fruitful	1st
23 Fri	Pisces	Water	Fruitful	1st
24 Sat 8:31 am	Aries	Fire	Barren	1st
25 Sun	Aries	Fire	Barren	1st
26 Mon 11:37 am	Taurus	Earth	Semi-fruitful	2nd 11:48 pm
27 Tue	Taurus	Earth	Semi-fruitful	2nd
28 Wed 5:36 pm	Gemini	Air	Barren	2nd
29 Thu	Gemini	Air	Barren	2nd
30 Fri	Gemini	Air	Barren	2nd
31 Sat 2:09 am	Cancer	Water	Fruitful	2nd

January Aspectarian/Favorable & Unfavorable Days

Date	Sun	Mercury	Venus	Mars	Jupiter	Saturn	Uranus	Neptune	Pluto
1		T	T			O		Q	
2							X		
3				T	X				
4	O						Q	T	O
5									
6		O	O			T			
7						T			
8				O	C	Q			
9							O	T	
10	T								
11						X			
12		T	T				O		Q
13	Q			T	X				
14		Q	Q					T	X
15	X				Q				
16				Q		C	Q		
17		X	X		T		T		
18				X				X	
19							Q		C
20	C					X			
21		C	C		O		X		
22				C		Q	C		
23									X
24	X					T			
25		X			T		C		Q
26	Q		X				X		
27		Q		X	Q				T
28			Q			O			
29	T	T		Q			X	Q	
30					X				
31			T					T	

Date	Aries	Taurus	Gemini	Cancer	Leo	Virgo	Libra	Scorpio	Sagittarus	Capricorn	Aquarius	Pisces
1		F		f	u	f		U		f	u	f
2	f		F		f	u	f		U		f	u
3	f		F		f	u	f		U		f	u
4	u	f		F		f	u	f		U		f
5	u	f		F		f	u	f		U		f
6	f	u	f		F		f	u	f		U	
7	f	u	f		F		f	u	f		U	
8	f	u	f		F		f	u	f		U	
9		f	u	f		F		f	u	f		U
10		f	u	f		F		f	u	f		U
11	U		f	u	f		F		f	u	f	
12	U		f	u	f		F		f	u	f	
13	U		f	u	f		F		f	u	f	
14		U		f	u	f		F		f	u	f
15		U		f	u	f		F		f	u	f
16	f		U		f	u	f		F		f	u
17	f		U		f	u	f		F		f	u
18	u	f		U		f	u	f		F		f
19	u	f		U		f	u	f		F		f
20	f	u	f		U		f	u	f		F	
21	f	u	f		U		f	u	f		F	
22		f	u	f		U		f	u	f		F
23		f	u	f		U		f	u	f		F
24	F		f	u	f		U		f	u	f	
25	F		f	u	f		U		f	u	f	
26		F		f	u	f		U		f	u	f
27		F		f	u	f		U		f	u	f
28		F		f	u	f		U		f	u	f
29	f		F		f	u	f		U		f	u
30	f		F		f	u	f		U		f	u
31	u	f		F		f	u	f		U		f

February Moon Table

Date	Sign	Element	Nature	Phase
1 Sun	Cancer	Water	Fruitful	2nd
2 Mon 12:41 pm	Leo	Fire	Barren	2nd
3 Tue	Leo	Fire	Barren	Full 6:09 pm
4 Wed	Leo	Fire	Barren	3rd
5 Thu 12:46 am	Virgo	Earth	Barren	3rd
6 Fri	Virgo	Earth	Barren	3rd
7 Sat 1:44 pm	Libra	Air	Semi-fruitful	3rd
8 Sun	Libra	Air	Semi-fruitful	3rd
9 Mon	Libra	Air	Semi-fruitful	3rd
10 Tue 2:05 am	Scorpio	Water	Fruitful	3rd
11 Wed	Scorpio	Water	Fruitful	4th 10:50 pm
12 Thu 11:46 am	Sagittarius	Fire	Barren	4th
13 Fri	Sagittarius	Fire	Barren	4th
14 Sat 5:24 pm	Capricorn	Earth	Semi-fruitful	4th
15 Sun	Capricorn	Earth	Semi-fruitful	4th
16 Mon 7:13 pm	Aquarius	Air	Barren	4th
17 Tue	Aquarius	Air	Barren	4th
18 Wed 6:47 pm	Pisces	Water	Fruitful	New 6:47 pm
19 Thu	Pisces	Water	Fruitful	1st
20 Fri 6:13 pm	Aries	Fire	Barren	1st
21 Sat	Aries	Fire	Barren	1st
22 Sun 7:28 pm	Taurus	Earth	Semi-fruitful	1st
23 Mon	Taurus	Earth	Semi-fruitful	1st
24 Tue 11:54 pm	Gemini	Air	Barren	1st
25 Wed	Gemini	Air	Barren	2nd 12:14 pm
26 Thu	Gemini	Air	Barren	2nd
27 Fri 7:50 am	Cancer	Water	Fruitful	2nd
28 Sat	Cancer	Water	Fruitful	2nd

February Aspectarian/Favorable & Unfavorable Days

Date	Sun	Mercury	Venus	Mars	Jupiter	Saturn	Uranus	Neptune	Pluto
1				T			Q		O
2						T			
3	O	O					T		
4					C				
5						Q		O	
6			O	O					T
7		T				X			
8								O	Q
9	T				X				
10		Q						T	
11	Q		T		Q				X
12		X		T		C			
13					T		T	Q	
14	X		Q	Q					
15							Q	X	C
16			X	X					
17		C				O	X	X	
18	C								
19						Q		C	X
20			C	C					
21		X			T	T	C		Q
22									
23	X	Q			Q			X	T
24									
25	Q	T	X	X		O		Q	
26					X		X		
27				Q				T	
28	T		Q				Q		O

Date	Aries	Taurus	Gemini	Cancer	Leo	Virgo	Libra	Scorpio	Sagittarius	Capricorn	Aquarius	Pisces
1	u	f		F		f	u	f		U		f
2	u	f		F		f	u	f		U		f
3	f	u	f		F		f	u	f		U	
4	f	u	f		F		f	u	f		U	
5		f	u	f		F		f	u	f		U
6		f	u	f		F		f	u	f		U
7		f	u	f		F		f	u	f		U
8	U		f	u	f		F		f	u	f	
9	U		f	u	f		F		f	u	f	
10		U		f	u	f		F		f	u	f
11		U		f	u	f		F		f	u	f
12	f		U		f	u	f		F		f	u
13	f		U		f	u	f		F		f	u
14	f		U		f	u	f		F		f	u
15	u	f		U		f	u	f		F		f
16	u	f		U		f	u	f		F		f
17	f	u	f		U		f	u	f		F	
18	f	u	f		U		f	u	f		F	
19		f	u	f		U		f	u	f		F
20		f	u	f		U		f	u	f		F
21	F		f	u	f		U		f	u	f	
22	F		f	u	f		U		f	u	f	
23		F		f	u	f		U		f	u	f
24		F		f	u	f		U		f	u	f
25	f		F		f	u	f		U		f	u
26	f		F		f	u	f		U		f	u
27	u	f		F		f	u	f		U		f
28	u	f		F		f	u	f		U		f

March Moon Table

Date	Sign	Element	Nature	Phase
1 Sun 6:34 pm	Leo	Fire	Barren	2nd
2 Mon	Leo	Fire	Barren	2nd
3 Tue	Leo	Fire	Barren	2nd
4 Wed 6:58 am	Virgo	Earth	Barren	2nd
5 Thu	Virgo	Earth	Barren	Full 1:05 pm
6 Fri 7:52 pm	Libra	Air	Semi-fruitful	3rd
7 Sat	Libra	Air	Semi-fruitful	3rd
8 Sun	Libra	Air	Semi-fruitful	3rd
9 Mon 9:10 am	Scorpio	Water	Fruitful	3rd
10 Tue	Scorpio	Water	Fruitful	3rd
11 Wed 7:30 pm	Sagittarius	Fire	Barren	3rd
12 Thu	Sagittarius	Fire	Barren	3rd
13 Fri	Sagittarius	Fire	Barren	4th 1:48 pm
14 Sat 2:40 am	Capricorn	Earth	Semi-fruitful	4th
15 Sun	Capricorn	Earth	Semi-fruitful	4th
16 Mon 6:14 am	Aquarius	Air	Barren	4th
17 Tue	Aquarius	Air	Barren	4th
18 Wed 6:58 am	Pisces	Water	Fruitful	4th
19 Thu	Pisces	Water	Fruitful	4th
20 Fri 6:28 am	Aries	Fire	Barren	New 5:36 am
21 Sat	Aries	Fire	Barren	1st
22 Sun 6:40 am	Taurus	Earth	Semi-fruitful	1st
23 Mon	Taurus	Earth	Semi-fruitful	1st
24 Tue 9:23 am	Gemini	Air	Barren	1st
25 Wed	Gemini	Air	Barren	1st
26 Thu 3:45 pm	Cancer	Water	Fruitful	1st
27 Fri	Cancer	Water	Fruitful	2nd 3:43 am
28 Sat	Cancer	Water	Fruitful	2nd
29 Sun 1:48 am	Leo	Fire	Barren	2nd
30 Mon	Leo	Fire	Barren	2nd
31 Tue 2:12 pm	Virgo	Earth	Barren	2nd

March Aspectarian/Favorable & Unfavorable Days

Date	Sun	Mercury	Venus	Mars	Jupiter	Saturn	Uranus	Neptune	Pluto
1									
2			T	T	C	T	T		
3		O							
4					Q			O	
5	O								T
6									
7				O		X			
8		T	O		X		O		Q
9									
10					Q			T	X
11	T	Q							
12					T	C	T	Q	
13	Q		T	T					
14		X						X	
15	X			Q				Q	C
16			Q			X			
17				X	O		X		
18		C	X			Q		C	
19									X
20	C					T			
21				C	T		C		Q
22			C					X	
23		X		Q					T
24	X				O			Q	
25		Q		X		X			
26				X					
27	Q		X				Q	T	O
28		T		Q					
29	T					T			
30			Q		C		T		
31				T				Q	

Date	Aries	Taurus	Gemini	Cancer	Leo	Virgo	Libra	Scorpio	Sagittarius	Capricorn	Aquarius	Pisces
1	u	f		F	f	u	f			U		f
2	f	u	f		F	f	u	f			U	
3	f	u	f		F	f	u	f			U	
4		f	u	f		F	f	u	f			U
5		f	u	f		F	f	u	f			U
6		f	u	f		F	f	u	f			U
7	U		f	u	f		F	f	u	f		
8	U		f	u	f		F	f	u	f		
9		U		f	u	f		F	f	u	f	
10		U		f	u	f		F	f	u	f	
11		U		f	u	f		F	f	u	f	
12	f		U		f	u	f		F	f	u	f
13	f		U		f	u	f		F	f	u	f
14	u	f		U		f	u	f		F	f	u
15	u	f		U		f	u	f		F	f	u
16	u	f			U		f	u	f		F	f
17	u	f			U		f	u	f		F	f
18	f	u	f			U		f	u	f		F
19	f	u	f			U		f	u	f		F
20	F	f	u	f			U		f	u	f	
21	F	f	u	f			U		f	u	f	
22		F	f	u	f			U		f	u	f
23		F	f	u	f			U		f	u	f
24	f		F	f	u	f			U		f	u
25	f		F	f	u	f			U		f	u
26	f		F	f	u	f			U		f	u
27	u	f		F	f	u	f			U		f
28	u	f		F	f	u	f			U		f
29	f	u	f		F	f	u	f			U	
30	f	u	f		F	f	u	f			U	
31	f	u	f		F	f	u	f			U	

April Moon Table

Date	Sign	Element	Nature	Phase
1 Wed	Virgo	Earth	Barren	2nd
2 Thu	Virgo	Earth	Barren	2nd
3 Fri 3:07 am	Libra	Air	Semi-fruitful	2nd
4 Sat	Libra	Air	Semi-fruitful	Full 8:06 am
5 Sun 3:04 pm	Scorpio	Water	Fruitful	3rd
6 Mon	Scorpio	Water	Fruitful	3rd
7 Tue	Scorpio	Water	Fruitful	3rd
8 Wed 1:08 am	Sagittarius	Fire	Barren	3rd
9 Thu	Sagittarius	Fire	Barren	3rd
10 Fri 8:47 am	Capricorn	Earth	Semi-fruitful	3rd
11 Sat	Capricorn	Earth	Semi-fruitful	4th 11:44 pm
12 Sun 1:44 pm	Aquarius	Air	Barren	4th
13 Mon	Aquarius	Air	Barren	4th
14 Tue 4:12 pm	Pisces	Water	Fruitful	4th
15 Wed	Pisces	Water	Fruitful	4th
16 Thu 5:00 pm	Aries	Fire	Barren	4th
17 Fri	Aries	Fire	Barren	4th
18 Sat 5:31 pm	Taurus	Earth	Semi-fruitful	New 2:57 pm
19 Sun	Taurus	Earth	Semi-fruitful	1st
20 Mon 7:28 pm	Gemini	Air	Barren	1st
21 Tue	Gemini	Air	Barren	1st
22 Wed	Gemini	Air	Barren	1st
23 Thu 12:25 am	Cancer	Water	Fruitful	1st
24 Fri	Cancer	Water	Fruitful	1st
25 Sat 9:13 am	Leo	Fire	Barren	2nd 7:55 pm
26 Sun	Leo	Fire	Barren	2nd
27 Mon 9:07 pm	Virgo	Earth	Barren	2nd
28 Tue	Virgo	Earth	Barren	2nd
29 Wed	Virgo	Earth	Barren	2nd
30 Thu 10:03 am	Libra	Air	Semi-fruitful	2nd

April Aspectarian/Favorable & Unfavorable Days

Date	Sun	Mercury	Venus	Mars	Jupiter	Saturn	Uranus	Neptune	Pluto
1								O	T
2		T							
3		O				X			
4	O				X			O	Q
5				O					
6					Q			T	X
7			O						
8						C		Q	
9	T	T			T		T		
10				T					
11	Q						Q	X	C
12		Q	T			X			
13				Q	O		X		
14	X	X	Q			Q			
15				X				C	X
16						T			
17			X		T			C	Q
18	C								
19		C		C	Q			X	T
20									
21			C		X	O		Q	
22								X	
23	X							T	
24		X		X		Q			O
25	Q					T			
26			X	Q	C			T	
27		Q							
28	T					Q	O		
29			Q	T					T
30		T				X			

Date	Aries	Taurus	Gemini	Cancer	Leo	Virgo	Libra	Scorpio	Sagittarius	Capricorn	Aquarius	Pisces
1		f	u	f		F		f	u	f		U
2		f	u	f		F		f	u	f		U
3	U		f	u	f		F		f	u	f	
4	U		f	u	f		F		f	u	f	
5	U		f	u	f		F		f	u	f	
6		U		f	u	f		F		f	u	f
7		U		f	u	f		F		f	u	f
8	f		U		f	u	f		F		f	u
9	f		U		f	u	f		F		f	u
10	u	f		U		f	u	f		F		f
11	u	f		U		f	u	f		F		f
12	u	f		U		f	u	f		F		f
13	f	u	f		U		f	u	f		F	
14	f	u	f		U		f	u	f		F	
15		f	u	f		U		f	u	f		F
16		f	u	f		U		f	u	f		F
17	F		f	u	f		U		f	u	f	
18	F		f	u	f		U		f	u	f	
19		F		f	u	f		U		f	u	f
20		F		f	u	f		U		f	u	f
21	f		F		f	u	f		U		f	u
22	f		F		f	u	f		U		f	u
23	u	f		F		f	u	f		U		f
24	u	f		F		f	u	f		U		f
25	f	u	f		F		f	u	f		U	
26	f	u	f		F		f	u	f		U	
27	f	u	f		F		f	u	f		U	
28		f	u	f		F		f	u	f		U
29		f	u	f		F		f	u	f		U
30	U		f	u	f		F		f	u	f	

May Moon Table

Date	Sign	Element	Nature	Phase
1 Fri	Libra	Air	Semi-fruitful	2nd
2 Sat 9:47 pm	Scorpio	Water	Fruitful	2nd
3 Sun	Scorpio	Water	Fruitful	Full 11:42 pm
4 Mon	Scorpio	Water	Fruitful	3rd
5 Tue 7:13 am	Sagittarius	Fire	Barren	3rd
6 Wed	Sagittarius	Fire	Barren	3rd
7 Thu 2:16 pm	Capricorn	Earth	Semi-fruitful	3rd
8 Fri	Capricorn	Earth	Semi-fruitful	3rd
9 Sat 7:22 pm	Aquarius	Air	Barren	3rd
10 Sun	Aquarius	Air	Barren	3rd
11 Mon 10:53 pm	Pisces	Water	Fruitful	4th 6:36 am
12 Tue	Pisces	Water	Fruitful	4th
13 Wed	Pisces	Water	Fruitful	4th
14 Thu 1:13 am	Aries	Fire	Barren	4th
15 Fri	Aries	Fire	Barren	4th
16 Sat 3:02 am	Taurus	Earth	Semi-fruitful	4th
17 Sun	Taurus	Earth	Semi-fruitful	4th
18 Mon 5:27 am	Gemini	Air	Barren	New 12:13 am
19 Tue	Gemini	Air	Barren	1st
20 Wed 9:56 am	Cancer	Water	Fruitful	1st
21 Thu	Cancer	Water	Fruitful	1st
22 Fri 5:42 pm	Leo	Fire	Barren	1st
23 Sat	Leo	Fire	Barren	1st
24 Sun	Leo	Fire	Barren	1st
25 Mon 4:52 am	Virgo	Earth	Barren	2nd 1:19 pm
26 Tue	Virgo	Earth	Barren	2nd
27 Wed 5:42 pm	Libra	Air	Semi-fruitful	2nd
28 Thu	Libra	Air	Semi-fruitful	2nd
29 Fri	Libra	Air	Semi-fruitful	2nd
30 Sat 5:34 am	Scorpio	Water	Fruitful	2nd
31 Sun	Scorpio	Water	Fruitful	2nd

May Aspectarian/Favorable & Unfavorable Days

Date	Sun	Mercury	Venus	Mars	Jupiter	Saturn	Uranus	Neptune	Pluto
1					X		O		Q
2		T							
3	O							T	
4				O	Q				X
5		O				C			
6						T	T	Q	
7			O						
8	T						Q	X	C
9			T		X				
10		T			O				
11	Q		Q				X		
12		Q	T			Q		C	
13	X								X
14		X	Q	X		T			
15						T	C		Q
16			X				X		
17					Q				T
18	C			C	O		Q		
19		C		X			X		
20									
21			C				Q	T	O
22	X					T			
23		X		X					
24					C		T		
25	Q					Q			
26		Q	X	Q				O	T
27						X			
28	T	T		T					
29			Q		X		O		Q
30									
31					Q			T	X

Date	Aries	Taurus	Gemini	Cancer	Leo	Virgo	Libra	Scorpio	Sagittarus	Capricorn	Aquarius	Pisces
1	U		f	u	f		F		f	u	f	
2	U		f	u	f		F		f	u	f	
3		U		f	u	f		F		f	u	f
4		U		f	u	f		F		f	u	f
5	f		U		f	u	f		F		f	u
6	f		U		f	u	f		F		f	u
7	f		U		f	u	f		F		f	u
8	u	f		U		f	u	f	F			f
9	u	f		U		f	u	f	F			f
10	f	u	f		U		f	u	f	F		
11	f	u	f		U		f	u	f	F		
12		f	u	f		U		f	u	f		F
13		f	u	f		U		f	u	f		F
14	F		f	u	f		U		f	u	f	
15	F		f	u	f		U		f	u	f	
16		F		f	u	f		U		f	u	f
17		F		f	u	f		U		f	u	f
18	f		F		f	u	f		U		f	u
19	f		F		f	u	f		U		f	u
20	u	f		F		f	u	f		U		f
21	u	f		F		f	u	f		U		f
22	u	f		F		f	u	f		U		f
23	f	u	f		F		f	u	f		U	
24	f	u	f		F		f	u	f		U	
25		f	u	f		F		f	u	f		U
26		f	u	f		F		f	u	f		U
27		f	u	f		F		f	u	f		U
28	U		f	u	f		F		f	u	f	
29	U		f	u	f		F		f	u	f	
30		U		f	u	f		F		f	u	f
31		U		f	u	f		F		f	u	f

June Moon Table

Date	Sign	Element	Nature	Phase
1 Mon 2:39 pm	Sagittarius	Fire	Barren	2nd
2 Tue	Sagittarius	Fire	Barren	Full 12:19 pm
3 Wed 8:50 pm	Capricorn	Earth	Semi-fruitful	3rd
4 Thu	Capricorn	Earth	Semi-fruitful	3rd
5 Fri	Capricorn	Earth	Semi-fruitful	3rd
6 Sat 1:02 am	Aquarius	Air	Barren	3rd
7 Sun	Aquarius	Air	Barren	3rd
8 Mon 4:16 am	Pisces	Water	Fruitful	3rd
9 Tue	Pisces	Water	Fruitful	4th 11:42 am
10 Wed 7:14 am	Aries	Fire	Barren	4th
11 Thu	Aries	Fire	Barren	4th
12 Fri 10:16 am	Taurus	Earth	Semi-fruitful	4th
13 Sat	Taurus	Earth	Semi-fruitful	4th
14 Sun 1:51 pm	Gemini	Air	Barren	4th
15 Mon	Gemini	Air	Barren	4th
16 Tue 6:51 pm	Cancer	Water	Fruitful	New 10:05 am
17 Wed	Cancer	Water	Fruitful	1st
18 Thu	Cancer	Water	Fruitful	1st
19 Fri 2:23 am	Leo	Fire	Barren	1st
20 Sat	Leo	Fire	Barren	1st
21 Sun 12:59 pm	Virgo	Earth	Barren	1st
22 Mon	Virgo	Earth	Barren	1st
23 Tue	Virgo	Earth	Barren	1st
24 Wed 1:41 am	Libra	Air	Semi-fruitful	2nd 7:03 am
25 Thu	Libra	Air	Semi-fruitful	2nd
26 Fri 1:57 pm	Scorpio	Water	Fruitful	2nd
27 Sat	Scorpio	Water	Fruitful	2nd
28 Sun 11:21 pm	Sagittarius	Fire	Barren	2nd
29 Mon	Sagittarius	Fire	Barren	2nd
30 Tue	Sagittarius	Fire	Barren	2nd

June Aspectarian/Favorable & Unfavorable Days

Date	Sun	Mercury	Venus	Mars	Jupiter	Saturn	Uranus	Neptune	Pluto
1			T			C			
2	O	O		O	T			Q	
3							T		
4								X	C
5						Q			
6		T	O			X			
7	T			T	O		X		
8		Q				Q		C	
9	Q			Q					X
10		X	T			T			
11	X			X	T		C		Q
12			Q						
13					Q			X	T
14		C				O			
15			X		X			Q	
16	C			C			X		
17								T	O
18						Q			
19		X				T			
20			C		C	T			
21	X			X		Q			
22		Q						O	T
23									
24	Q			Q		X			
25		T	X		X		O		Q
26				T					
27	T							T	X
28			Q		Q	C			
29								Q	
30		O	T		T		T		

Date	Aries	Taurus	Gemini	Cancer	Leo	Virgo	Libra	Scorpio	Sagittarius	Capricorn	Aquarius	Pisces
1		U		f	u	f		F		f	u	f
2	f		U	f	u	f		F		f	u	
3	f		U	f	u	f		F		f	u	
4	u	f	U		f	u	f		F			f
5	u	f	U		f	u	f		F			f
6	f	u	f		U		f	u	f		F	
7	f	u	f		U		f	u	f		F	
8		f	u	f		U		f	u	f		F
9		f	u	f		U		f	u	f		F
10	F		f	u	f		U		f	u	f	
11	F		f	u	f		U		f	u	f	
12		F		f	u	f		U		f	u	f
13		F		f	u	f		U		f	u	f
14		F		f	u	f		U		f	u	f
15	f		F		f	u	f		U		f	u
16	f		F		f	u	f		U		f	u
17	u	f		F		f	u	f		U		f
18	u	f		F		f	u	f		U		f
19	f	u	f		F		f	u	f		U	
20	f	u	f		F		f	u	f		U	
21	f	u	f		F		f	u	f		U	
22		f	u	f		F		f	u	f		U
23		f	u	f		F		f	u	f		U
24	U		f	u	f		F		f	u	f	
25	U		f	u	f		F		f	u	f	
26	U		f	u	f		F		f	u	f	
27		U		f	u	f		F		f	u	f
28		U		f	u	f		F		f	u	f
29	f		U		f	u	f		F		f	u
30	f		U		f	u	f		F		f	u

July Moon Table

Date	Sign	Element	Nature	Phase
1 Wed 5:11 am	Capricorn	Earth	Semi-fruitful	Full 10:20 pm
2 Thu	Capricorn	Earth	Semi-fruitful	3rd
3 Fri 8:21 am	Aquarius	Air	Barren	3rd
4 Sat	Aquarius	Air	Barren	3rd
5 Sun 10:23 am	Pisces	Water	Fruitful	3rd
6 Mon	Pisces	Water	Fruitful	3rd
7 Tue 12:38 pm	Aries	Fire	Barren	3rd
8 Wed	Aries	Fire	Barren	4th 4:24 pm
9 Thu 3:49 pm	Taurus	Earth	Semi-fruitful	4th
10 Fri	Taurus	Earth	Semi-fruitful	4th
11 Sat 8:16 pm	Gemini	Air	Barren	4th
12 Sun	Gemini	Air	Barren	4th
13 Mon	Gemini	Air	Barren	4th
14 Tue 2:14 am	Cancer	Water	Fruitful	4th
15 Wed	Cancer	Water	Fruitful	New 9:24 pm
16 Thu 10:15 am	Leo	Fire	Barren	1st
17 Fri	Leo	Fire	Barren	1st
18 Sat 8:47 pm	Virgo	Earth	Barren	1st
19 Sun	Virgo	Earth	Barren	1st
20 Mon	Virgo	Earth	Barren	1st
21 Tue 9:23 am	Libra	Air	Semi-fruitful	1st
22 Wed	Libra	Air	Semi-fruitful	1st
23 Thu 10:07 pm	Scorpio	Water	Fruitful	1st
24 Fri	Scorpio	Water	Fruitful	2nd 12:04 am
25 Sat	Scorpio	Water	Fruitful	2nd
26 Sun 8:24 am	Sagittarius	Fire	Barren	2nd
27 Mon	Sagittarius	Fire	Barren	2nd
28 Tue 2:47 pm	Capricorn	Earth	Semi-fruitful	2nd
29 Wed	Capricorn	Earth	Semi-fruitful	2nd
30 Thu 5:40 pm	Aquarius	Air	Barren	2nd
31 Fri	Aquarius	Air	Barren	Full 6:43 am

July Aspectarian/Favorable & Unfavorable Days

Date	Sun	Mercury	Venus	Mars	Jupiter	Saturn	Uranus	Neptune	Pluto
1	O		O					X	
2							Q		C
3						X			
4					O		X		
5		T	O	T		Q			
6	T							C	X
7		Q				T			
8	Q			Q			C		Q
9		X	T		T				
10				X				X	T
11	X		Q		Q	O			
12								Q	
13		X		X		X			
14								T	
15	C	C		C			Q		O
16						T			
17									
18			C		C	Q	T		
19								O	
20		X		X					T
21	X					X			
22									Q
23			X	Q	X		O		
24	Q	Q						T	
25				T					X
26	T	T	Q		Q	C			
27							T	Q	
28			T		T				
29								X	C
30					O		X	Q	
31	O	O							

Date	Aries	Taurus	Gemini	Cancer	Leo	Virgo	Libra	Scorpio	Sagittarus	Capricorn	Aquarius	Pisces
1	u	f		U		f	u	f		F		f
2	u	f		U		f	u	f		F		f
3	f	u	f		U		f	u	f		F	
4	f	u	f		U		f	u	f		F	
5		f	u	f		U		f	u	f		F
6		f	u	f		U		f	u	f		F
7		f	u	f		U		f	u	f		F
8	F		f	u	f		U		f	u	f	
9	F		f	u	f		U		f	u	f	
10		F		f	u	f		U		f	u	f
11		F		f	u	f		U		f	u	f
12	f		F		f	u	f		U		f	u
13	f		F		f	u	f		U		f	u
14	u	f		F		f	u	f		U		f
15	u	f		F		f	u	f		U		f
16	f	u	f		F		f	u	f		U	
17	f	u	f		F		f	u	f		U	
18	f	u	f		F		f	u	f		U	
19		f	u	f		F		f	u	f		U
20		f	u	f		F		f	u	f		U
21	U		f	u	f		F		f	u	f	
22	U		f	u	f		F		f	u	f	
23	U		f	u	f		F		f	u	f	
24		U		f	u	f		F		f	u	f
25		U		f	u	f		F		f	u	f
26	f		U		f	u	f		F		f	u
27	f		U		f	u	f		F		f	u
28	f		U		f	u	f		F		f	u
29	u	f		U		f	u	f		F		f
30	u	f		U		f	u	f		F		f
31	f	u	f		U		f	u	f		F	

August Moon Table

Date	Sign	Element	Nature	Phase
1 Sat 6:36 pm	Pisces	Water	Fruitful	3rd
2 Sun	Pisces	Water	Fruitful	3rd
3 Mon 7:24 pm	Aries	Fire	Barren	3rd
4 Tue	Aries	Fire	Barren	3rd
5 Wed 9:29 pm	Taurus	Earth	Semi-fruitful	3rd
6 Thu	Taurus	Earth	Semi-fruitful	4th 10:03 pm
7 Fri	Taurus	Earth	Semi-fruitful	4th
8 Sat 1:40 am	Gemini	Air	Barren	4th
9 Sun	Gemini	Air	Barren	4th
10 Mon 8:08 am	Cancer	Water	Fruitful	4th
11 Tue	Cancer	Water	Fruitful	4th
12 Wed 4:52 pm	Leo	Fire	Barren	4th
13 Thu	Leo	Fire	Barren	4th
14 Fri	Leo	Fire	Barren	New 10:53 am
15 Sat 3:46 am	Virgo	Earth	Barren	1st
16 Sun	Virgo	Earth	Barren	1st
17 Mon 4:23 pm	Libra	Air	Semi-fruitful	1st
18 Tue	Libra	Air	Semi-fruitful	1st
19 Wed	Libra	Air	Semi-fruitful	1st
20 Thu 5:24 am	Scorpio	Water	Fruitful	1st
21 Fri	Scorpio	Water	Fruitful	1st
22 Sat 4:41 pm	Sagittarius	Fire	Barren	2nd 3:31 pm
23 Sun	Sagittarius	Fire	Barren	2nd
24 Mon	Sagittarius	Fire	Barren	2nd
25 Tue 12:22 am	Capricorn	Earth	Semi-fruitful	2nd
26 Wed	Capricorn	Earth	Semi-fruitful	2nd
27 Thu 4:03 am	Aquarius	Air	Barren	2nd
28 Fri	Aquarius	Air	Barren	2nd
29 Sat 4:51 am	Pisces	Water	Fruitful	Full 2:35 pm
30 Sun	Pisces	Water	Fruitful	3rd
31 Mon 4:33 am	Aries	Fire	Barren	3rd

August Aspectarian/Favorable & Unfavorable Days

Date	Sun	Mercury	Venus	Mars	Jupiter	Saturn	Uranus	Neptune	Pluto
1			O		O	Q	X		
2								C	X
3				T		T			
4	T								Q
5		T	T	Q	T		C		
6	Q							X	T
7			Q			O			
8		Q		X	Q			Q	
9	X						X		
10		X	X		X				
11							Q	T	O
12				C		T			
13									
14	C		C			T			
15					C	Q		O	
16		C							T
17						X			
18				X					Q
19	X		X				O		
20				Q	X			T	
21			Q						X
22	Q	X			Q	C			
23				T				Q	
24		Q	T				T		
25	T				T			X	C
26								Q	
27		T				X			
28			O	O			X		
29	O				O	Q		C	
30									X
31		O				T			

Date	Aries	Taurus	Gemini	Cancer	Leo	Virgo	Libra	Scorpio	Sagittarus	Capricorn	Aquarius	Pisces
1	f	u	f		U		f	u	f		F	
2		f	u	f		U		f	u	f		F
3		f	u	f		U		f	u	f		F
4	F		f	u	f		U		f	u	f	
5	F		f	u	f		U		f	u	f	
6		F		f	u	f		U		f	u	f
7		F		f	u	f		U		f	u	f
8	f		F		f	u	f		U		f	u
9	f		F		f	u	f		U		f	u
10	u	f		F		f	u	f		U		f
11	u	f		F		f	u	f		U		f
12	u	f		F		f	u	f		U		f
13	f	u	f		F		f	u	f		U	
14	f	u	f		F		f	u	f		U	
15		f	u	f		F		f	u	f		U
16		f	u	f		F		f	u	f		U
17		f	u	f		F		f	u	f		U
18	U		f	u	f		F		f	u	f	
19	U		f	u	f		F		f	u	f	
20		U		f	u	f		F		f	u	f
21		U		f	u	f		F		f	u	f
22		U		f	u	f		F		f	u	f
23	f		U		f	u	f		F		f	u
24	f		U		f	u	f		F		f	u
25	u	f		U		f	u	f		F		f
26	u	f		U		f	u	f		F		f
27	f	u	f		U		f	u	f		F	
28	f	u	f		U		f	u	f		F	
29		f	u	f		U		f	u	f		F
30		f	u	f		U		f	u	f		F
31	F		f	u	f		U		f	u	f	

September Moon Table

Date	Sign	Element	Nature	Phase
1 Tue	Aries	Fire	Barren	3rd
2 Wed 5:02 am	Taurus	Earth	Semi-fruitful	3rd
3 Thu	Taurus	Earth	Semi-fruitful	3rd
4 Fri 7:48 am	Gemini	Air	Barren	3rd
5 Sat	Gemini	Air	Barren	4th 5:54 am
6 Sun 1:40 pm	Cancer	Water	Fruitful	4th
7 Mon	Cancer	Water	Fruitful	4th
8 Tue 10:36 pm	Leo	Fire	Barren	4th
9 Wed	Leo	Fire	Barren	4th
10 Thu	Leo	Fire	Barren	4th
11 Fri 9:56 am	Virgo	Earth	Barren	4th
12 Sat	Virgo	Earth	Barren	4th
13 Sun 10:41 pm	Libra	Air	Semi-fruitful	New 2:41 am
14 Mon	Libra	Air	Semi-fruitful	1st
15 Tue	Libra	Air	Semi-fruitful	1st
16 Wed 11:43 am	Scorpio	Water	Fruitful	1st
17 Thu	Scorpio	Water	Fruitful	1st
18 Fri 11:32 pm	Sagittarius	Fire	Barren	1st
19 Sat	Sagittarius	Fire	Barren	1st
20 Sun	Sagittarius	Fire	Barren	1st
21 Mon 8:33 am	Capricorn	Earth	Semi-fruitful	2nd 4:59 am
22 Tue	Capricorn	Earth	Semi-fruitful	2nd
23 Wed 1:51 pm	Aquarius	Air	Barren	2nd
24 Thu	Aquarius	Air	Barren	2nd
25 Fri 3:43 pm	Pisces	Water	Fruitful	2nd
26 Sat	Pisces	Water	Fruitful	2nd
27 Sun 3:29 pm	Aries	Fire	Barren	Full 10:51 pm
28 Mon	Aries	Fire	Barren	3rd
29 Tue 2:57 pm	Taurus	Earth	Semi-fruitful	3rd
30 Wed	Taurus	Earth	Semi-fruitful	3rd

September Aspectarian/Favorable & Unfavorable Days

Date	Sun	Mercury	Venus	Mars	Jupiter	Saturn	Uranus	Neptune	Pluto
1			T	T				C	Q
2	T				T			X	
3			Q	Q					T
4					Q	O		Q	
5	Q	T	X	X			X		
6									
7	X	Q			X			T	O
8						T	Q		
9									
10		X	C	C			T		
11					C	Q			
12								O	T
13	C						X		
14									
15		C	X				O		Q
16				X					
17			Q		X			T	X
18	X			Q		C			
19					Q			Q	
20		X	T				T		
21	Q			T				X	
22		Q			T		Q		C
23	T					X			
24		T					X		
25			O	O		Q			
26					O			C	X
27	O					T			
28		O					C		Q
29			T	T					
30					T			X	T

Date	Aries	Taurus	Gemini	Cancer	Leo	Virgo	Libra	Scorpio	Sagittarius	Capricorn	Aquarius	Pisces
1	F		f	u	f		U		f	u	f	
2		F		f	u	f		U		f	u	f
3		F		f	u	f		U		f	u	f
4	f		F		f	u	f		U		f	u
5	f		F		f	u	f		U		f	u
6	f		F		f	u	f		U		f	u
7	u	f		F		f	u	f		U		f
8	u	f		F		f	u	f		U		f
9	f	u	f		F		f	u	f		U	
10	f	u	f		F		f	u	f		U	
11		f	u	f		F		f	u	f		U
12		f	u	f		F		f	u	f		U
13		f	u	f		F		f	u	f		U
14	U		f	u	f		F		f	u	f	
15	U		f	u	f		F		f	u	f	
16		U		f	u	f		F		f	u	f
17		U		f	u	f		F		f	u	f
18		U		f	u	f		F		f	u	f
19	f		U		f	u	f		F		f	u
20	f		U		f	u	f		F		f	u
21	u	f		U		f	u	f		F		f
22	u	f		U		f	u	f		F		f
23	u	f		U		f	u	f		F		f
24	f	u	f		U		f	u	f		F	
25	f	u	f		U		f	u	f		F	
26		f	u	f		U		f	u	f		F
27		f	u	f		U		f	u	f		F
28	F		f	u	f		U		f	u	f	
29	F		f	u	f		U		f	u	f	
30		F		f	u	f		U		f	u	f

October Moon Table

Date	Sign	Element	Nature	Phase
1 Thu 4:03 pm	Gemini	Air	Barren	3rd
2 Fri	Gemini	Air	Barren	3rd
3 Sat 8:22 pm	Cancer	Water	Fruitful	3rd
4 Sun	Cancer	Water	Fruitful	4th 5:06 pm
5 Mon	Cancer	Water	Fruitful	4th
6 Tue 4:31 am	Leo	Fire	Barren	4th
7 Wed	Leo	Fire	Barren	4th
8 Thu 3:50 pm	Virgo	Earth	Barren	4th
9 Fri	Virgo	Earth	Barren	4th
10 Sat	Virgo	Earth	Barren	4th
11 Sun 4:45 am	Libra	Air	Semi-fruitful	4th
12 Mon	Libra	Air	Semi-fruitful	New 8:06 pm
13 Tue 5:38 pm	Scorpio	Water	Fruitful	1st
14 Wed	Scorpio	Water	Fruitful	1st
15 Thu	Scorpio	Water	Fruitful	1st
16 Fri 5:18 am	Sagittarius	Fire	Barren	1st
17 Sat	Sagittarius	Fire	Barren	1st
18 Sun 2:52 pm	Capricorn	Earth	Semi-fruitful	1st
19 Mon	Capricorn	Earth	Semi-fruitful	1st
20 Tue 9:38 pm	Aquarius	Air	Barren	2nd 4:31 pm
21 Wed	Aquarius	Air	Barren	2nd
22 Thu	Aquarius	Air	Barren	2nd
23 Fri 1:18 am	Pisces	Water	Fruitful	2nd
24 Sat	Pisces	Water	Fruitful	2nd
25 Sun 2:22 am	Aries	Fire	Barren	2nd
26 Mon	Aries	Fire	Barren	2nd
27 Tue 2:07 am	Taurus	Earth	Semi-fruitful	Full 8:05 am
28 Wed	Taurus	Earth	Semi-fruitful	3rd
29 Thu 2:24 am	Gemini	Air	Barren	3rd
30 Fri	Gemini	Air	Barren	3rd
31 Sat 5:09 am	Cancer	Water	Fruitful	3rd

October Aspectarian/Favorable & Unfavorable Days

Date	Sun	Mercury	Venus	Mars	Jupiter	Saturn	Uranus	Neptune	Pluto
1			Q	Q		O			
2	T	T			Q			Q	
3			X				X		
4	Q	Q		X	X			T	O
5							Q		
6		X						T	
7	X							T	
8			C				Q		
9				C	C			O	T
10									
11		C					X		
12	C							O	Q
13									
14			X	X	X			T	X
15									
16		X	Q			C		Q	
17				Q	Q		T		
18	X								
19		Q	T	T	T			X	C
20	Q						Q		
21		T				X			
22							X		
23	T					Q		C	X
24			O	O	O				
25						T			Q
26		O					C		
27	O							X	T
28			T	T	T				
29						O		Q	
30		T	Q	Q	Q		X		
31	T							T	

Date	Aries	Taurus	Gemini	Cancer	Leo	Virgo	Libra	Scorpio	Sagittarius	Capricorn	Aquarius	Pisces
1		F		f	u	f		U		f	u	f
2	f		F		f	u	f		U		f	u
3	f		F		f	u	f		U		f	u
4	u	f		F		f	u	f		U		f
5	u	f		F		f	u	f		U		f
6	f	u	f		F		f	u	f		U	
7	f	u	f		F		f	u	f		U	
8	f	u	f		F		f	u	f		U	
9		f	u	f		F		f	u	f		U
10		f	u	f		F		f	u	f		U
11	U		f	u	f		F		f	u	f	
12	U		f	u	f		F		f	u	f	
13	U		f	u	f		F		f	u	f	
14		U		f	u	f		F		f	u	f
15		U		f	u	f		F		f	u	f
16	f		U		f	u	f		F		f	u
17	f		U		f	u	f		F		f	u
18	f		U		f	u	f		F		f	u
19	u	f		U		f	u	f		F		f
20	u	f		U		f	u	f		F		f
21	f	u	f		U		f	u	f		F	
22	f	u	f		U		f	u	f		F	
23		f	u	f		U		f	u	f		F
24		f	u	f		U		f	u	f		F
25	F		f	u	f		U		f	u	f	
26	F		f	u	f		U		f	u	f	
27		F		f	u	f		U		f	u	f
28		F		f	u	f		U		f	u	f
29	f		F		f	u	f		U		f	u
30	f		F		f	u	f		U		f	u
31	u	f		F		f	u	f		U		f

November Moon Table

Date	Sign	Element	Nature	Phase
1 Sun	Cancer	Water	Fruitful	3rd
2 Mon 10:48 am	Leo	Fire	Barren	3rd
3 Tue	Leo	Fire	Barren	4th 7:24 am
4 Wed 9:22 pm	Virgo	Earth	Barren	4th
5 Thu	Virgo	Earth	Barren	4th
6 Fri	Virgo	Earth	Barren	4th
7 Sat 10:14 am	Libra	Air	Semi-fruitful	4th
8 Sun	Libra	Air	Semi-fruitful	4th
9 Mon 11:02 pm	Scorpio	Water	Fruitful	4th
10 Tue	Scorpio	Water	Fruitful	4th
11 Wed	Scorpio	Water	Fruitful	New 12:47 pm
12 Thu 10:14 am	Sagittarius	Fire	Barren	1st
13 Fri	Sagittarius	Fire	Barren	1st
14 Sat 7:21 pm	Capricorn	Earth	Semi-fruitful	1st
15 Sun	Capricorn	Earth	Semi-fruitful	1st
16 Mon	Capricorn	Earth	Semi-fruitful	1st
17 Tue 2:24 am	Aquarius	Air	Barren	1st
18 Wed	Aquarius	Air	Barren	1st
19 Thu 7:21 am	Pisces	Water	Fruitful	2nd 1:27 am
20 Fri	Pisces	Water	Fruitful	2nd
21 Sat 10:12 am	Aries	Fire	Barren	2nd
22 Sun	Aries	Fire	Barren	2nd
23 Mon 11:26 am	Taurus	Earth	Semi-fruitful	2nd
24 Tue	Taurus	Earth	Semi-fruitful	2nd
25 Wed 12:15 pm	Gemini	Air	Barren	Full 5:44 pm
26 Thu	Gemini	Air	Barren	3rd
27 Fri 2:27 pm	Cancer	Water	Fruitful	3rd
28 Sat	Cancer	Water	Fruitful	3rd
29 Sun 7:47 pm	Leo	Fire	Barren	3rd
30 Mon	Leo	Fire	Barren	3rd

November Aspectarian/Favorable & Unfavorable Days

Date	Sun	Mercury	Venus	Mars	Jupiter	Saturn	Uranus	Neptune	Pluto
1			X	X	X			Q	O
2		Q				T			
3	Q						T		
4									
5		X					Q	O	
6	X					C			T
7			C	C			X		
8								O	Q
9									
10								T	
11	C	C			X				X
12			X	X		C	Q		
13					Q		T		
14				Q					
15			Q					X	C
16	X	X				T	Q		
17			T	T	X				
18					X				
19	Q	Q				Q		C	
20				O					X
21	T	T		O		T			
22			O				C		Q
23								X	
24						T			T
25	O					O		Q	
26		O	T	T	Q		X		
27									
28				Q			Q	T	O
29			Q		X				
30	T			X		T			

Date	Aries	Taurus	Gemini	Cancer	Leo	Virgo	Libra	Scorpio	Sagittarius	Capricorn	Aquarius	Pisces
1	u	f		F		f	u	f		U		f
2	f	u	f		F		f	u	f		U	
3	f	u	f		F		f	u	f		U	
4	f	u	f		F		f	u	f		U	
5		f	u	f		F		f	u	f		U
6		f	u	f		F		f	u	f		U
7	U		f	u	f		F		f	u	f	
8	U		f	u	f		F		f	u	f	
9	U		f	u	f		F		f	u	f	
10		U		f	u	f		F		f	u	f
11		U		f	u	f		F		f	u	f
12	f		U		f	u	f		F		f	u
13	f		U		f	u	f		F		f	u
14	f		U		f	u	f		F		f	u
15	u	f		U		f	u	f		F		f
16	u	f		U		f	u	f		F		f
17	f	u	f		U		f	u	f		F	
18	f	u	f		U		f	u	f		F	
19		f	u	f		U		f	u	f		F
20		f	u	f		U		f	u	f		F
21	F		f	u	f		U		f	u	f	
22	F		f	u	f		U		f	u	f	
23		F		f	u	f		U		f	u	f
24		F		f	u	f		U		f	u	f
25		F		f	u	f		U		f	u	f
26	f		F		f	u	f		U		f	u
27	f		F		f	u	f		U		f	u
28	u	f		F		f	u	f		U		f
29	u	f		F		f	u	f		U		f
30	f	u	f		F		f	u	f		U	

December Moon Table

Date	Sign	Element	Nature	Phase
1 Tue	Leo	Fire	Barren	3rd
2 Wed 5:09 am	Virgo	Earth	Barren	3rd
3 Thu	Virgo	Earth	Barren	4th 2:40 am
4 Fri 5:34 pm	Libra	Air	Semi-fruitful	4th
5 Sat	Libra	Air	Semi-fruitful	4th
6 Sun	Libra	Air	Semi-fruitful	4th
7 Mon 6:26 am	Scorpio	Water	Fruitful	4th
8 Tue	Scorpio	Water	Fruitful	4th
9 Wed 5:25 pm	Sagittarius	Fire	Barren	4th
10 Thu	Sagittarius	Fire	Barren	4th
11 Fri	Sagittarius	Fire	Barren	New 5:29 am
12 Sat 1:46 am	Capricorn	Earth	Semi-fruitful	1st
13 Sun	Capricorn	Earth	Semi-fruitful	1st
14 Mon 7:59 am	Aquarius	Air	Barren	1st
15 Tue	Aquarius	Air	Barren	1st
16 Wed 12:45 pm	Pisces	Water	Fruitful	1st
17 Thu	Pisces	Water	Fruitful	1st
18 Fri 4:26 pm	Aries	Fire	Barren	2nd 10:14 am
19 Sat	Aries	Fire	Barren	2nd
20 Sun 7:13 pm	Taurus	Earth	Semi-fruitful	2nd
21 Mon	Taurus	Earth	Semi-fruitful	2nd
22 Tue 9:31 pm	Gemini	Air	Barren	2nd
23 Wed	Gemini	Air	Barren	2nd
24 Thu	Gemini	Air	Barren	2nd
25 Fri 12:27 am	Cancer	Water	Fruitful	Full 6:12 am
26 Sat	Cancer	Water	Fruitful	3rd
27 Sun 5:31 am	Leo	Fire	Barren	3rd
28 Mon	Leo	Fire	Barren	3rd
29 Tue 1:58 pm	Virgo	Earth	Barren	3rd
30 Wed	Virgo	Earth	Barren	3rd
31 Thu	Virgo	Eart	Barren	3rd

December Aspectarian/Favorable & Unfavorable Days

Date	Sun	Mercury	Venus	Mars	Jupiter	Saturn	Uranus	Neptune	Pluto
1		T	X					T	
2						Q		O	
3	Q	Q			C				T
4									
5	X			C		X			Q
6		X						O	
7			C					T	
8									X
9					X				
10						C	Q		
11	C			X	Q			T	
12		C	X					X	
13				Q	T		Q		C
14									
15			Q	T			X	X	
16	X								
17		X	T			Q		C	X
18	Q				O				
19		Q				T	C		Q
20	T			O					
21								X	T
22		T	O		T				
23						O		Q	
24					T	Q	X		
25	O							T	
26		O	T	Q	X		Q		O
27									
28						T	T		
29			Q	X					
30	T					Q		O	T
31					C				

Date	Aries	Taurus	Gemini	Cancer	Leo	Virgo	Libra	Scorpio	Sagittarus	Capricorn	Aquarius	Pisces
1	f	u	f		F		f	u	f		U	
2		f	u	f		F		f	u	f		U
3		f	u	f		F		f	u	f		U
4		f	u	f		F		f	u	f		U
5	U		f	u	f		F		f	u	f	
6	U		f	u	f		F		f	u	f	
7		U		f	u	f		F		f	u	f
8		U		f	u	f		F		f	u	f
9		U		f	u	f		F		f	u	f
10	f		U		f	u	f		F		f	u
11	f		U		f	u	f		F		f	u
12	u	f		U		f	u	f		F		f
13	u	f		U		f	u	f		F		f
14	f	u	f		U		f	u	f		F	
15	f	u	f		U		f	u	f		F	
16	f	u	f		U		f	u	f		F	
17		f	u	f		U		f	u	f		F
18		f	u	f		U		f	u	f		F
19	F		f	u	f		U		f	u	f	
20	F		f	u	f		U		f	u	f	
21		F		f	u	f		U		f	u	f
22		F		f	u	f		U		f	u	f
23	f		F		f	u	f		U		f	u
24	f		F		f	u	f		U		f	u
25	u	f		F		f	u	f		U		f
26	u	f		F		f	u	f		U		f
27	f	u	f		F		f	u	f		U	
28	f	u	f		F		f	u	f		U	
29	f	u	f		F		f	u	f		U	
30		f	u	f		F		f	u	f		U
31		f	u	f		F		f	u	f		U

2015 Retrograde Planets

Planet	Begin	Eastern	Pacific	End	Eastern	Pacific
Jupiter	12/8/14	3:41 pm	**12:41 pm**	4/8/15	12:57 pm	**9:57 am**
Mercury	1/21/15	10:54 am	**7:54 am**	2/11/15	9:57 am	**6:57 am**
Saturn	3/14/15	11:02 am	**8:02 am**	8/1/15		**10:53 pm**
				8/2/15	1:53 am	
Pluto	4/16/15	11:56 pm	**8:56 pm**	9/24/15		**11:57 pm**
				9/25/15	2:57 am	
Mercury	5/18/15	9:49 pm	**6:49 pm**	6/11/15	6:33 pm	**3:33 pm**
Neptune	6/12/15	5:09 am	**2:09 am**	11/18/15	11:31 am	**8:31 am**
Venus	7/25/15	5:29 am	**2:29 am**	9/6/15	4:29 am	**1:29 am**
Uranus	7/26/15	6:38 am	**3:38 am**	12/25/15	10:53pm	**7:53 pm**
Mercury	9/17/15	2:09 pm	**11:09 am**	10/9/15	10:57 am	**7:57 am**

Eastern Time in plain type, **Pacific Time in bold type**

	Dec 14	Jan 15	Feb	Mar	Apr	May	Jun	Jul	Aug	Sep	Oct	Nov	Dec	Jan 16
☿		▓				▓				▓				
♀									▓					
♂														
♃	▓	▓	▓											
♄				▓	▓	▓	▓	▓						
♅						▓	▓	▓	▓	▓	▓	▓		
♆							▓	▓	▓	▓	▓	▓	▓	
♇					▓	▓	▓	▓	▓					

Egg-Setting Dates

To Have Eggs by this Date	Sign	Qtr.	Date to Set Eggs
Jan 22, 7:48 am–Jan 24, 8:31 am	Pisces	1st	Jan 01, 2015
Jan 26, 11:37 am–Jan 28, 5:36 pm	Taurus	1st	Jan 05
Jan 31, 2:09 am–Feb 2, 12:41 pm	Cancer	2nd	Jan 10
Feb 18, 6:47 pm–Feb 20, 6:13 pm	Pisces	1st	Jan 28
Feb 22, 7:28 pm–Feb 24, 11:54 pm	Taurus	1st	Feb 01
Mar 27, 7:50 am–Mar 1, 6:34 pm	Cancer	2nd	Mar 06
Mar 20, 5:36 am–Mar 20, 6:28 am	Pisces	1st	Feb 27
Mar 22, 6:40 am–Mar 24, 9:23 am	Taurus	1st	Mar 01
Mar 26, 3:45 am–Mar 29, 1:48 am	Cancer	1st	Mar 05
Apr 3, 3:07 am–Apr 4, 8:06 am	Libra	2nd	Mar 13
Apr 18, 5:31 pm–Apr 20, 7:28 pm	Taurus	1st	Mar 28
Apr 23, 12:25 am–Apr 25, 9:13 am	Cancer	1st	Apr 02
Apr 30, 10:03 am–May 2, 9:47 pm	Libra	2nd	Apr 09
May 18, 12:13 am–May 18, 5:27 am	Taurus	1st	Apr 27
May 20, 9:56 am–May 22, 5:42 pm	Cancer	1st	Apr 29
May 27, 5:42 pm–May 30, 5:34 am	Libra	2nd	May 06
Jun 16, 6:51 pm–Jun 19, 2:23 am	Cancer	1st	May 26
Jun 24, 1:41 am–Jun 26, 1:57 pm	Libra	1st	Jun 03
Jul 15, 9:24 pm–Jul 16, 10:15 am	Cancer	1st	Jun 24
Jul 21, 9:23 am–Jul 23, 10:07 pm	Libra	1st	Jun 30
Aug 17, 4:23 pm–Aug 20, 5:24 am	Libra	1st	Jul 27
Aug 29, 4:51 am–Aug 29, 2:35 pm	Pisces	2nd	Aug 08
Sep 13, 10:41 pm–Sep 16, 11:43 am	Libra	1st	Aug 23
Sep 25, 3:43 pm–Sep 27, 3:29 pm	Pisces	2nd	Sep 04
Oct 12, 8:06 pm–Oct 13, 5:38 pm	Libra	1st	Sep 21
Oct 23, 1:18 am–Oct 25, 2:22 am	Pisces	2nd	Oct 02
Oct 27, 2:07 am–Oct 27, 8:05 am	Taurus	2nd	Oct 06
Nov 19, 7:21 am–Nov 21, 10:12 am	Pisces	2nd	Oct 29
Nov 23, 11:26 am–Nov 25, 12:15 pm	Taurus	2nd	Nov 02
Dec 16, 12:45 pm–Dec 18, 4:26 pm	Pisces	1st	Nov 25
Dec 20, 7:13 pm–Dec 22, 9:31 pm	Taurus	2nd	Nov 29
Dec 25, 12:27 am–Dec 25, 6:12 am	Cancer	2nd	Dec 04

Dates to Hunt and Fish

Date	Quarter	Sign
Jan 3, 8:08 pm–Jan 6, 6:03 am	2nd	Cancer
Jan 13, 6:44 pm–Jan 16, 3:01 am	4th	Scorpio
Jan 22, 7:48 am–Jan 24, 8:31 am	1st	Pisces
Jan 31, 2:09 pm–Feb 2, 12:41 pm	2nd	Cancer
Feb 10, 2:05 pm–Feb 12, 11:46 am	3rd	Scorpio
Feb 18, 6:47 pm–Feb 20, 6:13 pm	1st	Pisces
Mar 27, 7:50 am–Mar 1, 6:34 pm	2nd	Cancer
Mar 9, 9:10 am–Mar 11, 7:30 pm	3rd	Scorpio
Mar 11, 7:30 pm–Mar 14, 2:40 am	3rd	Sagittarius
Mar 18, 6:58 am–Mar 20, 6:28 am	4th	Pisces
Mar 26, 3:45 pm–Mar 29, 1:48 am	1st	Cancer
Apr 5, 3:04 pm–Apr 8, 1:08 am	3rd	Scorpio
Apr 8, 1:08 am–Apr 10, 8:47 am	3rd	Sagittarius
Apr 14, 4:12 pm–Apr 16, 5:00 pm	4th	Pisces
Apr 23, 12:25 am–Apr 25, 9:13 am	1st	Cancer
May 2, 9:47 pm–May 5, 7:13 am	2nd	Scorpio
May 5, 7:13 am–May 7, 2:16 pm	3rd	Sagittarius
May 11, 10:53 pm–May 14, 1:13 am	4th	Pisces
May 20, 9:56 am–May 22, 5:42 pm	1st	Cancer
May 30, 5:34 am–Jun 1, 2:39 pm	2nd	Scorpio
Jun 1, 2:39 pm–Jun 3, 8:50 pm	2nd	Sagittarius
Jun 8, 4:16 am–Jun 10, 7:14 am	3rd	Pisces
Jun 16, 6:51 pm–Jun 19, 2:23 am	1st	Cancer
Jun 26, 1:57 pm–Jun 28, 11:21 pm	2nd	Scorpio
Jun 28, 11:21 pm–Jul 1, 5:11 am	2nd	Sagittarius
Jul 5, 10:23 am–Jul 7, 12:38 pm	3rd	Pisces
Jul 7, 12:38 pm–Jul 9, 3:49 pm	3rd	Aries
Jul 14, 2:14 am–Jul 16, 10:15 am	4th	Cancer
Jul 23, 10:07 pm–Jul 26, 8:24 am	1st	Scorpio
Jul 26, 8:24 am–Jul 28, 2:47 pm	2nd	Sagittarius
Aug 1, 6:36 pm–Aug 3, 7:24 pm	3rd	Pisces
Aug 3, 7:24 pm–Aug 5, 9:29 pm	3rd	Aries
Aug 10, 8:08 am–Aug 12, 4:52 pm	4th	Cancer
Aug 20, 5:24 am–Aug 22, 4:41 pm	1st	Scorpio
Aug 22, 4:41 pm–Aug 25, 12:22 am	2nd	Sagittarius
Aug 29, 4:51 am–Aug 31, 4:33 am	2nd	Pisces
Aug 31, 4:33 am–Sep 2, 5:02 am	3rd	Aries
Sep 6, 1:40 pm–Sep 8, 10:36 pm	4th	Cancer
Sep 16, 11:43 am–Sep 18, 11:32 pm	1st	Scorpio
Sep 25, 3:43 pm–Sep 27, 3:29 pm	2nd	Pisces
Sep 27, 3:29 pm–Sep 29, 2:57 pm	2nd	Aries
Oct 3, 8:22 pm–Oct 6, 4:31 am	3rd	Cancer
Oct 13, 5:38 pm–Oct 16, 5:18 am	1st	Scorpio
Oct 23, 1:18 am–Oct 25, 2:22 am	2nd	Pisces
Oct 25, 2:22 am–Oct 27, 2:07 am	2nd	Aries
Oct 31, 5:09 am–Nov 2, 10:48 am	3rd	Cancer
Nov 9, 11:02 pm–Nov 12, 10:14 am	4th	Scorpio
Nov 19, 7:21 am–Nov 21, 10:12 am	2nd	Pisces
Nov 21, 10:12 am–Nov 23, 11:26 am	2nd	Aries
Nov 27, 2:27 pm–Nov 29, 7:47 pm	3rd	Cancer
Dec 7, 6:26 am–Dec 9, 5:25 pm	4th	Scorpio
Dec 16, 12:45 pm–Dec 18, 4:26 pm	1st	Pisces
Dec 18, 4:26 pm–Dec 20, 7:13 pm	2nd	Aries
Dec 25, 12:27 am–Dec 27, 5:31 am	2nd	Cancer

Dates to Destroy Weeds and Pests

Date	Sign	Qtr.
Jan 6, 6:03 am–Jan 8, 5:58 pm	Leo	3rd
Jan 8, 5:58 pm–Jan 11, 6:57 am	Virgo	3rd
Jan 16, 3:01 am–Jan 18, 7:04 am	Sagittarius	4th
Jan 20, 7:59 am–Jan 20, 8:14 am	Aquarius	4th
Feb 3, 6:09 pm–Feb 5, 12:46 am	Leo	3rd
Feb 5, 12:46 am–Feb 7, 1:44 pm	Virgo	3rd
Feb 12, 11:46 am–Feb 14, 5:24 pm	Sagittarius	4th
Feb 16, 7:13 pm–Feb 18, 6:47 pm	Aquarius	4th
Mar 5, 1:05 pm–Mar 6, 7:52 pm	Virgo	3rd
Mar 11, 7:30 pm–Mar 13, 1:48 pm	Sagittarius	3rd
Mar 13, 1:48 pm–Mar 14, 2:40 am	Sagittarius	4th
Mar 16, 6:14 am–Mar 18, 6:58 am	Aquarius	4th
Apr 8, 1:08 am–Apr 10, 8:47 am	Sagittarius	3rd
Apr 12, 1:44 pm–Apr 14, 4:12 pm	Aquarius	4th
Apr 16, 5:00 am–Apr 18, 2:57 pm	Aries	4th
May 5, 7:13 am–May 7, 2:16 pm	Sagittarius	3rd
May 9, 7:22 am–May 11, 6:36 am	Aquarius	3rd
May 11, 6:36 am–May 11, 10:53 pm	Aquarius	4th
May 14, 1:13 am–May 16, 3:02 am	Aries	4th
Jun 2, 12:19 am–Jun 3, 8:50 pm	Sagittarius	3rd
Jun 6, 1:02 am–Jun 8, 4:16 am	Aquarius	3rd
Jun 10, 7:14 am–Jun 12, 10:16 am	Aries	4th
Jun 14, 1:51 pm–Jun 16, 10:05 am	Gemini	4th
Jul 3, 8:21 am–Jul 5, 10:23 am	Aquarius	3rd
Jul 7, 12:38 pm–Jul 8, 4:24 pm	Aries	3rd
Jul 8, 4:24 pm–Jul 9, 3:49 pm	Aries	4th
Jul 11, 8:16 pm–Jul 14, 2:14 am	Gemini	4th
Jul 31, 6:43 am–Aug 1, 6:36 pm	Aquarius	3rd
Aug 3, 7:24 pm–Aug 5, 9:29 pm	Aries	3rd
Aug 8, 1:40 am–Aug 10, 8:08 am	Gemini	4th
Aug 12, 4:52 pm–Aug 14, 10:53 am	Leo	4th
Aug 31, 4:33 am–Sep 2, 5:02 am	Aries	3rd
Sep 4, 7:48 am–Sep 5, 5:54 am	Gemini	3rd
Sep 5, 5:54 am–Sep 6, 1:40 pm	Gemini	4th
Sep 8, 10:36 am–Sep 11, 9:56 am	Leo	4th
Sep 11, 9:56 am–Sep 13, 2:41 am	Virgo	4th
Sep 27, 10:51 pm–Sep 29, 2:57 pm	Aries	3rd
Oct 1, 4:03 pm–Oct 3, 8:22 pm	Gemini	3rd
Oct 6, 4:31 am–Oct 8, 3:50 pm	Leo	4th
Oct 8, 3:50 pm–Oct 11, 4:45 am	Virgo	4th
Oct 29, 2:24 am–Oct 31, 5:09 am	Gemini	3rd
Nov 2, 10:48 am–Nov 3, 7:24 am	Leo	3rd
Nov 3, 7:24 am–Nov 4, 9:22 pm	Leo	4th
Nov 4, 9:22 pm–Nov 7, 10:14 am	Virgo	4th
Nov 25, 5:44 pm–Nov 27, 2:27 pm	Gemini	3rd
Nov 29, 7:47 pm–Dec 2, 5:09 am	Leo	3rd
Dec 2, 5:09 am–Dec 3, 2:40 am	Virgo	3rd
Dec 3, 2:40 am–Dec 4, 5:34 pm	Virgo	4th
Dec 9, 5:25 pm–Dec 11, 5:29 am	Sagittarius	4th
Dec 27, 5:31 am–Dec 29, 1:58 pm	Leo	3rd

Time Zone Map

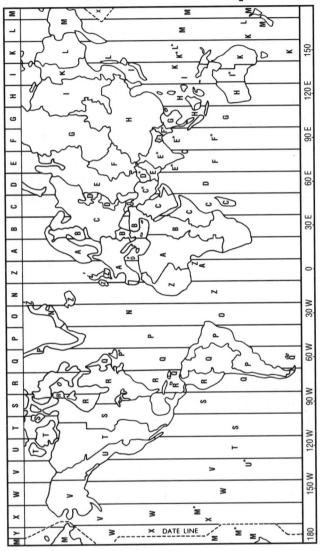

Time Zone Conversions

(R) EST—Used in book
(S) CST—Subtract 1 hour
(T) MST—Subtract 2 hours
(U) PST—Subtract 3 hours
(V) Subtract 4 hours
(V*) Subtract 4½ hours
(U*) Subtract 3½ hours
(W) Subtract 5 hours
(X) Subtract 6 hours
(Y) Subtract 7 hours
(Q) Add 1 hour
(P) Add 2 hours
(P*) Add 2½ hours
(O) Add 3 hours
(N) Add 4 hours
(Z) Add 5 hours
(A) Add 6 hours
(B) Add 7 hours
(C) Add 8 hours
(C*) Add 8½ hours

(D) Add 9 hours
(D*) Add 9½ hours
(E) Add 10 hours
(E*) Add 10½ hours
(F) Add 11 hours
(F*) Add 11½ hours
(G) Add 12 hours
(H) Add 13 hours
(I) Add 14 hours
(I*) Add 14½ hours
(K) Add 15 hours
(K*) Add 15½ hours
(L) Add 16 hours
(L*) Add 16½ hours
(M) Add 17 hours
(M*) Add 18 hours
(P*) Add 2½ hours

Important!

All times given in the *Moon Sign Book* are set in Eastern Time. The conversions shown here are for standard times only. Use the time zone conversions map and table to calculate the difference in your time zone. You must make the adjustment for your time zone and adjust for Daylight Saving Time where applicable.

Weather, Economic
& Lunar Forecasts

Forecasting the Weather

by Kris Brandt Riske

Astrometeorology—astrological weather forecasting—reveals seasonal and weekly weather trends based on the cardinal ingresses (Summer and Winter Solstices, and Spring and Autumn Equinoxes) and the four monthly lunar phases. The planetary alignments and the longitudes and latitudes they influence have the strongest effect, but the zodiacal signs are also involved in creating weather conditions.

The components of a thunderstorm, for example, are heat, wind, and electricity. A Mars-Jupiter configuration generates the necessary heat and Mercury adds wind and electricity. A severe thunderstorm, and those that produce tornados, usually involve Mercury, Mars, Uranus, or Neptune. The zodiacal signs add their energy to the planetary mix to increase or decrease the chance of weather phenomena and their severity.

In general, the fire signs (Aries, Leo, Sagittarius) indicate heat and dryness, both of which peak when Mars, the planet with a similar nature, is in these signs. Water signs (Cancer, Scorpio, Pisces) are conducive to precipitation, and air signs (Gemini, Libra, Aquarius) to cool temperatures and wind. Earth signs (Taurus, Virgo, Capricorn) vary from wet to dry, heat to cold. The signs and their prevailing weather conditions are listed here:

Aries: Heat, dry, wind
Taurus: Moderate temperatures, precipitation
Gemini: Cool temperatures, wind, dry
Cancer: Cold, steady precipitation
Leo: Heat, dry, lightning
Virgo: Cold, dry, windy
Libra: Cool, windy, fair
Scorpio: Extreme temperatures, abundant precipitation
Sagittarius: Warm, fair, moderate wind
Capricorn: Cold, wet, damp
Aquarius: Cold, dry, high pressure, lightning
Pisces: Wet, cool, low pressure

Take note of the Moon's sign at each lunar phase. It reveals the prevailing weather conditions for the next six to seven days. The same is true of Mercury and Venus. These two influential weather planets transit the entire zodiac each year, unless retrograde patterns add their influence.

Planetary Influences

People relied on astrology to forecast weather for thousands of years. They were able to predict drought, floods, and temperature variations through interpreting planetary alignments. In recent years there has been a renewed interest in astrometeorology. A weather forecast can be composed for any date—tomorrow, next week, or a thousand years in the future. According to astrometeorology, each planet governs certain weather phenomena. When certain planets are aligned with other planets, weather—precipitation, cloudy or clear skies, tornados, hurricanes, and other conditions—are generated.

Sun and Moon

The Sun governs the constitution of the weather and, like the Moon, it serves as a trigger for other planetary configurations that result in weather events. When the Sun is prominent in a cardinal ingress or lunar phase chart, the area is often warm and sunny. The Moon can bring or withhold moisture, depending upon its sign placement.

Mercury

Mercury is also a triggering planet, but its main influence is wind direction and velocity. In its stationary periods, Mercury reflects high winds, and its influence is always prominent in major weather events, such as hurricanes and tornadoes, when it tends to lower the temperature.

Venus

Venus governs moisture, clouds, and humidity. It brings warming trends that produce sunny, pleasant weather if in positive aspect to other planets. In some signs—Libra, Virgo, Gemini, Sagittarius—Venus is drier. It is at its wettest when placed in Cancer, Scorpio, Pisces, or Taurus.

Mars

Mars is associated with heat, drought, and wind, and can raise the temperature to record-setting levels when in a fire sign (Aries, Leo, Sagittarius). Mars is also the planet that provides the spark that generates thunderstorms and is prominent in tornado and hurricane configurations.

Jupiter

Jupiter, a fair-weather planet, tends toward higher temperatures when in Aries, Leo, or Sagittarius. It is associated with high-pressure systems and is a contributing factor at times to dryness. Storms are often amplified by Jupiter.

Saturn

Saturn is associated with low-pressure systems, cloudy to overcast skies, and excessive precipitation. Temperatures drop when Saturn is involved. Major winter storms always have a strong Saturn influence, as do storms that produce a slow, steady downpour for hours or days.

Uranus

Like Jupiter, Uranus indicates high-pressure systems. It reflects descending cold air and, when prominent, is responsible for a jet stream that extends far south. Uranus can bring drought in winter, and it is involved in thunderstorms, tornados, and hurricanes.

Neptune

Neptune is the wettest planet. It signals low-pressure systems and is dominant when hurricanes are in the forecast. When Neptune is strongly placed, flood danger is high. It's often associated with winter thaws. Temperatures, humidity, and cloudiness increase where Neptune influences weather.

Pluto

Pluto is associated with weather extremes, as well as unseasonably warm temperatures and drought. It reflects the high winds involved in major hurricanes, storms, and tornadoes.

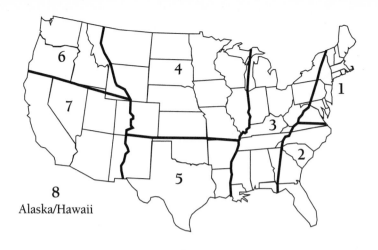

Weather Forecast for 2015

by Kris Brandt Riske

Winter 2015

Wind is a factor this winter in Zone 1, along with periods of heavy precipitation. Overall, though, the zone sees average weather with temperatures ranging from seasonal to above. In Zone 2, inland locations in central parts of the zone experience above-average precipitation as a result of storms moving in from the northwest; temperatures are seasonal to below with increased cloudiness. Northern areas of zone 3 also see heavy precipitation as a result of storms, along with below-average temperatures. The remainder of the Zone is generally seasonal, but southern areas have potential for major storms moving in from the Plains, along with a chance for severe thunderstorms.

Zones 4 and 5, the Plains states, see an above-average number of major storms that form in the northern part of Zone 4 and travel southeast, bringing abundant precipitation and resulting flood potential. Wind is an aggravating factor in the central areas, and throughout the zone, temperatures range from seasonal to below.

Zones 6 and 7 tend toward dryness with precipitation and temperatures closer to average in western parts of both zones. Much of the rest of Zones 6 and 7 experiences temperatures average to above, but with some notable winter storms in the central mountains.

In Zone 8, western and eastern Alaska receive an average amount of precipitation, while central parts of the state see an above-average number of major storms. Alaskan temperatures range from seasonal to below. Hawaii is windy and seasonal, with precipitation ranging from average to below.

Second Quarter Moon, December 28, 2014–January 3

Zone 1: The zone is partly cloudy to cloudy and windy with precipitation later in the week and heavier downfall in northern areas; temperatures are seasonal.

Zone 2: Wind and variably cloudy skies bring precipitation to much of the zone, and temperatures are seasonal.

Zone 3: Western areas could see stormy conditions later in the week, while eastern parts of the zone see precipitation earlier (some abundant; skies are variably cloudy and temperatures range from seasonal to below.

Zone 4: Much of the zone is windy under variably cloudy skies, temperatures are seasonal to below, and central areas could see abundant precipitation from stormy conditions.

Zone 5: Western and central parts of the zone are fair to partly cloudy with increasing cloudiness and wind in central and eastern areas, which have potential for stormy conditions later in the week; temperatures range from seasonal to below.

Zone 6: Temperatures are seasonal to below and western and central areas are windy later as a front brings precipitation; otherwise, the zone is mostly fair to partly cloudy with scattered precipitation east earlier in the week.

Zone 7: The zone is variably cloudy with precipitation west and central, which could be heavy in northern mountain areas; temperatures are seasonal.

Zone 8: Western parts of Alaska see abundant precipitation later in the week, eastern areas are windy with precipitation, and temperatures are seasonal under variably cloudy skies. Hawaii is mostly fair and seasonal.

Full Moon, January 4–12

Zone 1: The zone is stormy with high winds and below-average temperatures.

Zone 2: Northern areas are stormy, central and southern parts of the zone are partly cloudy with a chance for precipitation, and temperatures range from seasonal to below.

Zone 3: Temperatures are seasonal to below, the zone is variably cloudy and windy, western areas see precipitation later in the week, and eastern areas are stormy.

Zone 4: Skies are variably cloudy and the zone is windy and seasonal; precipitation in western areas moves across the zone.

Zone 5: Central and eastern areas see precipitation as a front advances from the west, and the zone is windy, seasonal, and variably cloudy.

Zone 6: Much of the zone is cloudy, especially central and eastern areas, which see precipitation (some abundant) under stormy conditions; temperatures are seasonal to below.

Zone 7: Western and central parts of the zone are windy with potential for stormy conditions and abundant downfall in northern coastal areas and central mountains, while eastern areas are partly cloudy; temperatures are seasonal to below.

Zone 8: Western Alaska is stormy, eastern parts of the state see precipitation, central skies are fair to partly cloudy, and temperatures are seasonal to below. Hawaii is fair to partly cloudy and seasonal.

Fourth Quarter Moon, January 13–19

Zone 1: The zone is partly cloudy with temperatures seasonal to below and scattered precipitation later in the week.

Zone 2: Temperatures are seasonal, skies are variably cloudy, and central and southern areas see precipitation.

Zone 3: The zone is partly cloudy to cloudy with scattered precipitation (some locally heavy, especially in central and eastern areas), and temperatures are seasonal; southern areas could see strong thunderstorms with tornado potential.

Zone 4: Western parts of the zone are overcast and stormy with abundant precipitation, central and eastern areas are variably cloudy with storm potential east and more cloudiness, and temperatures seasonal to below.

Zone 5: Temperatures are seasonal to above and skies are partly cloudy to cloudy with potential in southern central and eastern areas later in the week for strong thunderstorms and tornados and in northern areas.

Zone 6: Much of the zone sees precipitation under variably cloudy skies, and temperatures are seasonal to below.

Zone 7: Western and central parts of the zone see precipitation with a chance for precipitation in eastern areas later in the week, and skies are variably cloudy and windy with temperatures seasonal to below.

Zone 8: Central Alaska is cold and stormy, eastern areas see scattered precipitation, and western parts of the state are windy with precipitation later in the week; temperatures are seasonal in eastern and western parts of the state. Hawaii is windy with thunderstorms (some strong) and variably cloudy with temperatures seasonal to below.

New Moon, January 20–25

Zone 1: The zone is cloudy and windy, temperatures range from seasonal to below, and precipitation falls in northern areas.

Zone 2: Northern areas are windy with scattered precipitation, central and southern parts of the zone are variably cloudy with precipitation south, and temperatures are seasonal to below.

Zone 3: Western and central parts of the zone are windy with precipitation, much of the zone is cloudy, and temperatures are seasonal to below.

Zone 4: Much of the zone is windy and cloudy with precipitation (some abundant in the eastern Plains; temperatures are seasonal to below and much colder west and central.

Zone 5: The zone is fair to partly cloudy and windy with seasonal temperatures and precipitation in eastern areas.

Zone 6: Western parts of the zone are windy and cold, central and eastern areas more seasonal, and much of the zone is partly cloudy to cloudy; western and central areas see precipitation, some locally heavy.

Zone 7: The zone is windy and partly cloudy to cloudy west and central, fair to partly cloudy east, and temps are seasonal to below.

Zone 8: Western Alaska is windy with precipitation, central areas are partly cloudy with scattered precipitation, eastern parts of the state are cloudy with precipitation (some abundant), and temperatures are seasonal to below. Hawaii is windy and variably cloudy with seasonal temperatures and abundant precipitation in some western parts of the state.

Second Quarter Moon, January 26–February 2

Zone 1: The zone is windy, partly cloudy, and seasonal with scattered precipitation.

Zone 2: Skies are windy and variably cloudy with more cloudiness south along with precipitation (some heavy) in southern and central inland areas; temperatures are seasonal to below.

Zone 3: Western areas are stormy with abundant precipitation in some locations, the zone is windy and mostly cloudy with temperatures ranging from seasonal to below, and central and eastern areas see precipitation later in the week, some locally heavy.

Zone 4: Much of the zone is windy and fair to partly cloudy with temperatures seasonal to below, and eastern parts of the zone and the eastern Plains see precipitation, possibly abundant with blizzard potential.

Zone 5: Western areas are windy with precipitation later in the week, skies are variably cloudy, temperatures are seasonal to below, and eastern areas could see a major storm.

Zone 6: Western areas are windy with precipitation, central and eastern parts of the zone are mostly fair and windy with a chance for precipitation later in the week, and temperatures range from seasonal to below.

Zone 7: Northern coastal areas see precipitation later in the week, eastern parts are very windy with a chance for precipitation, and the zone is variably cloudy with temps seasonal to below.

Zone 8: Central Alaska is windy with precipitation (some abundant) under overcast skies; western areas are variably cloudy with scattered precipitation; eastern areas are overcast with precipitation; and temperatures are seasonal. Hawaii is variably cloudy, seasonal, and windy with precipitation, which is heaviest in central parts of the state.

Full Moon, February 3–10

Zone 1: Temperatures range from seasonal to below, northern areas are cloudy, and southern parts of the zone are partly cloudy.

Zone 2: Skies are windy and fair to partly cloudy with a chance for precipitation, and temperatures are seasonal to below.

Zone 3: The zone is windy with scattered precipitation in central areas, and temperatures are seasonal to below.

Zone 4: Western skies are cloudy, central and eastern skies are partly cloudy, and temperatures are seasonal to below.

Zone 5: The zone is windy and seasonal with a chance for precipitation in all areas.

Zone 6: Eastern and western parts of the zone are partly cloudy with a chance for precipitation, central areas are cloudy with precipitation, and temperatures range from seasonal to below.

Zone 7: The zone is partly cloudy and seasonal with a chance for precipitation.

Zone 8: Alaska is fair to partly cloudy and seasonal with precipitation in eastern areas. Hawaii is cloudy and seasonal with scattered precipitation.

Fourth Quarter Moon, February 11–17

Zone 1: Skies are variably cloudy and windy with precipitation, and temperatures are seasonal.

Zone 2: The zone is windy and partly cloudy to cloudy with seasonal temperatures and precipitation in northern areas.

Zone 3: Temperatures are seasonal, skies are partly cloudy to cloudy with scattered precipitation west and central and potential for windy conditions and abundant downfall east.

Zone 4: Skies are fair to partly cloudy, eastern areas see more cloudiness and precipitation, and temps are seasonal to below.

Zone 5: Eastern areas have a chance for precipitation, skies are fair to partly cloudy, and temps range from seasonal to below.

Zone 6: Western parts of the zone see precipitation that moves into central areas under variably cloudy skies, central and eastern areas are windy with more precipitation, and temps are seasonal.

Zone 7: Much of the zone sees precipitation as the week progresses with the highest levels in the mountains; western and central areas are very windy; and temperatures are seasonal.

Zone 8: Alaska is cloudy with seasonal temperatures and windy conditions and precipitation west. Hawaiian temperatures are seasonal, skies are fair to partly cloudy, and western areas see precipitation later in the week.

New Moon, February 18–24

Zone 1: Skies are fair to partly cloudy, temperatures are seasonal to below, and northern areas see scattered precipitation.

Zone 2: The zone is cloudy with precipitation (some locally heavy) and temperatures are seasonal.

Zone 3: Much of the zone is cloudy with significant precipitation, especially in central areas, and temps are seasonal to below.

Zone 4: Western and central skies are variably cloudy with scattered precipitation west, eastern areas see increasing cloudiness along with potential for significant precipitation later in the week, and temperatures are seasonal to below.

Zone 5: Western and central parts of the zone see precipitation under variably cloudy skies, eastern areas are fair to partly cloudy, and temperatures are seasonal to below.

Zone 6: Cloudy skies in western areas yield precipitation (some abundant) later in the week, central and eastern areas are windy and see precipitation under variably cloudy skies, and temperatures are seasonal.

Zone 7: The zone is mostly fair to partly cloudy with a chance for precipitation, and temperatures are seasonal to above.

Zone 8: Much of Alaska sees precipitation under variably cloudy skies and seasonal temps. Hawaii is fair to partly cloudy and seasonal with scattered precipitation in central parts of the state.

Second Quarter Moon, February 25–March 4

Zone 1: Northern areas are cloudy with precipitation, southern areas are partly cloudy with scattered precipitation, and temperatures are seasonal.

Zone 2: Northern parts of the zone are windy with precipitation, some locally heavy as a front advances; central and southern parts of the zone have a chance for precipitation and are mostly fair to partly cloudy; and temperatures are seasonal.

Zone 3: Western areas see precipitation (some locally heavy), central skies are fair to partly cloudy, temperatures are seasonal, and eastern parts of the zone are cloudy with abundant precipitation and flood potential.

Zone 4: Much of the zone sees precipitation as a front moves to the east, bringing locally heavy downfall in the central and eastern Plains; skies are variably cloudy and temperatures are seasonal.

Zone 5: Precipitation across the zone is abundant in eastern locations with more cloudiness east and seasonal temperatures.

Zone 6: Skies are variably cloudy west and central, eastern areas are fair, western parts of the zone see scattered precipitation, and temperatures are seasonal.

Zone 7: The zone is fair to partly cloudy with temperatures ranging from seasonal to above.

Zone 8: Alaska is variably cloudy and seasonal with precipitation central and east. Hawaii is fair and seasonal.

Full Moon, March 5–12

Zone 1: Skies are partly cloudy, temperatures are seasonal to below, and southern areas see precipitation.

Zone 2: Temperatures are seasonal under mostly fair skies central and south with a chance for thunderstorms, and northern areas are cloudy with precipitation.

Zone 3: Strong storms with tornado potential are possible across much of the zone, where temperatures are seasonal to below.

Zone 4: Stormy conditions could bring abundant precipitation to the western and central Plains, temperatures are seasonal, skies are partly cloudy to cloudy, and eastern parts of the zone see precipitation and have flood potential.

Zone 5: Skies are partly cloudy to cloudy with precipitation across much of the zone, some locally heavy; strong thunderstorms with tornado potential are possible in central areas, also with locally heavy precipitation; flood potential is higher in eastern areas; and temperatures are seasonal.

Zone 6: Temperatures are seasonal, skies are variably cloudy, western and central areas see scattered precipitation, and stormy conditions could develop later in the week.

Zone 7: Southern coastal and central parts of the zone have a chance for precipitation, eastern areas are windy, skies are variably cloudy, and temperatures are seasonal.

Zone 8: Central Alaska is stormy with precipitation that moves into eastern areas, western parts of the state are mostly fair, and temperatures are seasonal. Eastern Hawaii is windy with precipitation, and the state is variably cloudy with seasonal temperatures.

Fourth Quarter Moon, March 13–19

Zone 1: The zone is generally partly cloudy with precipitation north and seasonal temperatures.

Zone 2: Northern areas see precipitation, central and southern areas have a chance for precipitation, and the zone is variably cloudy and seasonal.

Zone 3: Strong thunderstorms with tornado potential along with locally heavy precipitation are possible in central parts of the zone, western and central areas are partly cloudy, eastern areas are cloudy with precipitation, and temperatures are seasonal.

Zone 4: Western areas are windy as a front moves through the area and into the central Plains with abundant precipitation, eastern skies are fair to partly cloudy, temps are seasonal, and southern areas could see storms with tornado potential.

Zone 5: The zone is partly cloudy to cloudy and seasonal, and storms with tornado potential are possible later in the week in central and eastern areas, some with locally heavy precipitation.

Zone 6: Locally heavy precipitation in western areas moves into central parts of the zone, eastern areas see scattered precipitation, skies are partly cloudy to cloudy, and temperatures are seasonal.

Zone 7: Eastern parts of the zone are fair to partly cloudy, western parts of the zone see precipitation, some locally heavy, that advances into central areas, and temps are seasonal to below.

Zone 8: Central and eastern Alaska see precipitation, western skies are partly cloudy, and temperatures are seasonal to below. Hawaii is mostly fair with temperatures ranging from seasonal to above with thunderstorms in eastern areas.

Spring

Zone 1 tends toward dryness and above-average temperatures this spring, as does much of Zone 2. Inland areas of central parts of Zone 2 see more precipitation and strong thunderstorms, although still below average. Zone 3 also tends to dryness, but with more precipitation in central areas, along with strong thunderstorms at times.

The eastern Plains of Zones 4 and 5 receive above-average precipitation, along with high potential for flooding and strong thunderstorms with tornados. Central areas also see abundant precipitation and have the same strong thunderstorm and tornado potential. Major storm systems develop over Minnesota and the Dakotas. Western parts of these zones also see stormy conditions but without the excessive precipitation. Temperatures in Zones 4 and 5 are seasonal to below.

Temperatures in Zone 6 are generally seasonal, with above-average periods, and this zone is windy. Zone 7 is mostly dry with temperatures ranging from seasonal to above and periodic storms that move through the central mountains from the northwest.

In Zone 8, eastern Alaska sees an above-average number of major storms and temperatures seasonal to below, while western and central areas of the state tend toward dryness and above-average temperatures. Central and eastern Hawaii see more cloudiness, and temperatures overall are seasonal to above with precipitation ranging from average to below.

New Moon, March 20–26

Zone 1: The zone is windy and partly cloudy to cloudy with precipitation south (some abundant with flood potential, and temperatures are seasonal); a Nor'easter is possible.

Zone 2: Northern areas see abundant precipitation with flood potential, possibly from a Nor'easter; strong thunderstorms with tornado potential are possible in central areas; and much of the zone is cloudy and windy with temperatures seasonal to below.

Zone 3: Eastern parts of the zone are windy with potential for abundant precipitation and flooding, western areas see precipitation, central parts of the zone are partly cloudy, and temperatures are seasonal.

Zone 4: Temps are seasonal to below and skies are partly cloudy to cloudy and windy with precipitation in western areas later in the week and scattered precipitation in central and eastern areas.

Zone 5: Western and central skies are windy and partly cloudy, eastern areas see more cloudiness and precipitation, and temperatures are seasonal.

Zone 6: The zone is windy and stormy with locally heavy downfall and temperatures ranging from seasonal to below.

Zone 7: Eastern areas see precipitation, the zone is windy, temperatures are seasonal to above, and western and central areas are partly cloudy.

Zone 8: Western and eastern Alaska see precipitation with high winds west, central areas are fair to partly cloudy, and temperatures are seasonal to below. Hawaii is windy with temperatures seasonal to below and scattered precipitation, some locally heavy.

Second Quarter Moon, March 27–April 3

Zone 1: The zone is windy with precipitation under variably cloudy skies with seasonal temperatures.

Zone 2: Much of the zone is windy with precipitation (some locally heavy), temperatures are seasonal, and skies are cloudy.

Zone 3: Temperatures are seasonal to below and the zone is windy with precipitation from thunderstorms (some strong with tornado potential).

Zone 4: Scattered thunderstorms are possible across much of the zone (some strong with tornado potential); eastern areas are partly cloudy; temperatures are seasonal; and flooding is possible in some western and central areas as a result of locally heavy downfall.

Zone 5: Skies are fair to partly cloudy, temperatures are seasonal, and strong thunderstorms with tornado potential are possible.

Zone 6: Precipitation moves across much of the zone under

partly cloudy to cloudy skies along with seasonal temps, and locally heavy downfall and flooding are possible in central areas.

Zone 7: The zone is fair to partly cloudy, windy east with a chance for precipitation, and temperatures seasonal to above.

Zone 8: Abundant precipitation is possible in central and eastern Alaska, western skies are mostly fair, and temperatures are seasonal. Hawaii is fair and seasonal, with showers developing in western and central areas later in the week.

Full Moon, April 4–10

Zone 1: Northern areas are fair to partly cloudy, central areas are partly cloudy to cloudy with precipitation, and temperatures are seasonal to below.

Zone 2: Temperatures are seasonal, northern areas are partly cloudy, and central and southern parts of the zone are windy with thunderstorms (some strong with tornado potential).

Zone 3: Much of the zone sees thunderstorms with tornado potential, and temps are seasonal under variably cloudy skies.

Zone 4: Western skies are fair, temperatures are seasonal, and central and eastern areas are variably cloudy with precipitation and thunderstorms (some strong with tornado potential).

Zone 5: Central and eastern areas see strong thunderstorms with tornado potential, temperatures are seasonal, and the zone is variably cloudy and mostly fair west.

Zone 6: Western and eastern areas are partly cloudy, central parts of the zone are windy with more cloudiness and scattered precipitation, and temperatures are seasonal.

Zone 7: Northern coastal areas see precipitation (some abundant), that moves into northern central parts of the zone; eastern areas are fair to partly cloudy; western and central areas are partly cloudy to cloudy and windy; and temperatures are seasonal to below.

Zone 8: Western and central Alaska are windy with scattered precipitation, eastern areas are cloudy with precipitation, and temps are seasonal. Hawaii is mostly partly cloudy and seasonal.

Fourth Quarter Moon, April 11–17

Zone 1: The zone is partly cloudy with a chance for precipitation south and seasonal temperatures.

Zone 2: Strong thunderstorms with tornado potential are possible in central and southern areas, along with locally heavy precipitation, and temperatures are seasonal under variably cloudy skies.

Zone 3: Western areas see precipitation (some abundant), skies are partly cloudy to cloudy, temperatures are seasonal, and strong thunderstorms with tornado potential are possible.

Zone 4: Precipitation later in the week in western parts of the zone moves into the western Plains and central areas, bringing abundant downfall and potentially stormy conditions along with temperatures ranging from seasonal to below; flooding is possible, as are strong thunderstorms with tornado potential.

Zone 5: Much of the zone sees precipitation and possible stormy conditions with the heaviest downfall in central areas; flooding is possible, as are strong thunderstorms with tornado potential; temperatures are seasonal.

Zone 6: Skies are variably cloudy, temperatures are seasonal to above, and western areas see precipitation later in the week, possibly as a result of stormy conditions; central and eastern areas have a chance for precipitation.

Zone 7: Northern coastal areas see precipitation later in the week, and the zone is mostly fair to partly cloudy with temperatures seasonal to above.

Zone 8: Alaska is partly cloudy and seasonal, with more cloudiness and precipitation in eastern areas. Hawaii is generally partly cloudy and seasonal with thunderstorms possible in eastern areas.

New Moon, April 18–24

Zone 1: Temperatures are seasonal to below, skies are cloudy and windy, and northern areas see precipitation, some locally heavy.

Zone 2: Northern parts of the zone are partly cloudy, central and southern areas are mostly fair with increasing windiness later in the week, and temperatures are seasonal.

Zone 3: Western and central areas see strong thunderstorms with tornado potential, conditions are windy under generally fair to partly cloudy skies, and temperatures are seasonal.

Zone 4: Temperatures range from seasonal to above under partly cloudy skies with strong thunderstorms with tornado potential in central and eastern areas.

Zone 5: Skies are windy and fair to partly cloudy with strong storms with tornado potential and locally heavy precipitation possible in eastern areas; temperatures are seasonal to above.

Zone 6: Much of the zone sees precipitation under partly cloudy to cloudy skies with locally heavy downfall in eastern areas; temperatures are seasonal to below.

Zone 7: Skies are variably cloudy, temperatures are seasonal to below, much of the zone sees precipitation, and central and eastern areas are very windy.

Zone 8: Central Alaska is overcast with locally heavy precipitation that moves into eastern areas, temperatures are seasonal, and western parts of the state are fair to partly cloudy. Hawaii is seasonal and partly cloudy to cloudy with scattered showers and thunderstorms.

Second Quarter Moon, April 25–May 2

Zone 1: Temperatures are seasonal and the zone is windy with scattered showers and thunderstorms.

Zone 2: Skies are variably cloudy, temperatures are seasonal, and the zone sees scattered showers and thunderstorms.

Zone 3: Partly cloudy skies and seasonal temperatures accompany scattered showers and thunderstorms.

Zone 4: Western areas are windy with precipitation (some locally heavy) at week's end, temperatures are seasonal to below, and central and eastern parts of the zone are partly cloudy.

Zone 5: Temps are seasonal to below, skies are variably cloudy, and western and central areas see thunderstorms (some strong) with locally heavy precipitation and tornado potential.

Zone 6: The zone is fair to partly cloudy and temperatures are seasonal to above with a chance for showers later in the week.

Zone 7: Central areas have a chance for precipitation, skies are fair to partly cloudy, and the zone is windy with temperatures seasonal to above.

Zone 8: Alaska is cloudy and windy with locally heavy precipitation in central areas later in the week as a front moves in from the west; temperatures are seasonal to below; and eastern areas see scattered precipitation. Hawaii is windy, skies are mostly fair to partly cloudy, temperatures are seasonal, and eastern areas see showers at week's end.

Full Moon, May 3–10

Zone 1: Fair to partly cloudy skies accompany seasonal temperatures, with precipitation (some locally heavy) in northern parts of the zone later in the week.

Zone 2: The zone is variably cloudy with scattered thunderstorms, some with locally heavy precipitation and tornado potential, and temperatures are seasonal to above.

Zone 3: Humid conditions and temperatures seasonal to above trigger scattered showers and thunderstorms (some strong with tornado potential) across the zone.

Zone 4: Temperatures are seasonal and the zone is variably cloudy with more cloudiness and precipitation (some locally heavy) in central areas.

Zone 5: Much of the zone sees showers and thunderstorms (some strong with tornado potential); skies are partly cloudy to cloudy, conditions are humid, and temperatures are seasonal.

Zone 6: Western and eastern parts of the zone are windy and partly cloudy, western areas see scattered precipitation, temperatures are seasonal, and central areas are cloudy with precipitation, some locally heavy.

Zone 7: Western skies are cloudy with precipitation (some locally heavy) that moves into central areas; eastern areas see scattered precipitation; and the zone is windy with temps seasonal to below.

Zone 8: Alaska is fair to partly cloudy and seasonal with a chance for precipitation east. Western Hawaii is windy, and the area is seasonal and fair to partly cloudy with a chance for showers.

Fourth Quarter Moon, May 11–17

Zone 1: The zone is fair to partly cloudy, windy, and seasonal with scattered precipitation.

Zone 2: Northern areas are generally partly cloudy with more clouds central and south, along with greater chance for precipitation; temperatures are seasonal to above.

Zone 3: The zone is humid and partly cloudy with more clouds east along with scattered showers; temps are seasonal to above.

Zone 4: Much of the zone sees showers and thunderstorms under variably cloudy skies with seasonal temperatures.

Zone 5: Temperatures are seasonal and skies partly cloudy to cloudy with scattered showers and thunderstorms; central areas could see strong thunderstorms with tornado potential.

Zone 6: The zone is generally fair to partly cloudy with more cloudiness in eastern areas, along with precipitation; temperatures are seasonal.

Zone 7: Skies are variably cloudy with precipitation in central and eastern areas; temperatures are seasonal to above.

Zone 8: Western and central Alaska are mostly fair and seasonal, eastern skies are cloudy with precipitation, and temperatures are seasonal to below. Hawaii is fair and seasonal with showers west and central later in the week.

New Moon, May 18–24

Zone 1: The zone is fair to partly cloudy with scattered thunderstorms and temperatures seasonal to above.

Zone 2: Partly cloudy skies accompany humid conditions, scattered thunderstorms, and temperatures seasonal to above.

Zone 3: Much of the zone sees showers and scattered thunderstorms (some strong with high winds and locally heavy precipitation later in the week); skies are variably cloudy, conditions are humid, and temperatures are seasonal to above.

Zone 4: Thunderstorms (some strong with tornado potential) across much of the zone accompany variably cloudy skies, humidity, and temperatures seasonal to above.

Zone 5: Locally heavy precipitation accompanies thunderstorms (some strong with tornado potential), variably cloudy skies, humid conditions, and temperatures seasonal to above.

Zone 6: Skies are fair to partly cloudy west and central, eastern areas see more cloudiness and wind with showers, and temperatures are seasonal to above.

Zone 7: Temperatures are seasonal and skies are generally partly cloudy; western and central areas see precipitation with some locally heavy in northern areas later in the week.

Zone 8: Precipitation in western and central Alaska moves into eastern areas, some of which receive abundant downfall; skies are variably cloudy, and temperatures are seasonal to below. Hawaii is mostly fair with temperatures seasonal to above.

Second Quarter Moon, May 25–June 1

Zone 1: The zone sees precipitation, with some locally heavy later in the week; conditions are humid, skies are variably cloudy, and temperatures are seasonal to above.

Zone 2: Variably cloudy skies accompany showers and thunderstorms (some strong with tornado potential), especially central and south; temperatures are seasonal to above.

Zone 3: Central parts of the zone see precipitation, some locally heavy, later in the week; western areas are partly cloudy; scattered showers and thunderstorms (some strong with tornado potential), are possible in eastern areas; and the zone is humid with temperatures seasonal to above.

Zone 4: Skies are fair to partly cloudy, conditions are humid, temperatures are seasonal to above, and the zone has a chance for thunderstorms.

Zone 5: The zone is mostly fair with temperatures seasonal to above and a chance for thunderstorms.

Zone 6: Western and central areas are cloudy with precipitation, eastern areas are partly cloudy with a chance for showers, and temperatures are seasonal to below.

Zone 7: Northern coastal areas see precipitation, some locally heavy, with a chance for showers in southern coastal and central parts of the zone; eastern areas are partly cloudy; temperatures are seasonal.

Zone 8: Western Alaska is cloudy with precipitation (some abundant), central and eastern areas are partly cloudy with scattered precipitation, and temperatures are seasonal. Hawaiian skies are mostly fair to partly cloudy with showers in western parts of the state and seasonal temperatures.

Full Moon, June 2–8

Zone 1: The zone is humid and cloudy with precipitation, some locally heavy, and temperatures are seasonal to below.

Zone 2: Northern areas are cloudy with precipitation (some locally heavy), central and southern parts of the zone have a chance for precipitation, and temperatures are seasonal.

Zone 3: Western areas see scattered thunderstorms, skies are fair to partly cloudy in western and central parts of the zone, and eastern areas are cloudy with precipitation and cooler than the rest of the zone, where temperatures are seasonal to above.

Zone 4: Conditions are humid with temperatures seasonal to above, western areas see precipitation, and central and eastern parts of the zone are mostly fair to partly cloudy with a chance for scattered precipitation.

Zone 5: The zone is humid and partly cloudy with temperatures seasonal to above, and eastern areas see scattered thunderstorms.

Zone 6: Much of the zone is cloudy and windy with showers and temperatures seasonal to below.

Zone 7: Western and central areas are cloudy, eastern areas are humid and partly cloudy, temperatures are seasonal to above, and much of the zone sees precipitation.

Zone 8: Central parts of Alaska are cloudy with abundant precipitation that moves into eastern areas, while western locations are mostly fair, windy, and seasonal. Hawaii is windy, seasonal, and variably cloudy with showers.

Fourth Quarter Moon, June 9–15

Zone 1: The zone is windy and cloudy with temperatures seasonal to below and precipitation (some abundant).

Zone 2: Northern areas are cloudy with precipitation, central and southern areas are mostly fair with a chance for thunderstorms, and temps are seasonal but cooler in northern parts of the zone.

Zone 3: Western and central parts of the zone are seasonal with scattered thunderstorms under fair to partly cloudy skies, and eastern areas are cloudy and cooler with precipitation.

Zone 4: Western skies are partly cloudy, central and eastern areas see showers and scattered thunderstorms along with fair to partly cloudy skies, and temperatures are seasonal to above.

Zone 5: The zone is partly cloudy to cloudy with showers and a chance for scattered thunderstorms in central and eastern areas; conditions are humid and temperatures seasonal to above.

Zone 6: Western areas are fair to partly cloudy, central and eastern parts of the zone see scattered thunderstorms along with windy conditions and cloudy skies, and temperatures are seasonal to below.

Zone 7: Skies are fair to partly cloudy in western areas, central and eastern parts of the zone see scattered showers and thunderstorms under variably cloudy skies, and temperatures are seasonal to below.

Zone 8: Central Alaska is cloudy and windy with abundant precipitation that moves into eastern areas of the state, while western skies are fair; temperatures are seasonal. Central and eastern Hawaii see precipitation (some locally heavy), western parts of the state are fair, and temperatures are seasonal to above.

New Moon, June 16–23

Zone 1: Southern areas see showers and thunderstorms, skies are variably cloudy, and temperatures are seasonal.

Zone 2: The zone is humid with showers north, temperatures seasonal to above, and variably cloudy skies; central and southern areas have a chance for scattered thunderstorms.

Zone 3: Temperatures are seasonal to above, conditions are humid, and skies fair to partly cloudy, and much of the zone has a chance for scattered showers and thunderstorms.

Zone 4: Skies are variably cloudy with more cloudiness west, much of the zone sees scattered showers and precipitation, eastern areas are humid with more precipitation later in the week along with strong thunderstorms with tornado potential, and temperatures are seasonal to above.

Zone 5: Skies are mostly fair to partly cloudy, central and eastern areas are humid, temperatures are seasonal to above, and much of the zone sees scattered thunderstorms with tornados possible at week's end.

Zone 6: Skies are fair to partly cloudy and windy with showers in central areas and temperatures seasonal to above.

Zone 7: Skies are variably cloudy, western and central areas see scattered showers, eastern parts of the zone are mostly fair, and temperatures are seasonal to above.

Zone 8: Eastern and central Alaska are fair, western parts of the state are cloudy with precipitation, and temperatures are seasonal. Fair to partly cloudy skies accompany temperatures seasonal to above in Hawaii, and western and central areas see showers later in the week.

Summer

Zone 1 sees average to above-average precipitation this summer along with more cloudiness and cooler temperatures. Zone 2 also tends toward cooler weather, and precipitation levels range from average to below. Western areas of Zone 3 see strong thunderstorms with tornado potential at times, but precipitation and temperatures are seasonal to below. Hurricane potential is low this summer.

Eastern and central parts of Zones 4 and 5 are especially prone to strong thunderstorms with tornados this summer, and hurricanes are more likely to occur in the Gulf areas of Zones 3 and 5 than in Zones 1 and 2. Temperatures range from seasonal to below, especially in western and central areas of Zones 4 and 5, where precipitation is average. Eastern areas see above-average precipitation.

Above-average temperatures are the norm for Zones 6 and 7, which tend toward dryness. The central areas of both zones see more precipitation than western and eastern areas.

In Zone 8, eastern Alaska is mostly cool, while central and western parts of the state are seasonal to above. Precipitation ranges from average in western areas to below in the rest of the state. Temperatures in Hawaii are seasonal to above with precipitation average to below.

Second Quarter Moon, June 24–30

Zone 1: The zone is partly cloudy, seasonal, windy, and humid with showers and thunderstorms.

Zone 2: Northern areas see showers and thunderstorms, central and southern parts of the zone are partly cloudy, and humidity accompanies seasonal temperatures.

Zone 3: Skies are fair to partly cloudy, temperatures are seasonal, and eastern areas see scattered showers and thunderstorms.

Zone 4: Western and central skies are cloudy with showers and thunderstorms (some strong with locally heavy precipitation and tornado potential); eastern areas are mostly fair; and seasonal temperatures accompany humidity.

Zone 5: The zone is humid and cloudy with temperatures ranging from seasonal to above, and much of the zone sees precipitation (some abundant) along with a chance for strong thunderstorms with tornado potential.

Zone 6: Skies range from fair to cloudy across the zone along with showers and thunderstorms in central and eastern areas; temperatures are seasonal to above.

Zone 7: Temperatures are seasonal, western and eastern skies are fair to partly cloudy, eastern areas have a chance for precipitation, and southern coastal and central parts of the zone see showers and storms under cloudy skies with locally heavy precipitation.

Zone 8: Western and central Alaska are variably cloudy and windy with precipitation, eastern areas are partly cloudy, and temperatures are seasonal. Hawaii is partly cloudy and seasonal, windy east, with a chance for precipitation west.

Full Moon, July 1–7

Zone 1: The zone is humid, seasonal, and partly cloudy to cloudy with a chance for thunderstorms.

Zone 2: Skies are fair to partly cloudy with more cloudiness north, central and southern areas see scattered showers and thunderstorms, and humidity accompanies seasonal temperatures.

Zone 3: Skies are variably cloudy with more cloudiness east, western and central areas see scattered showers and thunderstorms, and temperatures are seasonal to above but cooler east.

Zone 4: The zone is mostly fair and windy with temperatures seasonal to above; showers and strong thunderstorms with tornado potential are possible.

Zone 5: Humidity accompanies temperatures seasonal to above under variably cloudy skies, and strong thunderstorms with tornado potential are possible.

Zone 6: Temperatures ranging from seasonal to above accompany partly cloudy skies west and central, and central and eastern parts of the zone have a chance for showers and thunderstorms, with more cloudiness east.

Zone 7: The zone is mostly fair with temperatures seasonal to above, and eastern areas are humid, windy, and hot with a chance for thunderstorms.

Zone 8: Much of Alaska sees precipitation along with partly cloudy to cloudy skies and seasonal temperatures, and central parts of the state see abundant downfall. Hawaii is humid with temperatures seasonal to above and showers, some locally heavy.

Fourth Quarter Moon, July 8–14

Zone 1: Variably cloudy skies accompany humidity and seasonal temperatures, along with a chance for showers and thunderstorms, some with locally heavy downfall.

Zone 2: Central and southern areas are windy with thunderstorms and precipitation (some abundant), possibly from a tropical storm; northern areas have a chance for precipitation; and temperatures are seasonal.

Zone 3: Northern areas are generally fair with a chance for thunderstorms; southern areas, especially central, see precipitation and thunderstorms, some with abundant downfall, possibly from a tropical storm; and temperatures are seasonal to above.

Zone 4: Skies are fair and temperatures are seasonal to above.

Zone 5: Temps range from seasonal to above under fair skies.

Zone 6: Precipitation in western parts of the zone moves into central areas, eastern areas have a chance for precipitation, and temperatures are seasonal under variably cloudy skies.

Zone 7: Some western and central parts of the zone see showers, skies are fair to partly cloudy, temperatures are seasonal, and central and eastern areas are humid.

Zone 8: Alaska is mostly fair to partly cloudy and seasonal with scattered precipitation west. Hawaii is fair and seasonal.

New Moon, July 15–23

Zone 1: The zone is windy, cloudy, and seasonal with precipitation (some abundant), possibly from a tropical storm.

Zone 2: Northern areas are cloudy with abundant downfall, possibly from a tropical storm, and central and southern parts of the zone are partly cloudy to cloudy; temps are seasonal to below.

Zone 3: Temps range from seasonal to above, skies are fair to partly cloudy west and central, and eastern areas are cooler with abundant precipitation, possibly from a tropical storm.

Zone 4: The zone is generally fair to partly cloudy with temperatures ranging from seasonal to above, and central and eastern areas have a chance for thunderstorms, which could be strong with tornado potential.

Zone 5: Humidity accompanies temperatures ranging from seasonal to above, skies are fair to partly cloudy, and western parts of the zone have a chance for thunderstorms.

Zone 6: Windy skies and seasonal temperatures accompany showers and thunderstorms across the zone as a front advances, bringing locally heavy downfall to eastern areas.

Zone 7: Skies are variably cloudy, temperatures are seasonal to above, eastern areas are humid, and much of the zone sees scattered showers and thunderstorms.

Zone 8: Alaska is seasonal and partly cloudy to cloudy with abundant precipitation west and central. Much of Hawaii sees showers and thunderstorms with heavy downfall in some areas, along with humidity and temperatures seasonal to above.

Second Quarter Moon, July 24–30

Zone 1: Temperatures seasonal to above trigger storms (some strong with locally heavy precipitation), and the zone is windy.

Zone 2: Northern areas see precipitation (some abundant); central parts of the zone see scattered thunderstorms (some strong with tornado potential); southern areas have a chance for thunderstorms; and temperatures are seasonal to above under partly cloudy to cloudy skies; a tropical storm is possible.

Zone 3: The zone is windy and fair to partly cloudy with temperatures ranging from seasonal to above, and strong thunderstorms with tornado potential are possible along with abundant precipitation in eastern areas; a tropical storm is possible.

Zone 4: The zone is fair to partly cloudy, humid, and windy with temperatures ranging from seasonal to above and a chance for thunderstorms.

Zone 5: Temperatures range from seasonal to above under windy and fair to partly cloudy skies, along with humidity and a chance for thunderstorms.

Zone 6: Skies are partly cloudy to cloudy and temperatures seasonal to below, eastern areas have a chance for precipitation, and western and central parts of the zone see precipitation, some locally heavy.

Zone 7: Northern coastal areas see locally heavy precipitation, as do southern coastal and central parts of the zone, and skies are partly cloudy to cloudy with temperatures ranging from seasonal to above; eastern areas have a chance for precipitation.

Zone 8: Much of Alaska sees precipitation under variably cloudy skies with seasonal temperatures. Western Hawaii is fair, central and eastern areas see scattered showers and thunderstorms, and temperatures are seasonal.

Full Moon, July 31–August 5

Zone 1: The zone is mostly fair and seasonal.

Zone 2: Northern areas are partly cloudy, central and southern parts of the zone are mostly fair, and humidity accompanies seasonal temperatures.

Zone 3: Temperatures are seasonal and the zone is windy and variably cloudy with scattered thunderstorms, some strong with tornado potential.

Zone 4: Western areas are windy and fair; temperatures are seasonal but cooler east, which is windy with scattered thunderstorms; and central parts of the zone see more cloudiness with precipitation, some abundant.

Zone 5: Central and eastern areas have a chance for scattered showers and thunderstorms, some strong with tornado potential; western parts of the zone are windy with a chance for precipitation; and skies are variably cloudy with seasonal temperatures.

Zone 6: The zone is windy, seasonal, and partly cloudy with a chance for precipitation later in the week.

Zone 7: Skies are fair to partly cloudy and temperatures seasonal, and central and eastern areas are windy with a chance for scattered showers and thunderstorms.

Zone 8: Much of Alaska is windy and partly cloudy with scattered precipitation, eastern areas see more cloudiness and precipitation, some locally heavy; temperatures are seasonal to below. Hawaii is fair and seasonal.

Fourth Quarter Moon, August 6–13

Zone 1: Seasonal temperatures accompany variably cloudy skies and scattered showers and thunderstorms.

Zone 2: Northern areas see scattered showers and thunderstorms, central and southern parts of the zone are partly cloudy, and temperatures are seasonal.

Zone 3: Western and central parts of the zone are mostly fair and windy with a chance for strong storms in central areas at week's end, eastern areas see scattered showers and thunderstorms with more cloudiness, and the zone is humid and seasonal.

Zone 4: Northwest areas of the zone see precipitation (some abundant), and much of the rest of the zone is fair; strong thunderstorms with tornado potential are possible, along with locally heavy precipitation, later in the week in the eastern Plains and east; and the zone is humid with seasonal temperatures.

Zone 5: Much of the zone is fair with temperatures seasonal to above, central areas see more cloudiness, and central and eastern parts of the zone could see strong thunderstorms with locally heavy precipitation and tornados later in the week.

Zone 6: Western skies are partly cloudy, central parts of the zone are fair, eastern areas are windy with showers and thunderstorms, and temperatures are seasonal to below.

Zone 7: Temperatures are seasonal to above, eastern areas are humid with scattered showers and thunderstorms, central parts of the zone have a chance precipitation, and temperatures range from seasonal to above.

Zone 8: Alaska is windy and variably cloudy with scattered precipitation and temperatures seasonal to below. Hawaii is windy, partly cloudy, and seasonal with scattered precipitation.

New Moon, August 14–21

Zone 1: Northern areas could see locally heavy precipitation, southern areas see scattered precipitation, temperatures are seasonal to below, and skies are partly cloudy to cloudy.

Zone 2: Northern parts of the zone are partly cloudy, temperatures are seasonal, and central and southern areas are cloudy and windy with potential for locally heavy precipitation, possibly from a tropical storm.

Zone 3: Western areas have a chance for precipitation, the zone is humid, temperatures are seasonal, and abundant precipitation is possible in the Gulf states, possibly from a tropical storm.

Zone 4: Skies are fair to partly cloudy, seasonal temps accompany humidity, and the zone has a chance for showers and storms.

Zone 5: A chance for thunderstorms accompanies seasonal temperatures, humidity, and partly cloudy skies.

Zone 6: The zone is mostly fair and windy with temperatures seasonal to above and scattered thunderstorms west.

Zone 7: Western and central parts of the zone are windy, skies are mostly fair, temperatures range from seasonal to above, and eastern areas have a chance for thunderstorms.

Zone 8: Central Alaska is windy and partly cloudy, western parts of the state are fair, eastern areas are cloudy with precipitation, and temperatures are seasonal. Central Hawaii will have a chance for thunderstorms, and the state is windy, fair to partly cloudy, and seasonal to above.

Second Quarter Moon, August 22–28

Zone 1: Partly cloudy skies accompany temperatures ranging from seasonal to below, and the zone has a chance for showers and thunderstorms.

Zone 2: The zone has a chance for showers and thunderstorms under partly cloudy skies with temperatures seasonal to above.

Zone 3: Skies are partly cloudy and windy, temperatures are seasonal, and the zone has a chance for showers and thunderstorms with locally heavy precipitation possible in western areas.

Zone 4: The zone is variably cloudy and windy with precipitation, some locally heavy, possibly from a tropical storm, and temperatures are seasonal.

Zone 5: Temperatures range from seasonal to below under variably cloudy skies with precipitation, some locally heavy, possibly from a tropical storm.

Zone 6: The zone is mostly fair to partly cloudy with more cloudiness east and scattered precipitation, temperatures are seasonal, and western areas are windy with showers later in the week.

Zone 7: Western areas see scattered precipitation, central parts of the zone are fair and windy, eastern areas are cloudy with precipitation, and temperatures are seasonal.

Zone 8: Central Alaska is cloudy and windy with precipitation, western and eastern areas are partly cloudy, and temperatures are seasonal. Hawaiian temperatures are seasonal to above and the state is windy and partly cloudy with scattered precipitation in central areas.

Full Moon, August 29–September 4

Zone 1: Scattered thunderstorms accompany partly cloudy to cloudy skies and temperatures seasonal to above.

Zone 2: The zone is seasonal, northern areas are variably cloudy with scattered thunderstorms, and central and southern parts of the zone are mostly fair with a chance for thunderstorms.

Zone 3: Skies are partly cloudy to cloudy, temperatures are seasonal, and the zone sees thunderstorms, some with locally heavy precipitation.

Zone 4: Much of the zone is partly cloudy to cloudy with scattered showers and thunderstorms, some with locally heavy precipitation, and temperatures are seasonal.

Zone 5: Seasonal temperatures accompany cloudy skies and precipitation (some abundant), possibly from a tropical storm.

Zone 6: Temps are seasonal to above under partly cloudy skies with a chance for scattered showers and thunderstorms central.

Zone 7: Southern coastal and central areas see scattered showers and thunderstorms, western and central areas are partly cloudy to cloudy and windy, eastern parts of the zone are mostly fair with a chance for showers, and temperatures are seasonal to above.

Zone 8: Alaska is windy, seasonal, and partly cloudy to cloudy with scattered precipitation west and central. Hawaiian temperatures are seasonal to above and the state is humid and partly cloudy with precipitation.

Fourth Quarter Moon, September 5–12

Zone 1: Temperatures are seasonal to below and the zone is cloudy with locally heavy precipitation north.

Zone 2: Northern skies are cloudy and windy with precipitation, central and southern areas are windy with scattered precipitation, and temperatures are seasonal to below.

Zone 3: Temperatures are seasonal under variably cloudy skies with thunderstorms west and central (some strong with heavy precipitation), and eastern areas are windy with thunderstorms later in the week.

Zone 4: Much of the zone is fair to partly cloudy, eastern areas have more cloudiness and potential for strong thunderstorms and heavy precipitation, and temperatures are seasonal.

Zone 5: The zone is partly cloudy and seasonal with a chance for thunderstorms east.

Zone 6: Temps are seasonal to below, eastern areas have a chance for precipitation, and windy and wet conditions with storm potential in western areas advance into central parts of the zone.

Zone 7: Skies are partly cloudy to cloudy with a chance for precipitation east, while western and central parts of the zone are wind with showers and thunderstorms.

Zone 8: Much of Alaska is cloudy with precipitation (some abundant in western and central areas, and temperatures are seasonal. Hawaii is cloudy and seasonal with abundant precipitation, possibly from a tropical storm or typhoon.

2014 © daveallenphoto Image from BigStockPhoto.com

New Moon, September 13–20

Zone 1: Skies are fair to partly cloudy, temperatures are seasonal to above, and southern areas have a chance for precipitation.

Zone 2: Temperatures are seasonal to below, and skies are cloudy and windy with showers and thunderstorms, some with locally heavy precipitation central and south.

Zone 3: Wind and variably cloudy skies accompany seasonal temperatures and scattered showers and thunderstorms.

Zone 4: Western and central areas are partly cloudy, eastern areas see more cloudiness and humidity along with precipitation, and temperatures are seasonal.

Zone 5: The zone is mostly fair to partly cloudy, temperatures are seasonal to above, and eastern areas are windy with scattered precipitation.

Zone 6: Much of the zone is cloudy with abundant precipitation in eastern areas, and temperatures are seasonal.

Zone 7: Cloudy skies and precipitation (some abundant) prevail across the zone and temperatures are seasonal.

Zone 8: Western Alaska is windy with precipitation (some abundant), skies are partly cloudy to cloudy, and temperatures are seasonal. Hawaii is partly cloudy with temperatures seasonal to above and a chance for precipitation.

Autumn

An above-average number of storms will move through Zone 1, bringing abundant precipitation; temperatures tend to be below average. Temperatures are also seasonal to below in northern parts of Zone 2, but more seasonal in central and southern parts of the zone. Northern areas of Zone 3 also see more storms, while precipitation in central and southern areas is average. The rest of Zone 3 tends to dryness and temperatures that range from seasonal to above.

Temperatures in central and eastern areas of Zones 4 and 5 are generally above average and precipitation is below. These areas will see some major storms, however, that generate north of the Dakotas. Precipitation is average in western parts of Zones 4 and 5, where temperatures also tend to be above average. The exception is the northwestern part of Zone 4, which sees an above-average number of storms.

Storms follow a path from the Northwest through the eastern areas of Zones 6 and 7, bringing average precipitation. Western and central parts of Zones 6 and 7 see precipitation average to below and temperatures seasonal to above.

In Zone 8, temperatures in western and central Alaska are below average, while eastern parts of the state are more seasonal. Central areas see abundant precipitation with more cloudiness, while downfall is average in eastern and western parts of the state. Temperatures in Hawaii are seasonal to above with precipitation generally below average.

Second Quarter Moon, September 21–26

Zone 1: Abundant precipitation is possible across the zone with windy, cloudy skies and temperatures seasonal to below.

Zone 2: Northern areas are windy, cloudy, and stormy; central and southern areas are partly cloudy to cloudy with potential for strong thunderstorms; and temperatures are seasonal to below.

Zone 3: Eastern areas are stormy and windy, temperatures are seasonal to below, and western and central parts of zone see showers and thunderstorms.

Zone 4: The zone is fair to partly cloudy and seasonal with precipitation in eastern areas.

Zone 5: Temperatures are seasonal, eastern areas have a chance for precipitation, and skies are fair to partly cloudy.

Zone 6: Western skies are partly cloudy, eastern skies are fair, temperatures are seasonal, and central parts of the zone are partly cloudy to cloudy with precipitation.

Zone 7: The zone is partly cloudy with scattered precipitation west and central, eastern areas are humid with a chance for thunderstorms, and temperatures are seasonal to above.

Zone 8: Central and eastern Alaska are cloudy and stormy with abundant precipitation, western areas are mostly fair, and temps are seasonal. Hawaii is partly cloudy to cloudy, windy, and seasonal with locally heavy precipitation possible west and central.

Full Moon, September 27–October 3

Zone 1: Temperatures are seasonal to below and the zone is cloudy with locally heavy precipitation in northern areas.

Zone 2: Seasonal temperatures accompany cloudy, windy skies, and much of the zone sees precipitation, some locally heavy in southern areas.

Zone 3: Western areas are partly cloudy, central and eastern areas see more cloudiness with precipitation (some locally heavy), and temperatures are seasonal.

Zone 4: The zone is variably cloudy and seasonal, windy west and central, and central and eastern areas have a chance for precip.

Zone 5: Much of the zone has a chance for precipitation, especially central, and the zone is windy, seasonal, and partly cloudy.

Zone 6: Western and central parts of the zone are cloudy and windy with precipitation, eastern areas are partly cloudy with a chance for precipitation, and temperatures are seasonal to below.

Zone 7: Temperatures are seasonal to above, eastern areas are partly cloudy, and western and central parts of the zone are windy and partly cloudy to cloudy with precipitation.

Zone 8: Alaska is fair to partly cloudy and windy with temperatures seasonal to below. Hawaii is mostly fair and seasonal.

Fourth Quarter Moon, October 4–11

Zone 1: Skies are partly cloudy and temps seasonal to below.

Zone 2: Northern areas are partly cloudy, temperatures are seasonal, and central and southern areas are cloudy with potential for strong thunderstorms and abundant precipitation, possibly from a tropical storm or hurricane.

Zone 3: Temperatures are seasonal to below, western and central areas are cloudy with thunderstorms with tornado potential and heavy precipitation, possibly from a tropical storm or hurricane.

Zone 4: Western and central areas are partly cloudy, temperatures are seasonal to below, and eastern areas are cloudy with precipitation (some abundant.

Zone 5: Temperatures are seasonal to below, western and central areas are fair to partly cloudy and windy, and eastern parts of the zone are cloudy with precipitation.

Zone 6: Skies are partly cloudy, temperatures are seasonal, and the zone has a chance for precipitation.

Zone 7: Western and central parts of the zone are windy with scattered precipitation under partly cloudy to cloudy skies, and temperatures are seasonal to above.

Zone 8: Alaska is fair to partly cloudy and seasonal. Hawaii is mostly fair and seasonal.

New Moon, October 12–19

Zone 1: The zone is partly cloudy to cloudy and seasonal and northern areas are windy with precipitation, some locally heavy.

Zone 2: Variably cloudy skies accompany seasonal temperatures, central areas are windy, and central and southern parts of the zone see thunderstorms (some strong with tornado potential.

Zone 3: Temperatures are seasonal but cooler west, eastern areas are partly cloudy with scattered precipitation, and western and central parts of the zone are cloudy with precipitation.

Zone 4: Western skies are partly cloudy; central and eastern areas are cloudy, windy, and stormy with abundant precipitation in some locations; and temperatures are seasonal to below.

Zone 5: Temperatures are seasonal but cooler east, which is cloudy with precipitation, and western and central parts of the zone are partly cloudy.

Zone 6: Much of the zone is windy with temperatures ranging from seasonal to below, central and western skies are fair, and eastern areas are partly cloudy.

Zone 7: Temperatures are seasonal to below, eastern areas are windy and partly cloudy, and western central parts of the zone are mostly fair.

Zone 8: Western and central Alaska are fair to partly cloudy, eastern areas are cloudy with abundant precipitation, and temperatures are seasonal. Hawaii is seasonal and partly cloudy with a chance for precipitation.

Second Quarter Moon, October 20–26

Zone 1: Skies are mostly fair, temperatures are seasonal, and southern areas have a chance for precipitation.

Zone 2: Northern areas have a chance for precipitation, temperatures are seasonal to above, and central and southern parts of the zone see thunderstorms, some strong with tornado potential and locally heavy precipitation.

Zone 3: Temperatures are seasonal to below, eastern areas are partly cloudy with a chance for precipitation, and western and central parts of the zone are cloudy with precipitation, some locally heavy.

Zone 4: Much of the zone sees precipitation (some abundant in central areas); western parts of the zone are windy and partly cloudy, central and eastern areas are cloudy; and temperatures are seasonal to below.

Zone 5: Western skies are partly cloudy, central and eastern areas are cloudy with abundant precipitation, and temperatures are seasonal to below.

Zone 6: The zone is partly cloudy with temperatures seasonal to below and scattered precipitation central and east later in the week.

Zone 7: Temperatures are seasonal, the zone is windy, and there is a chance for showers and thunderstorms later in the week.

Zone 8: Western and central Alaska are partly cloudy, eastern areas are cloudy with precipitation (some abundant, and temperatures are seasonal to below. Hawaii is partly cloudy and seasonal.

Full Moon, October 27–November 2

Zone 1: Skies are fair to partly cloudy, northern areas are windy, and temperatures are seasonal.

Zone 2: Central and southern parts of the zone are mostly fair, northern areas are partly cloudy, and temperatures are seasonal to above.

Zone 3: The zone is fair to partly cloudy and seasonal with a chance for precipitation in western areas.

Zone 4: Much of the zone is cloudy, temperatures are seasonal to below, and western and central parts of the zone see precipitation, abundant in some areas.

Zone 5: Western and central areas are cloudy with precipitation (some locally heavy), temperatures are seasonal, and eastern skies are partly cloudy.

Zone 6: Partly cloudy and windy skies accompany temperatures ranging from seasonal to above.

Zone 7: Temperatures are seasonal to above and the zone is partly cloudy to cloudy.

Zone 8: Western Alaska is fair, temperatures are seasonal to below, and central and eastern parts of the state are cloudy with abundant precipitation in some areas. Hawaii is variably cloudy and seasonal with showers in eastern areas.

Fourth Quarter Moon, November 3–10

Zone 1: The zone is cloudy and seasonal with precipitation north.

Zone 2: Skies are fair to partly cloudy and the zone is seasonal.

Zone 3: Seasonal temperatures accompany partly cloudy skies, and central areas have a chance for precipitation.

Zone 4: The zone is variably cloudy and seasonal with precipitation in central and eastern areas.

Zone 5: Skies are variably cloudy and windy, temperatures are seasonal to below, and central and eastern areas see precipitation.

Zone 6: Stormy conditions could develop across much of the zone, especially central and east, with cloudy skies and temperatures seasonal to below as a front advances.

Zone 7: Much of the zone is windy with variably cloudy skies and temperatures seasonal to below. Central and eastern areas could see stormy conditions.

Zone 8: Western Alaska sees abundant precipitation, eastern areas are windy with precipitation, and central parts of the state are partly cloudy; temperatures are seasonal. Hawaii is partly cloudy and seasonal.

New Moon, November 11–18

Zone 1: The zone is seasonal and partly cloudy to cloudy with scattered precipitation, some locally heavy.

Zone 2: Central and southern areas are windy with a chance for precipitation, northern areas see scattered precipitation, skies are variably cloudy, and temperatures are seasonal.

Zone 3: Temperatures range from seasonal to below under partly cloudy to cloudy skies with precipitation east and central.

Zone 4: Skies are variably cloudy and temperatures seasonal to below, and central and eastern areas are windy with precipitation as a front advances.

Zone 5: Eastern parts of the zone are windy with precipitation, and the zone is generally partly cloudy and seasonal.

Zone 6: The zone is windy and seasonal with a chance for precipitation central and east.

Zone 7: Eastern skies are fair, western and central areas are partly cloudy with a chance for precipitation, and temps are seasonal.

Zone 8: Alaska is fair to partly cloudy and seasonal with precipitation in eastern areas later in the week. Hawaii is cloudy with showers, some locally heavy, and temperatures ranging from seasonal to below.

Second Quarter Moon, November 19–24

Zone 1: Seasonal temps accompany fair to partly cloudy skies.

Zone 2: Northern areas are mostly fair, central and southern areas are partly cloudy, temperatures are seasonal, and the zone has a chance for precipitation later in the week.

Zone 3: Western and central parts of the zone are cloudy with precipitation later in the week (some abundant), temperatures are seasonal to below, and eastern areas are partly cloudy with a chance for precipitation.

Zone 4: Much of the zone is fair to partly cloudy with more cloudiness east, along with potential for locally heavy precipitation later in the week and a chance for precipitation west and central; temperatures are seasonal to below.

Zone 5: The zone is windy and partly cloudy to cloudy with scattered precipitation in central and eastern areas (some locally heavy east), and temperatures seasonal to below.

Zone 6: Temperatures are seasonal under partly cloudy skies, and eastern areas have a chance for precipitation.

Zone 7: The zone is partly cloudy and seasonal with a chance for precipitation, and eastern areas are windy.

Zone 8: Central and eastern Alaska are windy with precipitation, western areas are partly cloudy, and temperatures are seasonal. Hawaii is partly cloudy, windy, and seasonal.

Full Moon, November 25–December 2

Zone 1: Southern areas are partly cloudy, northern areas are cloudy with abundant precipitation, and temps are seasonal.

Zone 2: Northern areas are partly cloudy with scattered precipitation, central and southern parts of the zone are windy with more cloudiness and locally heavy precipitation, and temperatures are seasonal to below.

Zone 3: Central areas could see locally heavy precipitation, skies are variably cloudy, eastern areas are windy, and temperatures are seasonal to below.

Zone 4: Increasing clouds bring precipitation to western areas and the western Plains later in the week, along with scattered precipitation in the rest of the zone; partly cloudy to cloudy skies accompany temperatures seasonal to below.

Zone 5: Western areas see precipitation later in the week, central and eastern areas are partly cloudy to cloudy with scattered precipitation, and temperatures are seasonal.

Zone 6: Much of the zone sees precipitation under cloudy, windy skies, and temperatures are seasonal to below.

Zone 7: Temperatures range from seasonal to below with precipitation under partly cloudy to cloudy skies.

Zone 8: Abundant precipitation in western Alaska moves into central areas under cloudy skies, while eastern areas are partly cloudy; temperatures are seasonal to below. Western Hawaii is cloudy with locally heavy precipitation, central and eastern areas are fair to partly cloudy with a chance for precipitation, and temperatures are seasonal.

Fourth Quarter Moon, December 3–10

Zone 1: The zone is windy and cloudy with precipitation and temperatures seasonal to below.

Zone 2: Temperatures are seasonal to below and much of the zone is windy and stormy; strong thunderstorms with tornado potential are possible central and south.

Zone 3: Western skies are partly cloudy; central and eastern areas are windy and stormy with precipitation and possible strong thunderstorms with tornado potential in southern areas; and temperatures are seasonal to below.

Zone 4: Western areas are windy and the zone is fair to partly cloudy and seasonal.

Zone 5: Seasonal temps accompany fair to partly cloudy skies.

Zone 6: The zone is variably cloudy with scattered precipitation, especially central and east, and temps are seasonal to below.

Zone 7: Western areas are windy and southern areas generally fair, while northern coastal and central areas see more cloudiness along with locally heavy precipitation in some locations; eastern parts of the zone are windy and partly cloudy with a chance for precipitation, and temperatures are seasonal to below.

Zone 8: Alaskan temperatures range from seasonal to below, western and central areas see precipitation and windy, and skies are partly cloudy to cloudy. Much of Hawaii sees showers under partly cloudy to cloudy skies and seasonal temperatures.

New Moon, December 11–17

Zone 1: The zone is partly cloudy to cloudy and seasonal with scattered precipitation north.

Zone 2: Temperatures are seasonal, skies are partly cloudy to cloudy, and central and southern areas see precipitation (some locally heavy), along with possible strong thunderstorms with tornado potential.

Zone 3: Fair to partly cloudy skies prevail west and central, eastern areas are cloudy with locally heavy precipitation, and scattered thunderstorms are possible south; temps are seasonal.

Zone 4: Western skies are cloudy with precipitation, central and eastern areas are partly cloudy and windy, and temps are seasonal.

Zone 5: Skies are windy and partly cloudy to cloudy with precipitation west and central and temperatures seasonal to below.

Zone 6: Temperatures are seasonal to below, skies are partly cloudy to cloudy, and western areas are windy with precipitation (some abundant).

Zone 7: Partly cloudy to cloudy skies accompany seasonal temperatures and precipitation east, with a chance for precipitation west and central.

Zone 8: Alaska is seasonal and variably cloudy with precipitation central and east. Hawaii is partly cloudy and seasonal with scattered precipitation central and east.

Second Quarter Moon, December 18–24

Zone 1: The zone is cloudy with precipitation (some locally heavy) and temperatures are seasonal to below.

Zone 2: Much of the zone sees precipitation under variably cloudy skies with seasonal temperatures.

Zone 3: Precipitation in western areas advances into central parts of the zone under very windy and variably cloudy skies; temperatures are seasonal to below.

Zone 4: Western skies are fair, central and eastern skies are partly cloudy to cloudy with precipitation, and temperatures are seasonal to below.

Zone 5: Temperatures ranging from seasonal to below accompany partly cloudy to cloudy skies central and east, where strong thunderstorms with tornado potential are possible, while western parts of the zone are mostly fair.

Zone 6: Western parts of the zone are windy and stormy, central and eastern areas are partly cloudy, and temps are seasonal to below.

Zone 7: Temperatures are seasonal to below and skies are partly cloudy to cloudy with precipitation across much of the zone and locally heavy downfall in central and northeastern areas.

Zone 8: Central Alaska is cloudy with abundant precipitation, western and eastern areas are fair to partly cloudy, and temperatures are seasonal. Hawaii is cloudy and seasonal with locally heavy precipitation.

Full Moon, December 25–31

Zone 1: The zone is windy with precipitation under partly cloudy to cloudy skies and temperatures seasonal to below.

Zone 2: Seasonal temps accompany fair to partly cloudy skies.

Zone 3: Skies are partly cloudy to cloudy with scattered precipitation and seasonal temperatures.

Zone 4: Western and central areas are windy with precipitation (some locally heavy), eastern areas are partly cloudy with a chance for precipitation, and temperatures are seasonal to below.

Zone 5: Temperatures are seasonal to below, skies are partly cloudy to cloudy, some western and central areas see locally heavy precipitation, and central and eastern parts of the zone could see strong thunderstorms with tornado potential.

Zone 6: Western skies are partly cloudy, central and eastern areas are windy with precipitation, and temps are seasonal to below.

Zone 7: Central and eastern parts of the zone see precipitation as a front moves through, western skies are partly cloudy, and temperatures are seasonal to below.

Zone 8: Western and central Alaska are windy, eastern areas are fair, and temperatures are seasonal to below. Hawaii is windy, fair, and seasonal.

About the Author

Kris Brandt Riske is the executive director and a professional member of the American Federation of Astrologers (AFA), the oldest U.S. astrological organization, founded in 1938; and a member of the National Council for Geocosmic Research (NCGR). She has a master's degree in journalism and a certificate of achievement in weather forecasting from Penn State. Kris is the author of several books, including Llewellyn's Complete Book of Astrology: The Easy

Way to Learn Astrology; Mapping Your Money; *and* Mapping Your Future; *and she is coauthor of* Mapping Your Travels and Relocation *and* Astrometeorology: Planetary Powers in Weather Forecasting. *Her newest book is* Llewellyn's Complete Book of Predictive Astrology. *She also writes for astrology publications and does the annual weather forecast for* Llewellyn's Moon Sign Book. *In addition to astrometeorology, she specializes in predictive astrology. Kris is an avid NASCAR fan, although she'd rather be a driver than a spectator. In 2011 she fulfilled her dream when she drove a stock car for twelve fast laps. She posts a weather forecast for each of the thirty-six race weekends (qualifying and race day) for NASCAR drivers and fans. Visit her at www.pitstopforecasting.com. Kris also enjoys gardening, reading, jazz, and her three cats.*

Economic Forecast for 2015: Accountability & Opportunity

by Christeen Skinner

Astro-finance is a fascinating subject offering a multitude of research opportunities. From considering the position of the Moon in a company's natal chart to monitoring the effect on different markets as the Moon moves through the zodiac to the discovery that a Moon-planet cycle has impact on particular commodity prices, evidence suggests that the Moon plays a key role in world financial affairs.

We can all see the obvious effect of the Moon on sea tides. Just as these tides ebb and flow, so too do world markets. Sometimes the waves between tides are high; other times they are gentle and weak, though appearance may well belie a deep strength.

Just as financial technical analysts monitor several cycles, so too the astro-trader must take into account the different rhythms of the Moon. We are all familiar with the regular New-Full-New cycle that marks the Moon's position relative to the Sun. Study of this—arguably the simplest of the lunar rhythms—supports theories that, in some markets, buying at the New Moon and selling at the Full yields profit; in other markets, it seems purchase at the Full Moon and sale at Fourth Quarter is a more workable trading system.

No less important is the rhythm of the Moon created by its apparent distance from Earth. Each month the Moon moves from apogee (farthest away from the Earth) to perigee (closest to Earth). These distances are not consistent: there are times when the Moon is closer to Earth than at others and times when distance from Earth is greater. When this distance rhythm coincides with that of the New-Full cycle—when perigee or apogee occurs within a day or so of either the New or Full Moon—it is not uncommon for there to be severe weather disturbance. When this happens—as, for example with Hurricane Katrina and the tsunamis in Japan in 2011—world markets may be impacted.

Yet world markets do not respond to this "distance effect" every time, since much depends on exactly where the natural disaster takes place and the extent to which commercial activity in the region is affected. Without doubt, however, should a natural catastrophe occur in a major trading zone, the impact on global markets is considerable.

On March 19, 2015, the Moon reaches a relatively close perigee of about 222,000 miles. The following day is the Vernal Equinox, when the Sun reaches 0 Aries. This degree (the Aries point) is of considerable importance to the world. This is when the Sun's path (the ecliptic) crosses the Celestial Equator. In the Northern Hemisphere, this marks the start of the natural year; a chart for this moment set for a capital city's location would offer clues as to how a country will experience the forthcoming year.

What is particularly special in 2015 is that between the lunar perigee and the Vernal Equinox, there is a solar eclipse at 29 Pisces.

This is the very last degree of the zodiac. Perhaps because of an apparent lack of energy before the Sun reaches the first of the cardinal signs (Aries), this degree is associated with sadness and tears and is sometimes termed "the weeping degree." Just a few days earlier, Uranus and Pluto reach the last of a series of five apparent right-angle positions to one another. It is entirely possible that the total effect of these various celestial phenomena will result in a pull on the Earth's crust or affect Earth's core in such a way that there is major calamity, which in turn could have an effect on global markets, bringing considerable volatility during that third week of March.

Solar eclipses also attract our astro-financial attention. In any year there are at least two and sometimes as many as five of these celestial spectacles. In 2015, there are just two. The second occurs on September 12 and takes place approximately thirty-six hours before the Moon reaches an apogee of 252,000 miles. This eclipse does not fall at the end of a sign but in the 21st degree of Virgo. You may know that each degree of the zodiac has an image associated with it. These are known as the Sabian Symbols. For 20 Virgo, this is a "girl's basketball team." This image of the active, challenging feminine force seen from the perspective of finance and economics may be indicative of a groundswell of female entrepreneurship. Certainly the chart for this eclipse suggests a fresh approach to business problem-solving with an accent on women working together.

Whilst solar eclipses (sophisticated New Moons) offer one kind of economic signpost, lunar eclipses, where the Moon is temporarily obscured from view by Earth's shadow, offer another.

Solar eclipses do not have to be accompanied by a lunar eclipse, but they often are. These accompanying eclipses can occur at the Full Moon either side of the solar eclipse and, occasionally, at both. In 2015, the March solar eclipse is accompanied by a lunar eclipse two weeks later; this lunar eclipse highlights the Aries-Libra axis.

The lunar eclipse accompanying the September solar eclipse again takes place two weeks after the solar eclipse and also falls across the Aries-Libra axis, though in a different degree.

Of particular importance is this second lunar eclipse on September 27, which coincides with another perigee. Just a few days later, Mercury reaches its inferior conjunction with the Sun—a common signal for change of direction in commercial activity—while Saturn prepares to leave Scorpio to move on into Sagittarius. (Note that Saturn first moves into Sagittarius in 2014 but crosses back into Scorpio for some months in 2015.) Once again, the combined effect of celestial activity suggests a natural incident beyond the control of mankind. This event could have singular impact on global markets, though, as we know, one man's disaster is another's opportunity!

These lunar eclipses across the Aries-Libra axis speak of shifting fortunes and quite possibly a change in the balance of power. The timing may well be cosmic poetry, as the two lunar eclipses of 2015 occur *after* the last of the squares between Uranus and Pluto; the angle between these two planets has been the backdrop for considerable social, political, and economic upheaval since the angle first formed in 2010.

Uranus entered Aries in 2010, bringing to an end a period of mutual reception with Neptune, when each travelled through a sign better suited to the other. Pluto was already present in another of the cardinal signs (Capricorn), but since Pluto travels so slowly, it had not made much progress into that sign. Allowing for an orb—a few degrees before an angle is exact—Uranus and Pluto were then moving toward forming their first right-angle since the two had conjoined in the mid-1960s. Analysis of the history of this planet cycle shows the two planets to be in hard aspect to one another at times of revolution and disharmony. Thus, it was to be expected there would be signs of social, political, and economic upheaval across the world with the two planets in loose right-angle phase from 2010 through early 2015. There has indeed been considerable market volatility.

The financial and banking industries have each had to fight for their survival in recent years. As the square between these two planes separates from March 2015 forward, the accent moves toward rebalance. Where the dominant phase of combined Uranus and Pluto forces raised the spectre of default and collapse, those companies and businesses that have stayed afloat should find prevailing economic winds to be more favorable. Against the backdrop of this rare aspect, the lunar node has continued to trace its cycle through the zodiac.

Over the course of 18.6 years, the lunar North Node moves through the signs of the zodiac in reverse order to the Moon's movement through the twelve signs. The nodal cycle is such that the node spends approximately eighteen months in each sign. Louise McWhirter, an extremely fine American astrologer of the twentieth century, found that an increase in business activity occurred when the lunar node was passing between the signs of Scorpio and Leo. This part of the nodal cycle began in 2013 and continues through 2017. Throughout 2015—and especially between the two lunar eclipses in April and late September—business activity should be on the rise, providing plenty of opportunity for investors.

Accountability: Jupiter-Saturn

Jupiter and Saturn conjoin every twenty years. Their next conjunction is due in 2020, when they will align in the sign of Aquarius. In 2015, Saturn, the slower-moving of the two planets, completes its transit of Scorpio before making its final crossing into Sagittarius in the last quarter of the year. Jupiter spends the first half of 2015 in Leo and moves into Virgo in August, with the exact 90-degree angle between Jupiter and Saturn taking place on August 3.

Jupiter represents expansion, while Saturn usually places a curb on raw optimism and so curtails excess and boundless optimism, demanding that it be replaced by careful planning and adherence to regulation. In the past, these two planets in so-called "hard" aspect (in square or opposition) put stress on the banking sector that led to the collapse of a bank. The square in 2015, occurring between two lunar eclipses in cardinal signs, makes it quite likely that a major bank will be found to be under-capitalised. It's also likely that the relevant governments will not be keen to step in and lend support, as they might perhaps have done in previous years.

Though such a collapse would no doubt dominate head-lines, other aspects suggest a business renaissance in the third and fourth quarters of the year. On August 11, Jupiter moves into Virgo and Saturn makes its Sagittarius ingress a few weeks later, on September 18. This suggests something very interest-ing indeed: that between August 11 and September 18 (which includes the September solar eclipse period), Jupiter will be in earthy Virgo for a few weeks while Saturn is in watery Scorpio. The blend of earth and water is often visible at times of intense and practical creativity, so that financial products and services brought to market over these few weeks may be worthy of con-siderable attention and perhaps investment. Lending a little more weight to this potential, it should be pointed out that Saturn and Pluto will still be in mutual reception (when each planet is in the sign more favorable to the other).

Partnerships and Takeovers: Venus

The lunar eclipses in Aries and Libra alert us to issues of rela-tionships, compromise, and balance—words that are also used in connection with Venus. Though Venus makes her apparent journey around the Earth annually, in some years this planet has retrograde motion. In 2015, Venus is retrograde between July 25 and September 6. For some of the period, there is an otherwise promising connection between Jupiter and Saturn. There are few companies that have withstood the test of time having been incorporated or reached IPO under Venus retrograde, suggesting that this is not a good time to launch a venture. Obviously joint ventures and takeovers are at risk. July 25 to October 12 should be considered risky for all joint financial partnership activity, especially where borrowing and external funding is required.

However, a more promising Venus period occurs in May, when Venus reaches maximum declination. As with the Moon and other planets, Venus does not keep a steady distance from the celestial equator. The angle between the planet's position and the celestial equator is known as declination. Over a period of years, the angle appears to create a wave-like pattern; some years have deeper and more extreme waves than others. In 2015, Venus moves to a declination degree of more than 27 degrees in May, while Mars makes a similar but less-extreme angle the following month. As these positions do not occur annually, when they do—and when those aspects are highlighted by the Moon or another planet—there is market reaction. At a simple level, we anticipate volatility from Mars at extreme angle and considerable talk of takeovers and other commercial relationships when Venus moves to extreme angle. Together with the Aries-Libra lunar eclipses, it is probable that 2015 will be marked first by talk of collaboration as Venus moves to extreme declination in May, then by market volatility in June as talks progress, and finally by collapse of these prices when deals come undone.

Opportunity: Jupiter and Chiron

Over a period of approximately twelve years, Jupiter moves through the zodiac, spending approximately a year in each sign. As mentioned earlier, Jupiter is the planet associated with expansion. As Jupiter moves through a sign, sectors associated with that sign tend to blossom. From mid-2014 to early-August 2015, Jupiter moves through fiery Leo, most likely boosting leisure-sector stocks: sports items and services, jewellery, weddings, holidays, and high-end fashion. Those who invested in these sectors prior to July 2014 will hopefully find they have made a tidy profit by July 2015.

By contrast, Jupiter's move into Virgo on August 11 should boost service and health sectors as well as data management, all cleaning stocks and services, and precision engineering. Clearly much will depend on the actual companies involved, but in general, these stocks should rise between August 2015 and mid-2016. (If Jupiter boosts sectors, then Saturn has the opposite effect. This planet's move into Sagittarius could dampen the price of travel-related stocks. It is also likely to bring chill winds to the publishing sector.)

So far unmentioned is Chiron, the planetoid whose orbit lies between Saturn and Uranus. For much of 2015, Chiron is very close to 0 declination: a highly sensitive area. Though mostly associated with healing, this planet is often prominent at times of accountability and audit. One of the major themes of 2015 will surely be restitution. The banking and financial sectors will likely be most affected in August, yet not exclusively. A shake-up to the health insurance industry should be apparent from September onward. Expect to see the rise of the "company doctor"—not simply a consultant brought in to identify weakness, but someone who maintains the general health of a corporation. Anticipate that the basic health checkup of companies will be broadened to include goodwill (or lack thereof) and general community standing as well as a healthy balance sheet.

2015 Quarterly Forecast

First Quarter

2015 opens with an opposition between Mars in Aquarius and

Jupiter in Leo. Investors tuning into this planetary combination will surely start the year with very definite strategies in mind. As the New York markets close on the Full Moon, Monday, January 5, Chiron will be at the midheaven. Chiron holds this position at close of trade in New York for just a few days every year. Each time it seems to mark a turning point. With this Full Moon at right angles to Uranus, this could be a day of surprise moves.

Each quarter of the year is dominated by major aspects and accented by the presence of one or more eclipses. The first key outer planet aspect of this first quarter occurs in the acknowledged wealth-creating cycle of Jupiter and Pluto. This quintile aspect is enhanced by the Moon on Tuesday, January 20, with a declination aspect between the Moon and Jupiter that coincides with the Sun's move from Capricorn to Aquarius. This is likely to be a day of considerable market reaction: a wealth-creating day. This begs the question as to which sectors are most likely to experience a surge of activity. With Jupiter in Leo and Pluto in Capricorn, gains may be made in high-end leisure stocks and perhaps in the price of diamonds. This would not be the moment to buy into these but, for some, may be the moment to sell and realize profit.

The early days of February are no less interesting, and we could witness extraordinary price moves between the last day of January and the Full Moon on February 3. Jupiter is conjunct the Moon as the New York market closes with Uranus at the midheaven, suggesting that sharp moves should be expected that day. On February 4, the Sun will be exactly halfway between the December Solstice and the March Equinox. It is not unusual for this date to coincide with significant trading activity. It would be quite in keeping with past records if commodities generally were to reverse trend on January 30 and (bearing in mind that Venus will be moving to maximum declination) for gold prices particularly to be on the move by February 4.

Coinciding with the February New Moon (February 18) and lunar perigee, Mars reaches the degree of the March solar eclipse and within a day moves into the sign in which it is said to have great impact: Aries. February 18 through 20 could see indices reach important resistance levels. Precious metal investors (especially silver traders) should be on alert for strong movements between February 15 and 18.

Mercury is at greatest elongation from the Sun on February 24. This is particularly noteworthy because experience suggests that such a position signals a change of direction in commercial activity. This is perhaps not a good day for signing financial contracts, however tempting bargains might appear to be.

Throughout January and February the lunar node is close to the position held by Saturn in July 1776: the "founding day" of the present USA. The US dollar could come under pressure, particularly in its relationship to sterling. We may also hear of corporate scandals that serve to undermine some of America's largest corporations. The potential for this is underscored by the Full Moon on March 5, which is aligned with Chiron and Uranus. The indications here are for a painful audit of some kind with a subsequent fall in share value. Since Uranus is part of this picture, it is perhaps most likely that it will be a company involved in technology that is most affected. This might not have serious effect on a whole index, but it will be headline news nevertheless.

The angular separation of Jupiter and Uranus is 120 degrees in early March, with the exact angle forming as the Moon lies close to both Jupiter and the fixed star Regulus. This could mark a period of extraordinary creativity for artists and perhaps spur scientific breakthroughs. Markets may reach new highs as the Moon approaches Full and apogee on March 4 and 5. As this Moon wanes, Mars moves to conjoin Uranus and square Pluto. This formation again indicates strong moves. It may be that some decide to take profits on March 11 and 12.

2014 © alexaldo Image from BigStockPhoto.com

Following the solar eclipse (March 20), both Saturn and Neptune hold key position in close-of-trade charts in New York. This is likely to be indicative of a fall in those prices or, at the very least, a leveling off for a few days. A rise is likely by March 25, when the declination cycles of the Moon and Jupiter meet.

Second Quarter

Arguably the most difficult period of the first half of 2015 will be the dates around the lunar eclipse on April 4. This is the accompanying eclipse to the solar, "weeping" eclipse of March 20. This lunar eclipse shows Uranus aligned with the Moon, and Pluto at right angles to both Sun and Moon. It would not be so surprising if there were protests similar to those in Paris in the mid-1960s, Beijing in 1989, or Brazil in 2013. Financial market turmoil is as likely as social disquiet.

April opens with a crossing of the declinations of Venus and Jupiter. Jupiter will be in Leo, a sign oft associated with gold. It would not be surprising—especially with the lunar eclipse just days away—if gold prices increased. With the Sun conjoining

Uranus on April 8 (a classic signature for instability), some investors may well move their investments from equities to precious metals.

Pluto makes its last station square to Uranus on April 17. Since 2010, the April station has coincided with significant movement in gold trading. In 2013, the moves were dramatic, with gold falling during times when we are near this Pluto station. 2015 is unlikely to see a repeat. Even so, great care should be taken—especially if the price has indeed risen sharply in the preceding period. The gold price could fall April 19 and 20.

The cosmic financial brakes may be applied to equities around the Full Moon (May 3). This lunation coincides with Mercury and Saturn reaching their opposition. To some traders it might seem that certain prices are just too high; trader sentiment will then result in the creation of a line of resistance, with prices then falling before recovering at the New Moon (May 17).

There is an oft-quoted statement that traders should "sell in May and go away." The planetary signals for adopting this strategy are suggested by Mercury's retrograde station on May 18, which coincides with the Sun's opposition to Saturn and is followed by the lunar declination alignments with Jupiter between May 23 and 25. Markets could indeed reach levels at which selling and pocketing profits seems a good start.

It seems another turning point will arrive in the last days of May, when Mercury arrives at inferior conjunction with the Sun, Saturn aligns with the Moon, and the next Full Moon begins to form. By June 2, global equity prices could indeed be on the wane.

Venus takes on astro-business prominence after June 6, when that planet reaches greatest elongation from the Sun and moves into Leo. As a bright evening star, those whose personal charts are affected by this Venus transit will no doubt be giving relationship matters their full consideration. Business-wise, entrepreneurs will surely give considerable thought to building alliances, and corporations are tempted to take over smaller businesses. As Venus turns retrograde in July, many of these ideas will prove lucrative—but only for those consultants assessing the viability of such moves, as it is probable that many of these would-be partnerships get no further than the drawing board. The intensity of these discussions should give business journalists much to write about in the days leading into the Gemini New Moon on June 16. Indeed, a war of words is probable in the Sunday papers released on June 14.

Saturn will then slip from Sagittarius back into Scorpio. A strong possibility is that shares in airlines and other travel companies will come under pressure. This may be due to threats that oil prices will rise significantly later in the year, prompting some companies to announce surcharges on flights and holidays. Even so, global indices could see a small rise near the solstice on June 21. This, one of the four most powerful days of the year, occurs soon after another of the promising alignments of the Moon with Venus and Jupiter; traders may respond by pushing prices higher.

Third Quarter

The third quarter of the year will start promisingly, with a likely rise into July 1 followed—as Mars squares the lunar nodes—by a fall on July 2. By the New Moon mid-month, as Mercury reaches its closest point to the Sun, commercial activity is likely to be high. Some investors may wish they had not withdrawn from the markets in May. However, they could feel reassured in late July. On July 25, retrograde Venus arrives in Virgo, signaling probable change. This could prove the start of a volatile few days, as Mercury also changes signs, and Mars and Uranus reach a quarter phase.

News of alliances coming undone, takeovers not going ahead, and difficulties in the banking sector could prompt negative reaction in traders. Equities may then fall in the early days of August. A bounce is likely over August 4 to 6, but even so, many investors will surely be happier not to trade during the first fortnight of August.

With Jupiter's move into Virgo on August 11, a significant mood change is probable. Though Jupiter will have left Leo, leisure stocks could experience a marked high in the last days of August before falling in September. As has been mentioned earlier, investors returning to the market might like to use the latter part of August and early September to research service sector stocks, particularly those related to either health or data management. Around this time a new industry could dawn based on the idea of a "digital death manager or agent"—someone who deep-cleans personal material from the Internet. This may prove a growth industry.

Investors might like to note that in the run-up to the second solar eclipse of 2015 (September 12), new industries may be announced. Those interested in getting in on the ground floor could find this to be a particularly profitable time.

Ahead of the actual Jupiter/Neptune opposition in October, these two planets form a contra-parallel aspect within a day of Saturn's Sagittarius ingress. Anticipate announcement of interest rate rises and strong movement in the price of oil. With equities struggling around the September equinox, it would not be surprising if the prices of precious metals—and gold especially— were to rise on September 25.

Fourth Quarter

The last quarter of 2015 promises to be of a very different hue than the first three quarters. From a political point of view, Socialism should dominate headlines as Saturn moves to its square with Neptune. Discussions about the redistribution of wealth will surely gather momentum. Public sector borrowing in many countries is likely to be on the rise from mid-November onward. Before then (but after the September eclipses), the accent will surely be on rising interest rates and taxes. With the business cycle carrying momentum, more than one government will surely deduce that its citizens can handle greater taxation.

Perhaps the dominating feature of this last quarter of the year will be natural disaster. There are three potentially critical periods: in the days leading up to the Libra New Moon on October 13, later that month around October 26, and between the solstice and Christmas, when the Moon is both Full and at perigee. In all cases, the Southern Hemisphere is most likely to be affected.

These matters aside, developments in both technical industries and biotechnologies should see the burgeoning of new industries that quickly accrue value (particularly in October). Investors may find interesting news items between October 8 and 10, which could prove optimum dates for buying into these shares.

Venus arrives at greatest elongation on October 25, slightly ahead of the perigee Full Moon, which could bring the disaster mentioned above. Over these same dates, the forging of a super-strong alliance—most likely in the pharmaceutical industry—may cause shares in this sector to reach new levels by the November New Moon (November 11).

Later that month Mars reaches its point farthest from the Sun on November 20, just ahead of the Sun's move into Sagittarius and its conjunction with Saturn on November 30. It would not be surprising if markets turned downward in the last days of November, having enjoyed a significant rise through November. Signs of recurring volatility may be apparent between December 5 and 11, when once again there is likely to be dispute over trade agreement. The arms industries may be involved.

Companies linked to service, health, and data management (whose share prices are expected to rise after August) seem set to fare well between December 11 and 14. Lunar perigee coincides with the solstice on December 21, just four days ahead of the Full Moon on December 25. As has been mentioned, this period could see excessive storms in the Southern Hemisphere. Storms of a different kind may be seen on the trading floors, with prices surging before the annual holidays, especially in the West. The indices are likely to be significantly higher at the close of 2015 than they were at the start of the year.

About the Author

Christeen Skinner is the author of Financial Universe *(2004), in which she forecast the banking crisis. She works in London, UK, and has a broad clientele—from City traders to entrepreneurs to private investors. She taught for the Faculty of Astrological Studies for a half-nodal cycle, was chair of the Astrological Association of Great Britain, and is a trustee of Urania Trust.*

2014 © creativa Image from BigStockPhoto.com

New and Full Moon Forecasts for 2015

by Sally Cragin

For 10,000 generations or so, our human species lived without electricity. Since Thomas Edison turned on the lights, we now can have bright light at night. Useful? Certainly. Disruptive to circadian rhythms? Absolutely. Humans evolved with a particularly rhythm of night-sky illumination. Half the month, it was dark. The other half, we had light—certainly enough for nocturnal agricultural practices or hunting.

Lately in my astrology classes, I've been preaching the virtues of "staying in tune with the Moon." If you understand the four phases, or at least the idea of "waxing and waning," you can be productive and kind to your own biorhythms.

Earth's shadow moves from right to left. Therefore, if you see the shadow on the right side of the Moon, the Moon is waning. If you see the shadow on the left side of the Moon, the Moon is waxing, and will be full before it wanes again. If that's too tricky to remember, how about parentheses as the shadow: (for waxing, and) for waning. Here's Romantic poet Christina Rossetti explaining the phenomena more elegantly: "O Lady Moon, your horns point toward the east: Shine, be increased; O Lady Moon, your horns point toward the west: wane, be at rest."

More important is understanding the meaning of phases and the best actions to take when the Moon is in a particular state. Are you starting a project? Take action when the Moon is waxing. Are you finishing a project? Do this during the period of the waning Moon. Farmers plant when the Moon is waxing; they weed or harvest during the waning period. The Full Moon is when excitement is building, and the New Moon is when it's hard to get energized. So projects, relationships, or life-passages that climax during the Full Moon are in tune with the Moon. If those same events conclude during the waning phase, they too are subject to lunar rhythms.

Of course, there are quirks to this system—for example, the day before the New Moon (and, for my money, the two days before that) is an accident-prone time. **The dark of the Moon** is when Luna is a thin crescent, disappearing as quickly as the Cheshire Cat's smile. If you start a project during this period, you may not have much enthusiasm to complete it a few days later.

And then there are the dreaded **eclipses**, which can put an extra layer of confusion into the mix. Many past world cultures interpreted eclipses to signify that a "fall from power" was imminent. Think of 1936—a year of six eclipses and three kings in Great Britain (George VI, Edward VIII, and George VII). Boasting or bragging during the time of an eclipse can bring down the wrath of the gods—a concept the Ancient Greek-speaking peoples well understood as "hubris"! Eclipses are generally more useful as phenomena to be simply observed, as opposed to a lunar phase, which has practical applications for your actions.

Void-of-course Moons are another lunar period to explore— once you are comfortable with the idea of the Moon changing phases and appearing to "grow" or "retreat." During void of course, which may last for a few minutes to a day or longer, the Moon ceases to make angles to other planets as it exits a sign (quick fact: the Moon changes sign every 2.5 days or so—and visits all twelve Sun signs during the course of a lunar month, 29.5 days). The VOC Moon is considered a questionable period: it's not a great time for making decisions, nor the best time to implement plans. However, artists and creative people can go to town during a VOC Moon.

The **New Moon** is all black, and a good time to begin a project or change your direction. The waxing crescent Moon is a thin sliver that gradually gets brighter from right to left. The **second-quarter Moon** is a great day for therapy or evaluating options. The Moon continues to get brighter, with the shadow diminishing on the left side. The **gibbous Moon** (the few days before and after a Full Moon) may as well be the **Full Moon** in terms of the "intensity" some people feel under its influence. As we said, the Full Moon is an excellent time to hit the high point in any endeavor; use the waning gibbous days to wrap up the project before the next New Moon.

Full Moon in Cancer, January 4

The Winter Moon is a time of stock-taking. In olden days, this is when you'd check your larder and see if you had sufficient food for getting your livestock and family through the season. In modern times, this period is helpful for getting clarity on your responsibilities, particularly for Capricorn folks. With the Sun in the sign of the goat, you may feel relationships or job dynamics are at a "turning point" (this can be a good thing, especially if you get some clarity on your responsibilities). Cancer: Build something new, if you can, as this is your Full Moon—a time of heightened skills and sensitivities. Others may seek you out. They don't mean to exhaust you, so it's up to you to "say when." All others: Remember what Barry Manilow told us—feeling are just feelings.

New Moon in Aquarius, January 20

This New Moon has one message loud and clear: make space for innovation. So set a place at the dinner table for your more eccentric friends, who may have a message that's not immediately readable, but which turns out to be absolutely spot-on (e.g., advice on health care or buying a tech stock). Leo: you may need to lick your wounds in public. Embarrassing? Temporarily—but drawing attention to yourself may prompt a larger group of empathetic friends. Aquarius: You're always one step ahead of others, but make a point of sitting still during this New Moon—you'll see exactly what's working in your life and what needs improvement. Others: If you're feeling like you have run out of ideas, it's time to start making lists of "what works" and "what should change."

February 3, Full Moon in Leo, eclipse

The Sun and Moon are in opposition during a Full Moon and could prompt feelings of being divided. This feeling can teach you more about your needs than you expect. Boastful statements are likely from all, and some folks (Leo, especially) can be charming, effective, and energetic. Even the quieter personalities will need to "roar" (the lion's prerogative). And it's also an excellent period for getting a really wild haircut. As Leo rules children and parties, are there any toys that would amuse you? Or perhaps amuse your boss, who may be feeling uncertain (eclipses traditionally signal a shift in status, or an actual fall from power). Aquarius: This isn't an easy time for you, so let others take the chances; you just take notes and carry the Band-Aids. Others: What new technology do you need? Do you need it right now?

February 18, New Moon in Pisces.

Do you love photographs or shoes? Look for bargains, and buy what amuses you or makes you think. And beware of secrets: confidential information is likely to come out. The sign of Pisces focuses on "hidden" themes, and New Moons encourage revelations, particularly about people from your past or ancestors. However, you may not hear the whole truth, and you may find people say one thing and mean another (completely unintentionally). Virgo: if you're getting insufficient information, investigate but be diplomatic. Other folks may have X-ray vision, particularly Pisces (those with sensitive souls). With Venus and Mars in your Sun sign for most of February, plan to make or deepen personal relationships. You're transmitting personal magnetism that will send compass needles spinning. Others: The danger is paranoia; the advantage is heightened perception. Decide what side you're more comfortable with.

Full Moon in Virgo, March 10

What happens when the sensitive Moon—signifier of the nurturing side of femininity—slips into clever and versatile Virgo? Fierce loyalties, abrupt changes of feeling, and possibly willful carelessness about others (from Pisces, usually so aware of others' temperaments). This Full Moon is also known as the Sap Moon, as in that stuff from maple trees that we turn into syrup. If you feel your own juices flowing, you're in tune with this lunation. Best activities include teaching, cleaning, and criticizing. Virgos have greater-than-usual abilities to split their focus and still be the sharpest person in the room. Therefore, this could be an excellent day for learning or being a student, whereas it could be a difficult day for teachers if too many questions throw you off your game. Health matters should also be addressed by all, and second opinions make sense for most signs.

New Moon in Aries, March 20

When the New Moon syncs up with the spring equinox, new projects get even more power to take flight. However, complexity is not the way to go. Keep your message short, sharp, and simple and stick to bullet points. With the Moon and Mars in sync, passionate arguments are on the menu, particularly for those "hot to trot." Energetic Aries falls into that category as you spring lambs get a fresh wind around your birthday. If you've put off a change of direction, this is your time to act—or to plan an action, since some Aries are more comfortable being methodical than being impulsive. Libra, on the other hand, may feel torn between what's old and comfortable and what's new and possibly discomfiting; find someone to commiserate with if you feel rudderless. All other signs should find an activity or project they can do quickly.

Full Moon in Libra, April 4

This Planter's Moon wants to bring unity, but some folks may resent specific direction to play nice. If you're negotiating a personal relationship this weekend, try to use open-ended prompts such as "What are you feeling?" or "Would you share your perspective?" This shifting perspective is Libra's most notable characteristic, although Libras could be forthright and passionate if some issue vexes or perplexes them. (Or, if they're hit with the love bug and realize belatedly, "This person is unsuitable!") Libra Moons can bring out vacillating behaviors, and Aries (usually so direct and confident) could be uncharacteristically tongue-tied. Well-evolved Rams will keep things light and make a joke of this. Spirited compromise could be the story for all other signs.

New Moon in Taurus, April 18

Plan your garden or plant it now—getting your hands dirty is key during this weekend's New Moon. And keep up with spring cleaning, disposing of items that are chipped, battered, or threadbare. Banking activities are favored—count your pennies to see if you can afford that summer vacation. However, some folks might be feeling possessive, but not fully aware of this (Scorpio, this could be you). So if your loved one is spruced up and looking glamorous, figure it's a tribute to your attractiveness and make a similar effort. Taurus: Need a makeover? From now until your birthday is the time. This is also an excellent day for beginning a project that needs consistency and staying power from you. No fly-by-night deals—instead, focus on the slow-and-steady pace that means an eventual payout. Patience will reward everyone.

Full Moon in Scorpio, May 3

We are close to Cinco de Mayo, and the Scorpio flavor brings an intensity to this festive holiday of Mexican independence. Yes, the Full Moon (also known as the Milk Moon) can make people fizz, especially since it's the weekend. Want some fun? Entertain folks who have strong opinions or passions. Gardeners should also be in a mood to rip out everything and start something new. Have you been craving a grotto, concealed fountain, or terraced garden? Scorpio: No one can say no to you (yes, that's intimidating—but useful). However, Scorpio also rules knives, so if you're getting a haircut, you may err on the side of "radical" and walk out with a "whiffle cut." Taurus could be feeling overlooked or underfunded. Right now, the Moon is urging you to lay low and let other folks sort things out (yes, that means relinquishing control). Go for the gusto, or at least an intense discussion.

New Moon in Gemini, May 18

Starting with the week with a New Moon gives everyone a fresh wind. Whatever wasn't working is easy to leave behind, and with the Moon in Gemini, it's easy to hear a variety of opinions and not feel like (a) you have to decide on anything right now, or (b) you need to control a discussion. Today will reward those who are charming and versatile, or those who work best in partnership situations. However, some folks may feel literally divided (that

"Janus twin" effect). If you find you are reversing your position more than once, it may be time to step out of the room. Sagittarius: You may not be seeing everything; if you're getting advice, wait a beat before following. Gemini: You should be at your best, since you multi-task so well; plant seeds now that you can reap in three months. There will be ups and downs, and startling new ideas for everyone during this time—the brave ones among you will trust your instincts.

Full Moon in Sagittarius, June 2

Rambunctious physical activities feel good, and even couch spuds want to kick off their slippers to put on some dancing shoes. This Full Moon is superb for planning (or embarking) on a lengthy journey, or exploring an exotic culture. Why not host a barbecue with a variety of international spicy sauces? Higher education is also emphasized, and since this is graduation week for many schools, even the most sick-of-it-all students may think about further studies. Sagittarius: Your personality will dazzle others—enjoy being the center of attention, and try not to let the coins go flying from your pockets in an effort to keep the party going! Gemini: If others are setting (needless) limits with you, keep your temper and ignore; the danger for you right now is loose lips, which can sink ships. All others: Head in a direction you don't usually consider—north for lovers of the sunny South, or inland for those who live for the beach.

New Moon in Cancer, June 16

This New Moon has but one mission: enhancing your desire for solitude and loyal companions, and making you aware of your own vulnerabilities. Restless spirits will be soothed by familiar environments, and if you're hearing a lot of phrases that start with "I feel," you're in the right place; Cancer makes us emotionally raw while helping us figure out exactly what it is we're feeling, so self-knowledge is the goal. Cancer will feel fragile, yet appear to others to be strong and determined. Meanwhile, you're accessing your circle of folks and asking, "Is this person or that person okay?" Cancer: Use this New Moon to make a wish list for the year that includes a list of people who always make you feel better. Capricorn: The Sun and Moon may be far away from you, which could put you on guard, particularly if others don't have your best interests at heart; be skeptical, but don't tip your hand too soon. All others: Enjoy the urge to confess, but choose your recipient wisely.

Full Moon in Capricorn, July 1

The Thunder Moon encourages us all to focus on the structure in our lives. Whether it's patching a ceiling, mending a fence, or finding a practical solution to an emotional problem, this Full Moon illuminates a narrow path. So wear sturdy shoes and don't rush into anything, particularly Cancers, who could be feeling underappreciated and overwrought. Some folks might sound more certain of matters than they are. Others (mainly the free spirits among us) may be craving commitment. If you're surprised at your need for consistency, you're in tune with this Moon. This is when you smile and say, "So that's what I'm feeling!" Capricorn: You'll be attractive to others, which could bring delightful social opportunities; this isn't the time to continue on that "lone maverick" journey—rather, open the door, and invite others in. All others: It's okay to do things the hard way.

New Moon in Cancer, July 15

Vulnerability could be a danger—or a pleasure, if you enjoy writing poetry. This Moon could find many people needing to rest, particularly if there's been a lot of emotional flare-ups in your life. Cancer Moons focus on the mother, or the nurturing impulse. If you've been bruised, this is when you can heal, and if you've been operating on impulse, this is your time to listen to your instincts. Cancer signs, of course, have an advantage, as they feel everything through their gut. So if you're a Cancer overwhelmed with the needs of others, find a safe rock to hide behind. Capricorn: From the energetic heights prompted by the Full Moon, you may find your energy level and even ambition has dissipated. You might face resistance from normally accommodating quarters this month. All others: Subtlety is the key, as is consistency; it's okay if you don't feel like making a change about something right now.

Full Moon in Aquarius, July 31

If you've been feeling cornered, or that you lacked options, then you'll love this Dog Day Moon, when you can get your pack together and howl in harmony. If you've been suffering from envy or those feelings of "shoulda-woulda-coulda," this Aquarius Moon is excellent for promoting goodwill on a broader level. Put aside pettiness and focus on the betterment of humanity, even if this means contributing to your local youth club so the youngsters will have a good summer. Aquarius: frankness in friendships could be risky right now, but today you'll see the truth of a lot of situations. Leo: With Mars and Venus moving toward your sign, you can't believe anyone could tell you no and mean it; today they can. All others: Fantasy fulfills subconscious desires, so explore yours!

New Moon in Leo, August 14

Four planets are in Leo, and Jupiter and Mercury just exited Leo. The lion likes to roar, but the New Moon is saying "Shhh." So even if you have a sensational piece of information, consider who may be hearing it. Self-indulgence is a temptation, such as overeating or fussing with your hair. Leo Moons tend to make everyone feel more dignified, yet in need of amusement. Embellishment could be attractive, in everything from a story you're telling to the decorations on your bathing suit. And don't forget how useful the New Moon is for finishing a project or starting something new. Leo Moons can put us in touch with our childish desires, which could mean popsicles for dinner. Leo: You'll find the easy way out comes naturally; if you're looking for support and not finding it, consider that others may be looking to you to take the lead. Aquarius: You could be tempted to get into trouble "just because." All others: If you aren't invited to the party, have one of your own.

Full Moon in Pisces, August 29

The Chinese called this the Chrysanthemum Moon, and it's an exciting time for photographers, radiologists, and those who work with the incarcerated or otherwise incapacitated. It's a fine day for making art, and for shopping for shoes (always satisfying!). Water Moons are usually an affectionate time for all, and if you're in a nostalgic mood, it will be easy to imbue the past with a rosy glow. This is a period when hidden secrets come to light, and trust will be a two-way street. Some folks (perhaps Virgo) may see matters as worse or more hopeless than they are, but the wiser ones will rest and do some productive zoning-out (meditation or yoga). Pisces: Your intuition is sharpened, and your ability to see many steps beyond where you are is heightened; if you're procrastinating, it's understandable. Others: The sensitive folks will want to share their innermost thoughts, but there's no need to provide feedback—just have patience.

New Moon in Virgo, September 13

Precision and versatility are the hallmarks of the Virgo New Moon. Health matters get a focus, as do new methods of healing. Are your caregivers good at what they do? Are you satisfied with your own habits of eating, exercise, and sleep? The Virgo New Moon brings all kinds of efficiencies, particularly with a focus on the body and mind. However, care must be taken so that perfectionism doesn't get in the way of forward movement. Everyone should ask themselves what they can grow better. Virgo: With Jupiter in your Sun sign and Mars close behind (from now through late 2016), it's your time to reap rewards due since the early 2000s. Pisces: You may feel it's your job to fix or clean up a situation—or maybe this is your way of coping when others get too demanding; during this New Moon, be gentle with yourself and recognize trifles as not worth your attention. Others should look for opportunities to show their versatility.

Full Moon in Aries, September 27

Here comes the Harvest Moon, and it's easy to shine on or start a project you can finish quickly. This is an excellent day for a cook-out with friends from childhood or the new neighbors. Learning a new game that requires quick reflexes and the ability to shift mental gears quickly is favored. This Full Moon may feel like the last hurrah for some, and Aries Moons can bring out impatience. The phrase "What did you mean by that?" could spring to Libra's lips. However, hot and spicy food, along with some social improvisation, will keep life interesting. Aries: If you're the kind of person who loves excitement, this is your Full Moon; don't hesitate if things get more complicated—you can do it all. Others: You may get excited about something that's a short-term pleasure. That's no reason not to enjoy, but be mindful of "sell-by" dates.

New Moon in Libra, October 12

Seeing both sides is a useful exercise and one that comes (too?) easily for some folks. Work on the issues that get in the way of having a strong partnership. It may be easy to exaggerate, whether it's woes or triumphs. Seeing things clearly will come easily to Libras, who are in a mood to be charmed. However, Aries signs may be plagued by someone afflicted with the dithers (you like forward momentum, always). Since Libra is ruled by Venus (as is Taurus), it's a fine day for renewing friendship or freshening your fall wardrobe. Libra: Your habit of seeing both sides could be useful today, but hold off before making a decision; emotionally, it's wiser to take a pause. Others: Since Libra Moons can prompt people to see contrasts more sharply than usual, take a pause if you find ambivalence is shifting to adoration or disgust.

Full Moon in Taurus, October 27

This Hunter's Moon will bring out your acquisitive impulse. Want it? Get it—and since this is the second major Moon phase in a sign ruled by Venus (Libra being the other), your desire for beauty will be intoxicating. Taurus: You're in full-steam-ahead mode, and your toughness will be helpful if you feel resistance from others. Changing banks or savings accounts is a temptation for all, but Leo and Aquarius need to be wary of "get-rich quick" schemes. Value for money is what we all want right now, and the smart signs will take their time with investments. Scorpio: Be gentle with yourself and avoid situations that require you to take care of others. This Full Moon makes you think you can do it all, but there are limits. Others: it's okay to take your time—especially if you need more time than you think. Just be clear about communicating that, as Taurus Moons can bring out selective deafness in others.

New Moon in Scorpio November 11

Scorpio Moons are sexy, but they can also have high stakes psychologically. Making tough decisions, cutting spending, or starting a project from scratch is in the cards. Scorpio Moons can also bring out toughness in others, so if you've been at a crossroads but reluctant to move in a particular direction, this New Moon will make those choices more easily. Scorpio: Sometimes compromise is the best choice—and it doesn't make you weak. Taurus: This New Moon could prompt you to jump to conclusions, or see that red cape and charge. Own that impulse, and try to wait a day or two before taking action. All others: This New Moon is helpful for getting back to nature or exploring a (hidden?) erotic side. Have fun!

Full Moon in Gemini, November 25

The Beaver Moon brings out a chatty impulse, and even the most silent, stoic types will have plenty to say. Give others the benefit of the doubt, and you'll get your own benefit in the form of deepened partnerships and improvements in your communication style. Writing, editing, and sharing are favored activities. Be pithy in your communications, as overexplaining can cost valuable time or make you seem as if you are underinformed. The advantages of this Full Moon are many. This is an excellent period for investing in sibling relationships or for learning something quickly. Sagittarius: You may have that "walk on hot coals" impulse, and if there's an audience, you'll do anything to amuse; just make sure you have the last laugh. Gemini: If you're explaining things, make sure others are keeping up with you—your understanding of many complex matters is deep. All others: Restlessness is a sign to watch. Is it time to switch gears?

New Moon in Sagittarius, December 11

Justice and humor have equal impact during this New Moon, and infatuation comes easily. It may be an accident-prone time for some, or a period when you take on more responsibilities than you intended. However, Sagittarius Moons really encourage everyone to have a good time and not take things so seriously.

Mediation could be a focus, as could the unplanned journey. Gemini: You could take the long way around without meaning to, and distractions are highly likely for you during this New Moon. Sagittarius: The magic word is *simplify*. Not so easy, but worth pursuing, especially since your essential self is a truly free spirit. All others: Stick with the folks who make you laugh or who can keep things light.

Full Moon in Cancer, December 25

Perfect timing for the most "family-oriented" holiday in the year, Cancer Moons emphasize loyalty and good cooking, nurturing through food, and massage. This Wolf Moon could prompt some to howl, especially Capricorn, who will need to be frank with all. Cancer: Your "homebound" feelings need to be acknowledged, but be patient with those who do not share your need for connection. Cancer Moons prompt reflectiveness and an ability to think deeply about feelings and relationships. This Yule, think about those who have nurtured you and who have been supporters of your own growth and development. Others: Be mindful of those who need more attention, and don't force relationships that don't feel completely natural.

About the Author

Sally Cragin is a teacher and the author of Astrology on the Cusp *for people whose birthdays are at the end of one Sun sign or the beginning of the next. Her first book was* The Astrological Elements, *both with Llewellyn Worldwide. She has written the astrological forecast "Moon Signs" for the* Boston Phoenix, *syndicated throughout New England. Reelected to the Fitchburg, MA, School Committee, she is the only professional astrologer holding elected office in New England. She also provides forecasts for clients that are "cool, useful and accurate." More at Moonsigns.net.*

2015
Moon Sign Book
Articles

The Dark Side of Your Moon

By Amy Herring

Smile at a baby, "aww" at a puppy, or share a personal secret with a new friend, and you're in the Moon's territory. Simply put, the Moon is your heart—your tender, vulnerable insides. Your natal Moon sign is the central place to look in your chart for clues on how to understand your emotional needs, as well as the experiences and types of environments that feel nurturing to you. The Moon also, in part, governs your instinctual self. The Moon isn't about thinking but simply feeling and responding. Our hearts instinctively open when we feel encouraged and loved, and close or shut down when we feel unsafe or insecure.

Understanding your Moon sign can give you insight into how to nurture and support yourself so you can feel free to express your most loving and open-hearted self. However, understanding your needs doesn't mean you'll always get them met; when they're not, you can feel unsupported, sad, and emotionally closed off. Identifying why those feelings are present can be instrumental in turning your frown upside down, but in order to do so, you sometimes have to be willing to explore the "dark side" of your Moon sign.

Astronomically speaking, the dark side of the Moon is the side of the Moon that always faces away from Earth. Because of a phenomenon called tidal locking, the Moon rotates around the Earth in about the same length of time it takes to spin on its axis, so the same hemisphere of the Moon is always facing Earth. The dark side of the Moon is more accurately referred to as the "far side" of the Moon, because it is actually not dark. The far side receives the same amount of light as the near side, but we never see it. Therefore, it is "dark" to us—unknown and distant.

Metaphorically speaking, the Moon is a doorway into our unconscious—the part of us that exists independently of our conscious awareness and that sometimes urges each of us to act or react in ways that we don't understand. When we are acknowledging, identifying, and purposefully acting on our feelings, we have left the realm of the Moon for the conscious territory of thought-processing Mercury or action-oriented Mars. But it's the Moon that symbolizes and takes us into the deep territory.

The phrase "dark side" usually conjures up the impression of something bad, evil, or undesirable. Cultural symbols and stories abound about the goodness of light and the evil of the dark. But wholeness and balance, not self-denial or suppression of negative feelings, is the key to understanding and embracing the dark side of your Moon. Our unconscious is inherently an unknown place, and it can feel frightening to let loose the feelings that aren't easy to control or don't have an appropriate outlet. We may be reluctant to explore them and, as a result, suppress them to the point where they become what psychologist Carl Jung called the "shadow," where we have little control or knowledge about what lurks within. But our shadow is always a part of us, and it makes itself known in subtle and not-so-subtle ways, especially the harder we try to deny it.

The dark side of our Moon can show up in our lives when it's time for us to acknowledge something that we may be afraid to see or admit. One of the most common reasons for this is our own neglect. Falling out of touch with your emotional self doesn't have to come about because of a big tragedy; in fact, it's often the mundane that slowly numbs us. Life can become and stay overwhelmingly busy, with demands from every direction and overloaded to-do lists, and suddenly we are responding to our life with the enthusiasm of a robot—if we're not outright breaking down in tears. Sometimes the motivation for neglect can be denial, where staying busy is not just a response to an overwhelming schedule but also a way to escape the things we don't want to feel or are scared to feel. However, "What you resist, persists," and it will grow until it becomes too big of a problem to ignore.

If we ignore our emotional needs, we may find ourselves throwing the equivalent of a temper tantrum. This is often an early warning device that can be useful in letting us know we are out of balance and should remedy the situation as soon as possible. We all get temporarily overwhelmed by life, but if we neglect or ignore our emotional needs as a matter of course, the problem can get bigger and we become more stuck. A routine can feel safe and our Moon likes safety, but an overwhelming or numbing routine is unsustainable and may also cause our dark Moon to rise.

While too much safety can cause us to sleepwalk through our life, too little safety can also draw down the dark Moon. Prolonged periods in our lives where we feel unsafe can also take their toll. Living in deadening situations or situations that constantly provoke fear, anger, or sorrow can prompt us to find coping mechanisms if we are unable to remedy the situation. Sometimes there are obvious situations where there is no simple fix, such as living with a dying or sick loved one, or the aftermath of a tragedy whose effects we cannot escape. Other times we may be deeply engaged in situations where we feel trapped and cannot or do not dare to see a way out. Again, tragedy doesn't have to strike for this to happen. We may feel stuck in a job, relationship, or living situation that would cause great upheaval or uncertainty to change. To cope, we may act out or eventually emotionally withdraw altogether, losing our ability to be open or empathetic to anyone, including ourselves.

Whatever the cause may be, to manage your dark Moon, first you have to identify the behaviors or thoughts that might start creeping into your life when the dark Moon is on the rise and tend to have an undesired impact on your life. Then, look beyond the symptoms to embrace what is inside of you that's trying to get your attention. Look for these symptoms as clues that your dark Moon may be rising and what to do about it. Find your natal Moon sign by entering your birth date, time, and location at astro .com under "Free Horoscopes" and "Astro Click Portrait."

The Fire Signs: Aries, Leo, and Sagittarius

Although your Moon sign is not astrologically water, the symbolic Moon and feelings in general are often associated with the water element, because of its depth and changing currents, like moods. What does fire do when it meets water? It blows off steam. When your dark Moon rises, so may your temper, from frequent impatience or irritability to outbursts of unprovoked or disproportionate anger. Not all fire Moons have hot tempers, though. If the rest of your chart is not very demonstrative or extroverted, you may find your impatience or frustration smoldering rather than exploding. You may also find yourself attempting to simply shrug off heavier emotions like sorrow or disappointment because they seem to threaten to drag you down or drown your fire altogether. But in doing so, these are the ones that may persist, especially if they are connected to something that needs resolution, not evasion.

Your dark Moon can also rise when your flame has gone out. Fire is the liveliest of the four elements and it needs frequent renewal, operating on a cycle. The fuel of inspiration sparks (creative) expression, and when that fuel source burns out, another must be created and new inspiration sought. Your passion for life does not generate out of nowhere, but out of spirit, and since you carry your fire in your heart, you must light your fire from within. Mythologist Joseph Campbell once said that we aren't really seeking the meaning of life, "what we are seeking is an experience of being alive"—a sentiment especially true for fire-sign Moons.

Light a robust fire and it wants to spread. At your core, you have an instinctive need for space and the freedom to move and do your own thing, to participate in this emotional renewal cycle as an individual. Stagnancy or confinement can rapidly take its toll. The bossiness of an Aries Moon, the diva-like behavior of a Leo Moon, or the restless evasion of the Sagittarius Moon can often be dark Moon symptoms of the need to claim their space.

The Air Signs: Gemini, Libra, and Aquarius

If you have an air Moon, you may have been told that you "think" your feelings rather than feel them; it's not that you don't feel them, but that you tend to manage your feelings by funneling them through your mental processes. Pure feeling is hard to understand in the rational mind, as feelings are irrational, which can leave you vulnerable to taking the quick leap into interpreting them as useless interference and dismissing them multiple times before taking them seriously.

The existing social constructs around feelings can also exert control over how you manage your feelings. It seems easier to understand that you feel sad because a loved one died or you just got dumped, and it seems reasonable that you would respond to winning the lottery with giddy happiness. But while feelings are often the effect of a cause, that cause may not always be obvious. Furthermore, if you are an Aquarius Moon, you may find that your genuine emotional reactions deviate from expected norms. If you are a Libra Moon, you may find it all too easy to hide any of the emotions that aren't easy to accept in response to social pressure. However, you have a strong need for emotional equilibrium and don't like to feel unbalanced by strong emotions, especially toward others, so the pressure to suppress or skip over the hotter emotions may also come from within.

You can be a little too good at convincing anyone of anything, including yourself, especially if you are a Gemini Moon. You have the ability to grasp an objective perspective from multiple angles better than most without necessarily getting emotionally attached to any one viewpoint. This is one of your talents, but it can also be fertile ground for the dark Moon. If you are too good at convincing yourself nothing is wrong, talking yourself out of feeling the way you do, or scolding yourself for of your irrational reaction altogether, the internal pressure can keep building. This is a subtle method of denial, because you seem to be acknowledging your feelings and moving on, but you may be doing so without really taking in the depth of their impact on your inner state.

Sometimes you may find that you don't realize how strongly you feel about something until you begin talking about it. Talking can be a good way to tap into the true depth of your dark Moon, but beware: it's also the route back to rationalizing your feelings and ignoring them.

The Earth Signs: Taurus, Virgo, and Capricorn

If you're an earth-sign Moon, you may not necessarily need to be in charge, but you feel most comfortable when you are in control to some extent. If it feels like your life or something in your surroundings is spiraling out of control, your dark Moon may rise.

The need to remain stable and in control can often be the source of a Taurus Moon's stubbornness, Virgo Moon's fussy nitpicking, or Capricorn Moon's excessive stoicism.

If you are a Taurus Moon, you may dig in your heels at change in direct proportion to how much you feel put upon or that life (or someone else) thrust it on you. You feel most secure in moving when and if you decide to move, not just wherever the wind takes you, and you deeply resent feeling pushed around or overrun. If you are a Virgo Moon, you may find that your attempts at controlling everything around you rise in direct proportion to how much you feel out of control. The more anxiety you feel at being unable to control the uncontrollable—such as the surprise elements in life and the chaos that other people bring—the more you may try to relieve that anxiety by controlling something small, even if it's inconsequential. If you are a Capricorn Moon, your stoic ability to see something through to the end and put your duty before your comfort does have a limit; if that's crossed, you may become the cold, robotic type that pop astrologers often accuse you of being.

A good way to defuse the tension in an earth-sign Moon's heart is through the material world, whether it's through pleasing the senses to help a Taurus Moon relax or putting something in order (the bedroom closet, the schedule, or the to-do list) to downsize anxiety for the Virgo Moon. The archetype of the hermit suits a Capricorn Moon well; it's easiest to calm your urge to put everything on your shoulders if no one is there to remind you that you should.

The Water Signs: Cancer, Scorpio, and Pisces

As a water Moon sign, your emotional life tends to be closer to the surface than some, so the earliest sign that you need a break may be tears, especially when you can't quite pinpoint a cause. Finding an outlet to explore the emotional depths where you feel safe, often when you're alone, can help you catch up to yourself.

However, you may tend toward keeping your emotions private to avoid feeling even more vulnerable, which can just keep them churning over themselves like a water wheel, exacerbating your inner state. A trusted confidante can provide you with an outlet that helps you air out your feelings, so you can get some objectivity rather than just drowning in them.

If your Moon is in Pisces or Cancer, you may find yourself escaping into an outlet that takes you away from the everyday world, which can be a good temporary release until you feel more emotionally stable to handle the source of the issue. However, chronic or prolonged avoidance in response to a situation that won't get better on its own can cause more problems. If your Moon is in Scorpio, you may still be inclined to escape, but since you tend to be friendlier with the "hotter" emotions, you may not be as prone to escape from them as much as escape into them. Power (or the perceived lack of it) can really spin your insides for a loop. If you are in a situation where you feel like you have been robbed of your power, you are vulnerable to letting yourself become consumed with thoughts of how to get it back. This is often an illusion but a powerful motivation for the dark Moon.

Dreams are a great way to access the unconscious, and strong feelings tend to find expression in dreams when our conscious defenses are down. This is true for everyone, but as a water Moon sign, you can attune yourself more easily to the sometimes-confusing symbolism that can show up in dreams. Dreams are symbolic, not rational, so their communication has to be put in symbolic context and personalized, but they can provide a wealth of insight about what's really hurting.

About the Author

Amy Herring is an Evolutionary and Jungian-oriented astrologer who uses astrology to support people in becoming whole. She has been studying, writing, teaching, and reading for clients as an astrologer for almost two decades. Her book, Astrology of the Moon, is available from Llewellyn. See her website www.heavenlytruth.com for more information about her services.

2015 Diet & Fitness Horoscope

By Michelle Perrin, Astrology Detective

Our Sun signs and solar-house horoscopes are a reflection of our outer ego—the force that drives us externally and helps us mold our surroundings to our inner will. Our Sun signs help us function by using our external awareness to mindfully find solutions to life's problems. Our Moon signs, on the other hand, represent the forces that bubble up from deep within, lingering just below the surface of our inner psyches. They are highly emotional impulses that drive us in an uncontrolled, incognizant way. Food and exercise are often strongly related to our unconscious mind and automatic behaviors, with habits we pick up from childhood, culture, or as a response to external stress guiding our decisions.

These diet and fitness horoscopes are for your natal Moon sign and will help you become alert to the subconscious reasons for your lifestyle approach, so that you can find the best dates in 2015 to modify dietary behavior, implement healthy eating regimes, gain or lose weight, and get physically active. These lunar-house horoscopes set your natal Moon in the first house and the subsequent signs in subsequent houses. (e.g., Taurus natal moons will have Taurus in the first house, Gemini in the second, Cancer in the third, and so on.) Find your natal Moon sign by entering your birth date, time, and location at Astro.com under "Free Horoscopes" and "Astro Click Portrait."

House Key Words

1. Identity
2. Money, Self-Esteem
3. Communication
4. Home
5. Creativity, Pleasure
6. Health and Wellness, Chores

7. Partnerships, Love
8. Transformation, Sex
9. Travel, Ideals
10. Career
11. Friends
12. Psychology, Secrets

Wellness Moons

New Moons in your wellness sector are the most auspicious times to implement changes in your diet and exercise regimen. New habits and wellness projects undertaken on these days will be easy to implement and set the tone of your well-being for the year ahead, as well as having a lifting effect on your emotional state.

Full Moons in your wellness zone are the best dates to end bad habits—from smoking to that high-calorie afternoon snack—and regain the emotional control that comes from a true mind/body balance.

Aries

Uranus's extended transit of your natal Moon Sign is putting your moods on a non-stop rollercoaster ride: one day up, one day down. You may feel like you have lost control of your entire persona, leaving you facing the world with anxiety and dread. While this pent-up nervous tension helps burn calories, a more balanced emotional life can be achieved through regular exercise, which will help calm you down. An especially auspicious time to implement new workout regimens is when Mars transits your sign from February 19 to March 31. Feel-good Jupiter also comes to the rescue on August 11, when it enters your health and wellness sector (Virgo) for its once-every-twelve-year stay.

The upcoming year is an excellent period to get in shape —it will be easier and more effortless than ever before. Jupiter has a tendency to overdo things, so you may throw yourself into a new exercise or dietary regimen with so much enthusiasm that you burn out just as quickly, especially when Mars enters Virgo from September 24 to November 12. It is better to take a more moderate approach to wellness matters by implementing new, small daily routines as opposed to intense, sweeping, and hardcore health initiatives; the long-term effects will be far more noticeable and sustainable. You may also fall off the nutrition wagon when Jupiter opposes Neptune and Chiron in your psychology zone (Pisces): September 17 and November 3, respectively. You may go on an eating binge to escape the stresses of life, so be especially conscious during these days.

Wellness New Moon, September 13; Wellness Full Moon, March 5

Taurus

Neptune's extended transit through your friendship sector (Pisces) is bringing social relationships marked by confusion, delusion, and maybe even deception into your life. Your best path to emotional and physical wellness in 2015, therefore, can be found in your own personal bullpen surrounded by family and kin; sharing home-cooked meals will especially help you recharge your batteries and destress. Jupiter in your home sector (Leo) until August 11—along with Venus's super-long transit of the same sector from June 5 to July 18 and July 31 to October 8—will allow you to pamper yourself in your own little nest. This care will counteract all that pent-up nervous tension you are carrying around due to high-strung Uranus's transit of your psychology zone (Aries). Even though you may be wound up like a top, all that anxiety will suppress your appetite and help you burn off unwanted calories.

Mars's once-every-two-year transit through your identity sector (Taurus) from March 31 to May 11 is a great time to implement long-term fitness regimens. You may want to take it easy at the lunar eclipse on April 4 in your health and wellness sector (Libra), however, as Mars may have you feeling so invincible that you overexert yourself and suffer a minor injury. Another great period to get in shape and eat well is when Mars enters your health sector (Libra) on November 12 until the end of the year. Even though Venus nearby may see you indulging near Thanksgiving, you will be able to burn off excess calories easily, so enjoy holiday indulgences—just be sure to get some exercise in.

Wellness New Moon, October 12; Wellness Full Moon, April 4

Gemini

Saturn's once-every-thirty-year transit through your sector of health and chores (Scorpio) for the past two years has also been taking its toll on your normally exuberant vitality. The end is now in sight, as Saturn makes one brief final appearance in this zone from June 14 to September 17, allowing your effervescent character to shine once more—and your epicurean enthusiasm to make a hedonistic comeback. Saturn has been serving as a natural appetite suppressant the last two years; you were running around taking care of duties and other people to such an extent that you either didn't have the time, were too tired, or just plain forgot to eat.

If you want to lose weight, utilize the summer months to make rational eating choices and implement a long-term dietary plan, while gaining weight can be done more easily during the other times of the year. You will be feeling especially vibrant when Mars is in your Moon sign from May 11 to June 24, a great time to enact a new exercise plan. Once Jupiter moves into your home sector on August 11 (joined by Venus and Mars in October), you may become a bit of a lazy, self-indulgent couch potato. Still, after taking care of everyone else the past few years, you deserve to just relax for a moment. With decadent Venus in your wellness zone (Scorpio) most of December, you can fully partake in the high life—and high-calorie food and drink—during the holiday season; Mars will help you burn off the extra calories in January 2016.

Wellness New Moon, November 11; Wellness Full Moon, May 3

Cancer

Your Moon is in a deeply emotional sign that has a similarly emotional attachment to food. Sustenance is linked not only to bodily functioning, but also to psychological concepts such as nurturing, acceptance, and belonging. Rationalist Saturn entered your wellness zone (Sagittarius) in late December 2014, and will remain in this sector until June 14, and then again from September 17 until the end of 2017, causing the intense, intimate relationship you have with food to cool off and transform into something more detached, objective, and (most of all) controllable. Saturn will allow you to re-establish the boundaries that life's epicurean delight's have with your psyche. Instead of being used as a psychological crutch, food will be relished for its nutritional value and as a source of fuel for your body. You will no longer be in the mood for comfort food, but instead can achieve a sense of grounding through the pursuit of a balanced diet filled with healthy comestibles. Include organic fruits, vegetables, and meats in your diet so that you can get the most nourishment and taste from your daily rations. This is also a good time to enroll in a cooking course so you can learn new recipes that will form the basis of your eating regimen for years to come. This new, balanced approach to eating will help you feel better, lose weight, and be more in control of yourself and your feelings. Finally, a great time to exercise and get in shape is when Mars transits your identity zone (Cancer) from June 24 to August 8.

Wellness New Moon, December 11; Wellness Full Moon, June 2

Leo

The hedonistic planets Jupiter and Venus are both lingering in your natal Moon sign this year, causing you to be glamorously indulgent and a wee bit lazy. All that high living, while intoxicating and energizing, can also wear you down after a while. Jupiter is in your sign until August 11, joined by Venus from June 5 to July 18. Be particularly careful to check your weight regularly, because this combination could pack on the pounds quickly—champagne and caviar are not low-cal treats! By the time Venus retrogrades back into your sign from July 31 to October 8, you will know it is time to clean up and rebeautify after the past year's non-stop binge of decadence. During this time you will not want to push yourself too hard, but instead pamper your body with fresh, nutritious, organic foods and low-impact exercise. Luckily, Jupiter's entry into your money zone (Virgo) on August 11 will give you the means to buy top-quality foods, take on a personal trainer, and visit the day spa.

Jupiter will remain in Virgo, the zodiac sign that rules nutrition, for the next year, and your level of confidence will greatly be enhanced by a balanced, sensible diet. It is time to return to seeing food as a fuel as opposed to luxury item, as you have done for the past year. Additionally, Saturn moves out of your home zone (Scorpio) on September 17 after a two-year transit, and you will be out and about in the world more, helping you lose weight naturally through the motions of your daily routine.

Wellness New Moon, none (occurs in the final days of 2014 and first days of 2016); Wellness Full Moon, July 1

Virgo

Virgo is the zodiac sign that rules nutrition, so you normally have a controlled and sensible approach to food. But when Jupiter enters your Moon sign on August 11 for a one-year transit, emotional triggers could be explosively set off, causing you to lose touch with your usual rational and practical approach to diet— and leading to binge-eating based on mood. The upside of this is that Jupiter will do wonders for your confidence, so these spontaneous emotions will largely be positive ones; indulging in a bit of luxuriant, decadent eating will help you connect with the exuberance of life and loosen up your normally rigid, restrictive nature. Your indulgent epicurean ways could lead to sudden weight gain, however. Keep a scale handy, so that you are consciously aware of when to rein it in.

When Venus retrogrades into your sector of inner-psychology and recuperation (Leo) from July 31 to October 8, you will feel a bit lazy and in no mood for physical exertion. Luckily, there will be two New Moons in your exercise and wellness sector on January 20 and February 18, giving you the rare double opportunity to implement an effective, calorie-fighting workout regimen early in the year. If you get super fit during the first half of the year, you will be able to absorb the indulgences of the latter months of 2015. Moreover, these New Moons will sandwich Mercury's retrograde transit of your health zone (Aquarius) from January 21 to February 11, allowing you to put long-held fitness plans into practice.

Wellness New Moon, January 20 and February 18; Wellness Full Moon, July 31

Libra

Family drama could be draining you and undermining your feelings of self-confidence, especially when Saturn is finishing up the last leg of its two-year transit of your self-esteem zone (Scorpio) from June 14 to September 17. Fighting for control within your own four walls could also be seriously zapping you of your inner vitality. In your quest for wellness, you could be seduced by fad diets, weight-loss pills, and get-in-shape gimmicks due to Neptune's extended transit of your health zone (Pisces); instead opt for a balanced, nutritious diet. Neptune also rules addictions, and you may be particularly beguiled by escapist pleasures that wreak havoc on your body and weight over time. Stay away from addictive substances, such as cigarettes, alcohol, and drugs; you will notice a subsequent improvement to your self-esteem as you give up these emotional crutches that just serve to hide your real feelings.

With Jupiter in your social zone (Leo) until August 11, you may be lured into a party-hearty life with friends that will temporarily revitalize; however, over time, all the alcohol and buzzing around will take its toll on your overall sense of well-being. Once Jupiter moves into your solitary/psychological zone (Virgo) on August 11, you will be ready to cut back on the social whirl, along with bad habits such as too much drinking and dining out. The best time of the year to get in shape is when Mars transits your health sector (Pisces) from January 12 to February 20. Beware of the Pisces solar eclipse on March 20, when bad eating or substance choices could leave lasting harmful effects.

Wellness New Moon, March 20; Wellness Full Moon, August 29

Scorpio

The planets have been on your side for the past two years in terms of weight loss. Saturn in your Moon sign has been working as an appetite suppressant, keeping you so busy and burdened that you just didn't have the time, nor the desire, to eat. Saturn will be making the final transit of your sign from June 14 to September 17, after which its restrictive nature will be removed and your appetite can

make a full comeback. You are not the world's biggest gourmand, having a tendency to eat because you have to, without paying much attention to the quality or nutrition of the food you consume. Once Saturn moves into your money sector (Sagittarius), you may additionally wish to cut your food budget to make ends meet. The resultant consumption of cheap, yet highly calorific, prepared food can lead to weight gain. Moreover, Jupiter's move into your social sector (Virgo) on August 11 could see you jump back into the social whirl after several years of isolation, which includes dining out at restaurants and drinking lots of alcohol.

Uranus's continued influence will help you burn off the calories but may also create an erratic relationship to nutrition. Try to make a conscious effort to eat whole foods and home-cooked meals on a regular basis; this will have a steadying effect on your nerves. When Mars transits your wellness sector (Aries) from February 19 to March 31, take a cooking class, join a gym, or see a nutritionist to set a long-term eating plan.

Wellness New Moon, April 18; Wellness Full Moon, September 27

Sagittarius

Saturn entered your Moon sign in late December 2014, and, while this may not be the most amusing transit, it does help take the weight off. You are now taking tentative baby steps back into the big, wide world after a few years of self-imposed isolation and self-assessment. You may subsequently have a lot of burdens and various responsibilities to juggle that will help burn calories; even if you don't you put your mind to losing weight, it may just happen naturally. Over the course of the next two years, it is important to take a rational approach to eating. Saturn can bring with it a feeling of decreased vitality, and getting takeout because you are too tired to cook will only exasperate your fatigue, especially if that "food" is just empty calories. If you implement a sensible eating regimen filled with healthy fruits, organic vegetables, whole grains, and lean meats, you will not only become leaner yourself, but also feel balanced and energetic. Saturn briefly retrogrades back into your psychology zone (Scorpio) from June 14 to September 17, and you may use calorie restriction to add a sense of control and order to your world. This is not a healthy approach, and you should resist this temptation—with the aid of a trained dietitian, if necessary. Physically fit Mars enters your wellness zone (Taurus) on March 31; if you make an effort to incorporate exercise as part of your weekly routine, you will keep up the workouts even after Mars leaves this zone on May 11.

Wellness New Moon, May 18; Wellness Full Moon, October 27

Capricorn

Which came first: your family's tendency to rebel against your every wish, your friends' ever-increasing distancing from you, or your need to control and dominate every situation? In fact, a synergy may be at play here, and as the people surrounding you grow ever more beyond your grasp, your need to control as much as you can becomes increasingly stronger—and that includes your own physical body. With long-term transits from domineering, compulsive Pluto in your outer identity zone (Capricorn) and restrained Saturn's recent entry into your psychology sector (Sagittarius), you may feel like isolating yourself from life's spontaneous, hedonistic pleasures, including food. You may feel you can control your body image by controlling your caloric intake, but beware of becoming too thin or nutrient deficient, as both Pluto and Saturn have a hard time taking the blinders off. If you have a tendency towards conditions such as anorexia, seek qualified help at the earliest warning sign.

Saturn may also make you a secret eater, which may exasperate already frayed relations with family members, who will miss you at mealtimes. Mars will be in your wellness zone (Gemini) from May 11 until June 24, which is a great time to get in shape or join a gym, while Mercury's simultaneous retrograde in this sector from May 18 to June 11 will allow you to take a time-out from your mental compulsions and objectively get a grip on negative health and dietary patterns, as well as draw up a sensible long-term eating and fitness plan.

Wellness New Moon, June 16; Wellness Full Moon, November 25

Aquarius

Even though you are the postcard of perfect health on the outside, inside you are at battle with a non-stop onslaught of inner demons, due to obsessive, brooding Pluto's long-term transit of your psychology zone (Capricorn). In order to feel fully fit in 2015, you need to do some subconscious gymnastics to maintain a balanced equilibrium, otherwise you may end up snapping at those around you with strangely erratic communication. One of the problems is expansive Jupiter's transit of your love and intimacy zone (Leo) all year. You have a hard time setting boundaries, since you want to meld as one with those around you, but you end up feeling lost, confused, and unconfident. Dedicating time each day to your physical wellness will help build physical boundaries that protect your currently oversensitive emotions.

There are two extremely auspicious periods for implementing long-term workout goals: when Mars transits your Moon sign from January 1 to 12, and your health sector (Cancer) from June 24 to August 8. Your energy reserves will be at a two-year high, which will help boost your self-esteem. Just be careful not to over-exert yourself on July 15, when Mars opposes Pluto, or you may end up with a minor injury. Diet is just as important as working out; during these phases, try implementing a long-term healthy eating strategy. And remember: what you eat is as important as with whom who you eat, so surround yourself with supportive, inspiring company at mealtimes and give overly traditional, close-minded people a wide berth.

Wellness New Moon, July 15; Wellness Full Moon, January 5

Pisces

Neptune in your Moon sign is draping your world in a hazy, rose-colored fog, and it may be difficult at times to delineate with clarity what is real and what is a fairy-tale-like illusion, putting your sense of self-esteem on a rollercoaster ride of unpredictability due to Uranus's long-term presence in your confidence zone (Aries). There will be at least one aspect of your existence that you can get a firm handle on: your sense of physical wellness. Jupiter is making its once-every-twelve year transit of your health sector (Leo) until August 11, and during this time you can easily get into tip-top shape with little effort on your part. From exercise to diet, if you put your mind to it, you will be able to implement healthy new regimens that last far into the future. Just be careful not to overdo it. At times, your desire for physical wellness could almost overwhelm you as you overcompensate for the confusion in your life. This is especially true when Mars transits your wellness zone (Leo) from August 8 to September 24. Exercising or dieting too much can be as harmful as being totally lazy, so work out with a personal trainer or collaborate with a certified dietitian so that you can get the sensible, objective perspective on your health that may be hard for you to achieve on your own. Focusing on optimizing your physical wellness can also boost your self-esteem at the rare and harmonious trines of Jupiter and Uranus on March 3 and June 22.

Wellness New Moon, August 14; Wellness Full Moon, February 3

About the Author
A contributor to the 2014 Moon Sign book, Michelle writes the "Love – Money – Health" monthly horoscope column for Dell Horoscope Magazine and is a regular contributor of articles and blogposts at astrology.com. You can visit her site at astrologydetective.com

How the Moon Influences Your Astrology Consultation

By Alice DeVille

The phone rings and a frantic client calls, alarmed. Her teenage daughter is missing and she thinks the girl met with foul play. Her daughter was last seen the previous evening but did not show up for breakfast and was not in the home. Friends and neighbors search the neighborhood and phone calls go out to her daughter's network. Disruption has occurred in the mother's Fourth House of home and family, where her natal Moon resides with Mercury, the planet that often represents communication matters related to themes affiliated with that particular house. Simultaneously transiting Mars and Uranus are conjunct the mother's Moon/Mercury placements, lending a sense of drama and possibly anger to the disappearance. The transiting Moon is in its gibbous phase, meaning that activity surrounding this matter is highly charged and intense, adding urgency to the problem and prompting the phone call to set an appointment with me ASAP.

I quickly construct a horary chart for the time of my client's phone call to see what hidden information comes to light, and there is plenty. The chart reveals that the mother, who was gone for several hours that night, was oblivious to what was going on in the household (a stellium of planets in the Twelfth House of secrets). I advised her to talk with every person in the home to find out what kind of disagreement may have taken place in her absence. She learned that her daughter and her stepfather got into an argument over money; he struck the girl and ordered her to her room. The transiting Moon on the cusp of the Fifth House of children was square Saturn (often representative of a father figure) in the Seventh House, and the Second House of money and resources held four planets that were square to the chart's Part of Fortune. The Eleventh House of friendship held Neptune, Mercury, and Chiron in tight conjunction with one another. That was all I needed to figure out the daughter left of her own volition in a fit of anger and went to a friend's house to seek refuge; that someone already questioned the friend, who denied knowledge of the daughter's whereabouts; and that my client's daughter would be home as soon as they figured out which one of her friends was lying and harboring the fugitive.

And it all came to pass.

This example illustrates one way in which the Moon influences the desire for an astrology consultation. In this case, the mother's natal Moon was strongly affected by a transiting personal planet (Mars) and the outer planet Uranus making harsh contact in her Fourth House of family matters. While not all consultation seekers need trauma to request an appointment, this article examines some of the factors involving the Moon that drive the desire to request a consultation.

The Lunar Foundation

The sign of the Moon in your natal chart is a strong indicator of your emotional temperament, while the house position of the Moon shows how you focus these emotions. Your inner feelings, awareness, sensitivities, and understanding are the drivers that prompt you to seek balance and answers in your world. The house location of your Moon is important because you deal with recurring lunar conditions that build the tension from which you seek relief. A lunar month takes approximately 29.5 days to cycle through every sign, while it covers each of eight lunar phases: New (first quarter), waxing crescent, waxing half (second quarter), waxing gibbous, Full (third quarter), waning gibbous, waning half (fourth quarter), and balsamic.

A lunation represents the amount of time it takes to go from one new Moon to the next, approximately 29.26 to 29.80 days, due to the effects of the Sun's gravity on the Moon's orbit. Astrology articles often direct readers to check the houses of their charts to determine where the lunation will occur and what conditions may emerge. A chart calculated for your time of birth indicates the Moon's sign, house location, degree, aspects, and lunar phase. Each month, the transiting Moon shows up in one of the eight lunar phases in the house your natal Moon occupies. Throughout your life, themes associated with your Moon sign emerge in the form of concerns or problems when you experience this mini lunar return. Sensitivity heightens if other planets reside in the house along with your Moon, especially if transiting planets and/ or eclipses are making connections to your Moon's house. It's not surprising that when these aspects occur, you contact your astrologer to sort things out.

A Call to Action

In New Moon phases, I typically receive calls from clients who interested in beginning new ventures. They may be applying for jobs, starting a business, initiating a new project, or seeking planning information to firm up meeting schedules or book travel. Patients undergoing medical procedures ask for advice on when to schedule surgery, begin a treatment, or look for medical professionals. Individuals experiencing newly evolving life developments want to know what gives! Romance is another topic that seems to blossom during the first quarter phase, when clients book appointments to discuss the potential of budding relationships, gain insight into the new person, or talk about their dating history and why this one might be different.

In the second quarter or gibbous phase, I get calls from clients working on projects who have personnel issues, need advice on changing workplace dynamics, making decisions on the direction to take in choosing a new job, relocating to another city, changing the dates for surgery or dental work, or managing emerging issues in lawsuits. The energy is more intense and commands attention because the Full Moon is approaching; people will generally fare better if they handle problems without drama.

Once the Full Moon beams its commanding and attention-seeking light, it is not unusual to hear from a client who just broke up with her Significant Other and wants to know if they will get back together. The tension has been mounting in any given scenario and has come to a head for those who have been coping, struggling, working hard, or denying that change is in the wind. Family revelations or unexpected announcements trigger other requests for an appointment at this time. If the client was also born in the Full Moon phase, the craving for attention is even stronger.

Fourth quarter clients frequently express boredom about key areas of their lives and annoyance with relationships. The Moon's influence is waning, and they may be scratching their heads asking why they got into the relationship/took the job/started the project/spent so much money in the first place. During this phase,

I get questions about home renovation contractors who haven't started or finished the job. The last few days of this phase seem to attract clients with tax questions, ranging from when to file and what expenses are deductible to where to find a good accountant. I also hear from individuals worn out from the stress of pending projects; they want to know how to wrap things up. I advise that this phase is the perfect time to chill, work on a problematic facet of your project, clean out or organize files, return phone calls, and table action until the next New Moon phase.

Solar and Lunar Eclipses

The influence of the Moon on your consultation would not be complete without acknowledging the importance of eclipses. I have noted that eclipses drive the need for a consultation. Each year, four to six eclipses of the Sun and Moon occur in pairs, two weeks apart. If a New Moon solar eclipse occurs, a lunar eclipse will manifest at the time of a Full Moon two weeks later. The influence of each is six months to a year. Eclipses heighten awareness of matters that need attention, often what you have been putting off or denying. A client whose chart is receiving strong aspects to the Sun, Moon, or other planets from an eclipse is undergoing major life changes. When a client calls for an appointment, my initial prep work involves checking the activity of current eclipses. Usually I find planets grabbing the spotlight due to heightened attention from one or more eclipses that are affecting important life directions. If this scenario sounds familiar, it's time to schedule your consultation.

Sources and Further Reading

All reference material in this article is from my personal consulting/ client files/writing; years ago I studied lunar phases at workshops conducted by the late astrologer Robert "Buzz" Meyers of Cleveland, Ohio.
DeVille, Alice. "2013 Eclipses—Will They Affect Your Career?" *Llewellyn's 2013 Moon Sign Book.* Woodbury, MN: Llewellyn, 2013.

————. "An Astrologer's Guide to Quirky Clients." *Llewellyn's 1999 Sun Sign Book*. St. Paul, MN: Llewellyn, 1999.

————. "How To Find The Right Astrologer." *Llewellyn's 1999 Sun Sign Book*. St. Paul, MN: Llewellyn, 1999.

Pottenger, Rique. *The American Ephemeris for the 21st Century*. San Diego, CA: ASC Publications, 1996.

About the Author

Known internationally as an astrologer, consultant and writer, Alice DeVille also has the pleasure of working as an executive coach integrating spiritual insight while meeting the needs of clients in the corporate, government, and small-business worlds. Alice specializes in relationships of all types that call for solid problem-solving advice to get to the core of issues and gives clients options for meeting critical needs. Her clients seek solutions in business practices, career and change management, real estate, relationships, and training. She has developed and presented more than 160 workshops and seminars related to her fields of expertise. The Star IQ, Astral Hearts, Llewellyn, Meta Arts, Inner Self, ShareItLiveIt, Twitter, and numerous websites and publications feature her articles. Quotes from her work on relationships appear in books, publications, training materials, calendars, planners, audio tapes, and Oprah's website. Alice is available for writing books and articles for publishers, newspapers, or magazines and conducting workshops and radio or TV interviews. Contact Alice at DeVilleAA@aol.com.

The Moon and Rainfall

By Bruce Scofield

Astrometeorology—the study of correlations between weather and the Sun, Moon, and planets—dates back to the origins of Western astrology some four thousand or more years ago. Because astrology originated in the early agricultural centers of the Near East, there was great interest in knowing what the weather might be like in the future, as the success of crops was of vital importance. Over time, sky watchers in the great cities of the region, such as Babylonia, observed and recorded correlations with the moving planets, Sun, and Moon. These early observations were the start of a long tradition that was documented by Ptolemy, the famous scientist of the early Roman period, more than a thousand years later. Five to seven hundred years after Ptolemy, the great Arab astrologers of the Middle Ages sought ways to predict rain using astrology; a thousand years after that, the almanac writers of the Renaissance issued forecasts based on astrometeorology for years ahead. Today, a few atmospheric scientists are busy rediscovering the Moon's effects on the weather.

In his great work on astrology from about 150 CE called the *Tetrabiblios*, Ptolemy described a way of predicting weather that was based on close scrutiny of the New or Full Moons that occur near the equinoxes or solstices, the markers of the four seasons. The methodology he recorded was to chart the time of these special New or Full Moons and note what signs they fell in and how they related to the other planets. With this information, a forecast for the season's weather could be made. Ptolemy also had some insights into a kind of lunar tidal effect on the atmosphere. He compared the ebb and flow of the tides (which he correctly attributed to the phases of the Moon), to the changes in air currents that occur when the Sun or Moon were rising, setting, or directly overhead or under the Earth.

Arab learning during the height of the Islamic Empire (c. 630–900 CE) was extensive and included astrometeorology as a subject of central importance. For religious reasons, Arab astrology concerned itself primarily with those parts of astrology that did not deal with individuals. Natal astrology was not practiced, but astrometeorology was a major theme, as was astrology applied to history, interrogations and elections, and the medical field. The contents of a work by the great Muslim philosopher Al-Kindi (800–873), titled *De Mutatione Temporum* (*On the Changes of the Weather*), are almost exclusively practical techniques and methodologies for predicting weather, especially rains—which makes good sense given the dry nature of the eastern and southern Mediterranean region. According to Al-Kindi, the probability for rain in the Middle East becomes greater near a New or Full Moon when all the planets are retrograde in a specific quadrant of the year, usually winter. Also, the motion of the planets must be moving in the zodiac toward the Sun and Moon. Further details amplify or decrease the possibility of rain. Other techniques, including zodiacal sign positioning, aspects between planets, aspects to the quarters of the Moon (which naturally involve the Sun), and ingresses into the equinoctal sign Libra all contribute to the art of forecasting rain.

During the Renaissance, almanac writers nearly always included weather forecasts for the year. Leonard Digges was the author of a popular almanac first published in 1553, *The Prognostication Everlasting of Right Good Effect.* It contained the standard astrological methodology for predicting the weather in England. With this almanac came an ephemeris of the year's planetary positions along with a "do-it-yourself" manual. Digges noted that "the conjunction, quadrature and opposition of the Moon with the Sunne in moist signes, rayny weather: the more if the Moon go from the Sunne to Saturne." He said one should look to the quarters of the Moon and pay attention to what signs they occur in, as this will tell you how much rain will fall. The moist signs are the water and air signs. He also said the chances for rain increase after the New, Full, and quarter Moons if the Moon's next aspect is to Saturn.

In 1686, John Goad (1616–1687) published a major work on astrology entitled *Astro-Meteorologica, or Aphorisms and Discourses on the Bodies Celestial, their Natures and Influences. Astro-Meteorologica* is a comprehensive work of over five hundred pages, many of them samples of his weather log. His book was probably the most scientific work that focused on astrometeorology, and certainly the most ambitious, to appear during the entire seventeenth century. After a lengthy introduction covering his basic principles, Goad examined the various Sun-Moon aspects. Beginning with the conjunction (New Moon), he analyzed its correlations with the weather over a seven-year period of eighty-seven conjunctions. He next considered the opposition between the

Sun and Moon (Full Moon). Next were the quarters (90 degrees), the trines (120 degrees), and the sextiles (60 degrees). Goad sought to examine the frequencies of various kinds of weather patterns occurring during the range of time that he thought each aspect was effective. If there was a correlation between aspect and weather pattern more than half the time, he maintained that the influence of the aspect was proved.

At the conclusion of his study of the five Sun-Moon aspects, Goad summarized his findings in a table. His records for the Full Moon showed that some form of moisture was recorded in 75 of the 87 aspect events during the seven-year period. His weather record suggested that there were more wet days at the Full Moon than at the New Moon, and that the second half of the Sun-Moon cycle (the later trine, square, and sextile) were generally warmer than the first half. He noted there was much rainfall at the first sextile (60 degrees after the New Moon) and the second trine (60 degrees after the Full Moon). This result, more rain about five days after the New and Full Moon, surprised him; he had expected that the traditionally more powerful aspects—the conjunction and the opposition—would account for the most moisture.

Goad's observation of rainfall peaks five days after New and Full Moons was confirmed to some extent by a study done in the 1960s, published in the prestigious journal *Science*. The lead author of the paper was Donald A. Bradley, known to the astrological community as Garth Allen. Under his pseudonym, Bradley published several books (some released by Llewellyn) and numerous articles in astrology magazines such as *American Astrology* during the later 1940s through the 1960s. He was best known in the astrological community as an advocate of sidereal astrology and has left a considerable legacy in that regard. But he was also an engineer and self-taught scientist who had a paper published (co-authored with Max A. Woodbury) in 1962 that examined precipitation data over the continental United States for a fifty-year period (1900–1949). They found that maximum precipitation appears to be related to the Sun-Moon cycle.

Bradley and Woodbury's study took into account only major rainfall events in a twenty-four-hour period thoughout the continental United States. These were graphed and compared to the lunar cycle over a fifty-year period and analyzed statistically. What they found was a strong tendency for extreme rainfalls near the middle of the first and third weeks of the lunar cycle; that is, the third to the fifth days after New Moon and Full Moon. This result is almost exactly what John Goad had found three hundred years earlier—that rain was more abundant at the first sextile and second trine, which are about five days after New Moon and Full Moon, respectively. In the same issue of the journal *Science*, Bradley and Woodbury's paper was followed by a report from researchers in New Zealand that they had found the same correlation between heavy rainfalls and the lunar cycle in that part of the world as well.

In 1964 Bradley co-authored a paper (with Glenn Brier of the U.S. Weather Bureau) published in *The Journal of Atmospheric*

Sciences that reported a 14.75-day cycle found in precipitation data—obviously a lunar connection, as that figure is exactly half the full 29.5-day cycle of the Moon. But this was only the beginning of the modern rediscovery of extraterrestrial effects on the Earth's atmosphere. Since the 1960s, many other scientific papers have been published in leading scientific journals that have demonstrated strong correlations between the Moon and atmospheric phenomena such as thunderstorm frequency, atmospheric pressure changes, hurricanes, cloudiness, and surface temperatures.

A connection between the Moon's phases and the frequency of thunderstorms was reported in 1970 in *The Journal of Geophysical Research*. Mae DeVoe Lethbridge, a meteorologist at Pennsylvania State University, analyzed thunderstorm data for twenty-eight years in the United States and compared it to the days when the Moon was at maximum declination and for the days around the Full Moon. What was found was a peak of thunderstorm frequency two days after the Full Moon, and also when the Moon was at maximum north declination. When these astronomical events combined, a very high increase in thunderstorm frequency occurred. The Moon's declination is always high when it is in Gemini and Cancer, so the Full Moons near the time of the Winter Solstice are the ones to watch. Lethbridge suggests that the cause behind this phenomena could be the Moon passing through the Earth's magnetic tail, the part of the magnetic field that is blown back into space by the solar wind. The Moon passes through this tail every Full Moon; the disruption could cause electrical changes leading to the formation of thunderstorms.

In 1995 atmospheric scientists and geographers at Arizona State University began publishing scientific papers about the influence of the Moon on weather. Robert C. Balling and Randall S. Cerveny reported in the journal *Science* that there is a correlation between lunar phase and daily global temperatures. They used daily temperature data from polar-orbiting satellites that cover the entire Earth and compared fifteen years of data with the lunar cycle. It wasn't much of a difference that they found, but they are very confident that the data shows global temperatures to be a little bit warmer at the Full Moon. Exactly how this occurs is not known, but the authors note that the Full Moon reflects a small amount of infrared light back to the Earth, and this causes warming on the Earth. They suggest that this mechanism, a very subtle heating, may also account for the correspondences between lunar phase and precipitation, cloudiness, and storms.

More recently, in 2011, another paper from the group at Arizona State University was published that showed a correlation between the monthly lunar declination extremes and the circulation of the lower atmosphere, the part where our weather occurs. Because the Moon's orbit is tilted relative to Earth's orbit around the Sun, the Moon swings north and south of the celestial equator every month as it orbits Earth. The distance north and south of the equator is measured in degrees of declination, a factor used by astrologers when reading charts. What the scientists found was evidence of greater atmospheric tides in the higher latitudes when declination was high. These tides are apparently strong enough to modulate atmospheric pressure, which could affect the formation of storms that bring rain.

. . . .

Close observers of the Moon, a group that includes astrologers and scientists, have recognized for over four thousand years that its motions coincide with weather changes including rainfall, though this varies according to the specific climate of a region. The fact that large rainfalls tend to occur a few days after New and Full Moon, and that thunderstorm frequency rises two days after a Full Moon (especially so in the winter months, when the Full Moon has a high declination), is something useful to know and should help us in predicting the weather.

References

Balling, Robert C., and Randall S. Cerveny. "Influence of Lunar Phase on Daily Global Temperatures." *Science* 267 (1995):1481–1483.

Bos, Gerrit, and Charles Burnett. *Scientific Weather Forecasting in the Middle Ages: The Writings of Al-Kindi.* London: Kegan Paul, 2000.

Bradley, DA, MA Woodbury, and GW Brier. "Lunar Synodical Period and Widespread Precipitation." *Science* 137 (1962):748–750.

Goad, John. *Astro-meteorologica, or Aphorism and Discourses of the Bodies Celestial, their Natures and Influences.* London: J. Rawlins, 1686.

Krahenbuhl, Daniel S., Matthew B. Pace, Randall S. Cerveny, and Robert C. Balling, Jr. "Monthly lunar declination extremes' influence on tropospheric circulation patterns." *Journal of Geophysical Research: Atmospheres* 116, issue D23 (2011).

Lethbridge, Mae DeVoe. "Relationship between Thunderstorm Frequency and Lunar Phase and Declination." *Journal of Geophysical Research* 75, no. 27 (1970): 5149–5154.

Ptolemy, Claudius. *Tetrabiblos.* Trans. F. E. Robbins. Cambridge, MA: Harvard University Press, 1940.

About the Author

Bruce Scofield is a practicing astrologer who's maintained a private practice as an consultant and conference speaker for over forty years. He is the author of seven books and hundreds of articles. He has served on the education committee of the National Council for Geocosmic Research since 1979 and was that organization's national education director from 1998 to 2003. He holds a master's degree in history and a PhD in geosciences and currently teaches at Kepler College and the University of Massachusetts. Scofield and Barry Orr maintain a website, www.onereed.com, which contains articles and an online calculation program on Maya and Aztec astrology.

Eating Local for Immune Health

by Robin Ivy Payton

Note: This article is not meant to diagnose, treat, prescribe, or substitute consultation with a licensed health-care professional.

Eating local has become newsworthy. More fine restaurants show their pride in preparing meals with fresh, seasonal produce; meat from animals raised on nearby farms; and seafood from nearby waters. Bloggers and authors write about their experiences with the 100-Mile Diet, in which all foods consumed are grown, harvested, or raised within 100 miles of home. Buying and consuming food from local farms, cooperatives, community gardens, and your own backyard earns you bragging rights in some circles. Keeping chickens for eggs and bees for honey for your household or neighborhood seems to be in fashion.

Whether it's healthier for us to eat locally grown foods is a topic of conversation, debate, and nutritional and medical studies.

Some people support and some debate or question the value and cost/benefit of local and seasonal eating.

In 2007, the word *locavore* was named Word of the Year in the *Oxford American Dictionary* after only three years in existence. *Locavore* describes an individual as well as a movement. Locavores believe there are a host of reasons to consume as much food as possible that is produced within a 100-mile radius of where you live. This includes foods grown and harvested close by and also foods you can, freeze, or pickle for the part of the year when fresh fruits and vegetables are not seasonally available. Rationales for going to the trouble of eating locally include fossil fuel consumption from shipping food, supporting and sustaining your local economy, unknown facts about food from distant sources (such as what animals were fed while being raised or what pesticides might have been used), the sense of community fostered by knowing your local farmer and seller, and also benefits to health.

Food eaten soon after being harvested or grown in the environment of the consumer may have health benefits over older produce, including additional nutritional value and a healthy boost to the immune system. Among the "Top Twelve Reasons to Eat Locally" listed on the Locavore community website are freshness, taste, nutrition, purity, and variety—all of which can impact health. For example, better taste and variety can increase the amount of fruits, herbs, and vegetables you'll want to eat! Eating more veggies and fresh foods is something most people should strive for since they contain more vitamins, fiber, and minerals than processed foods.

Freshness and purity are important and often unknown or absent factors in many grocery foods, which may be shipped from long distances and even other countries. Some of these grocery store foods need treatment so they'll look appetizing on store shelves! Conversely, local fruits and vegetables are usually harvested within twenty-four hours of purchase. If you live in

New York, for example, and buy produce from California, it lacks freshness and possibly purity. Many Americans are concerned about food safety, including the use of pesticides and fungicides and the residue of these substances that remains on and in food. If you know the source of your food or even your farmers, or if your produce is grown organically and certified, you have more assurance that your food is pure and chemical-free. Perhaps most notable in the health-based aspect of Locavore philosophy is that nutritional content is likely to be higher in foods from nearby since nutritional value declines, often dramatically, as more time passes between harvest and consumption.

As with any health topic, there is debate about whether eating local is truly better for you. One strong point is that what you eat is more important than how far it has traveled. Eating organic produce, dairy, or meat could be better than eating meat, dairy, or produce from nearby that is farmed or fed using pesticides or other chemicals. Local and small farms may spray pesticides or plow from road to road, decreasing the purity of crops. Others argue that limiting dairy and wheat or beef is a more nutritionally sound practice—regardless of whether they are local or organic sources—because of food sensitivities and an abundance of fat in our diets. Some believe the statements of journalist and sustainable-agriculture guru Michael Pollan in his recent book, *In Defense of Food*, to be more relevant. He suggests a common-sense guide to eating ethically and well: "Eat food. Not too much. Mostly plants."

However, many people live in areas where produce cannot be grown throughout the year, and important nutrients could end up missing from their diets for many months if only local produce is consumed. Bananas are often imported to America, and they contain potassium and are a good source of fiber. Would it be wise to ban the banana from our diet if it's not grown in our region? That's just one example of a food that many would never enjoy or reap the health benefit from if they ate only from a 100-mile range. The effects and consequences of eating locally versus eating a similar diet of nonlocal foods has not been as widely studied as it could be, so there's plenty of room for interpreting the facts.

A 2008 *New York Times* article summed it up well: "There's not real evidence that eating locally farmed food is better for you. But there are many reasons to think it might be. By definition, locally farmed food is not going to come from large commercial food companies, so people who eat locally aren't going to consume as much processed food, which typically contains lots of refined carbohydrates, sugar, fat, and preservatives." The WebMD website, one of many reputable resources on immunity, says consuming foods high in sugar and fat suppresses immune system cells that attack bacteria. According to this source, 75 to 100 grams of a sugar solution (equivalent to 24 ounces of sodas) "reduces the ability of white blood cells to overpower and destroy bacteria" for at least a few hours after consumption. In the same article, WebMD points out that getting more antioxidants is one of the greatest immune boosters, as they help neutralize free radicals, which cause damage. Antioxidants fight infection and reduce the risk of cancer and heart disease. These immune boosters include vitamins C, E, zinc, and beta carotene and are found in richly colored fruits and vegetables. Eating an abundance of these increases the body's resistance to disease.

Eating locally adds another dimension to immune boosting and vitamin consumption, since you are likely getting more vitamins in fresh food that has not been moved far and was harvested recently. Produce begins to change as soon as it's plucked, and vitamins such as C, E, A, and thiamine begin to decrease rapidly.

"Over time, vitamin stability decreases," according to Erika Ichinose, program coordinator for the Farmers Market Nutrition Program at Cornell University Cooperative Extension in New York City. "Temperature changes, exposure to air and artificial

light all wreak havoc, robbing fruits and vegetables of nutrients."
(Ramirez, "Farm Fresh") Yet, according to the National Resources
Defense Council, most of the produce grown in the United States
travels an average of 1,500 miles before it is sold in the grocery
store.

Our immune systems thrive with phytochemicals like carotenoids and anthocyanin found in blueberries, propolis (bee
resin), allicins that come from garlic, and beta glucans found in
mushrooms. As Lisa Fernandez of Maine Permaculture informed
me, "Some of the food highest in antioxidants and anthocyanins
are ones that are not always commercially available and [are] best
grown locally anyway, such as elderberry, aronia, seaberry, and
others. Those immune-building properties are at their strongest
as close to harvest as possible." Fernandez also acknowledged
that local versus nonlocal is not the be-all indicator when it comes
to healthy, immune-enhancing foods, since any farm could practice extractive agriculture where produce may lack in nutritional
value though it looks good on the surface. This happens when
the soil is not replenished with nutrients by composting and
adding seaweeds and other ocean matter, rich manure, or green
plant matter periodically. Chemical fertilizing cannot give the
food we eat high quality, like the immune-boosting power found
in vitamins and antioxidants of produce grown in soil amended
with fresh organic matter each season. Lisa Fernandez adds that,
"Knowing your farmer means being able to ask the right questions, find reliable sources, and be as informed as possible about
the value and source of your foods."

Mushrooms

If you're looking for immune-boosting foods and searching local
sources and farmers' markets or considering growing your own,
there are some particular foods to consider. Mushrooms, for
example, can be grown fairly easily at home, and studies on ani-

mals have shown anti-tumor and anti-virus effects. Mushrooms like shiitake and even the most common button varieties are high in beta glucans, which are believed to fight cancer and infections. "Beta glucan is believed to stimulate the immune system and activate certain cells and proteins that attack cancer, including macrophages, T-cells, natural killer cells... In laboratory studies, it appears to slow the growth of cancer in some cell cultures and in mice." (cancer.org/treatment) Mushrooms contain potassium and selenium, known for its antioxidant properties, which has been tested for its ability to combat prostate cancer and cardiovascular disease.

The primary reason to buy local may be for the freshness of your mushrooms, so the immune-fighting properties have not been diminished by light, time, and other factors. Dan Agro—a mushroom expert based in Portland, Maine—believes that the shorter time between harvest and consumption will always benefit the medicinal and nutritional effects of the mushroom. "The mushroom 'animal', mycelium, is the force that produces the mushroom's beneficial components, most of which are immune system based. While the mushroom is still connected to its mycelium parent(s), it is being pumped full of all the medicinal components it needs to ward off outside attacks from bacteria, viruses, and other fungi. Once the mushroom either drops its spores or is picked, that connection is lost and the medicinal contents start to wear off," Agro explains. A geographer by trade, Agro firmly believes that fungi that live and breath in the same environment as we do develop immune systems specific to the environment. He says, "We hold an evolutionary lineage with the fungi kingdom, which means we [humans] have to fight off the same things the fungi do to survive. When we consume a healthy mushroom from our local ecosystem, we can rest assured that the connected fungi network had already developed mechanisms to ward off much of the same competitions that we are working to fight off."

Honey

Honey is believed to help pollen allergies, and if you plan to try a honey regimen to combat yours, local honey may be the best choice. There is little scientific evidence solid enough to prove that local honey will significantly ease your seasonal allergies, but proponents suggest the nearer your honey bees worked to produce it, the better result. Adding honey to your daily diet for allergy relief is a form of immunotherapy, wherein the body slowly builds resistance as it becomes accustomed to the presence of the allergy-inducing spores. Close proximity to honey production means the flowering plants and grasses stimulating the allergy trouble will be the ones the bees used to make that honey. If you consume honey with spores from a type of flower that grows in the Northwest and you suffer from allergies in the Southeast, for example, the honey is less likely to make a positive impact on your symptoms. Try consuming local honey regularly to see if your condition can improve with this natural remedy.

Berries

Berries contain flavonoids, which give them their rich colors. Nature may have bestowed that power so we would find berries appealing to eat, thereby benefiting from their anti-inflammatory properties and their ability to enhance the effect of vitamin C. While spinach, onions, and black beans are among other foods in the flavonoid category, blueberries, raspberries (both red and black), strawberries, and other less common berry varieties have the highest concentration of a type of flavonoid called anthocyanins. Anthocyanin-rich herbs, vegetables, and fruits have a long history of use and effective reputation in folk medicine all over the world; in the laboratory, they have been found to inhibit some human tumor cells.

One less-common example of a berry being grown and used for immune health in recent years is the elderberry. The medicinal

use of elderberry goes way back in European history, both to treat wounds and respiratory illnesses. Now, tinctures and syrups are found on whole food store shelves as more people take elderberry preventatively to ward off colds and flu, or use it periodically to boost the immune system and reduce the duration of symptoms when illness sets in. David Hoffmann, author of *The Complete Illustrated Holistic Herbal*, calls elder a "virtual medicine chest". Hoffman praises the flowers and suggests using them to treat respiratory congestion, hayfever, and sinusitis. According to his research, elderflowers are high in flavonoids and the berries are high in vitamin C. Like honey, the power of elderberry for immunity may increase if it's grown nearby, since there are many types of elderberry. Berries or elderflowers from your area may be more effective for allergies and sinus-related ailments, in particular, since they contain the pollen and properties of the area where the irritants originated. Add local honey to elderberries and create your own syrup! Remember: raw elderberries are not to be consumed since they can be toxic. Their taste isn't appealing in the first place, which is one of nature's built-in messages! Elderberries must be boiled or used to infuse an elixir and then strained out. There are many good recipes for taking elderberries from your own bush, removing the stems, and adding ingredients like honey and ginger to create your own at home.

Other berries that are edible raw, like blackberries and strawberries, are at their best when fresh and local, with the highest concentration of the flavonoids present at picking time.

. . . .

So will you be more vital and resilient if you choose local foods? There's only a small amount of research proving that food grown and harvested near your home will provide better immune function and overall health. However, we do know that fresher is almost always healthier, and that fruits and vegetables lose nutritional value rapidly in shipping process. Also, knowing the sources of your produce, meat, and dairy and being able to ask questions and investigate the quality of your farmer, market, or cooperative makes you a more informed consumer. If what you seek is more reliably chemical-, GMO-, and pesticide-free food that provides the highest concentrations of antioxidants, vitamins, and nutrients, eating close to the source and soon after harvest increases the chance of reaching that goal. Ask questions, be informed, try things out, and see how you feel. Your instinct is always your best guide.

Sources

Pollan, Michael. *In Defense of Food: An Eater's Manifesto*. New York: Penguin Press, 2008.

Hoffman, David. *The Complete Illustrated Holistic Herbal: A Safe and Practical Guide to Making and Using Herbal Remedies*. Rockport, MA: Element Books, 1996.

Online Sources, accessed September 2013

Painter, Frank M. "Anthocyanins." The Chiropractic Resource Organization. www.chiro.org/nutrition/FULL/Anthocyanins.shtml.

Clark, Josh. "Can You Fight Allergies with Local Honey?" Discovery Communications. http://health.howstuffworks.com/diseases-conditions/allergies/allergy-treatments/local-honey-for-allergies.htm

Natural Resources Defense Council. "Green Eating Guide: Eat Local Foods." http://www.nrdc.org/health/food/eatlocal.asp

Parker-Pope, Tara. "Boosting Health with Local Food." New York Times. http://well.blogs.nytimes.com/2008/06/06/boosting-health-with-local-food/?_r=0

Ramirez, Lisa. "Farm Fresh: The Benefits of Buying Local Produce." Record Online. www.recordonline.com/apps/pbcs.dll/article?AID=/20080723/HEALTH/807230315/-1/HEALTH05

WebMD. "10 Immune System Boosters and Busters." www.webmd .com/cold-and-flu/10-immune-system-busters-boosters

Other Sources

Portland Maine Permaculture Meetup Group: www.portlandmaine permaculture.com

AgroMyCo: www.agromyco.com

Post Carbon Designs: http://www.postcarbondesigns.com/

Resilient Roots Permaculture. http://www.resilientroots.com/

About the Author

Robin Ivy Payton is known for her radio forecast and Robin's Zodiac Zone for the past fifteen years. In her role as yoga teacher, Robin created RoZoYo, a fusion of astrology and yoga. Based in Tampa, Florida, she leads weekly classes and specialty workshops from Florida to Maine. Robin teaches and presents at events large and small and is available for intuitive tarot and astrology readings. Find her at www.RoZoYo.com and Robin's Zodiac Zone and Yoga on facebook.

Spring, Summer, or Fall Garden

by Penny Kelly

I f you love gardening, fresh vegetables, and the fabulous physical benefits of working in a garden, you might like to try extending your gardening season a little. The most important differences between spring, summer, and fall gardens will be in your choice of what to plant and when to plant it; differences in when and how much to water; the tools and supporting materials you will need in order to keep things going smoothly; and the shape of the garden that you plant.

What to Plant

Knowing whether a plant likes cool, warm, hot, or downright cold weather is the first thing you need to know to begin extending your garden season. Anyone who has tried to grow lettuce in the heat of summer knows that it will quickly change from a sweet green thing with tender, ruffled leaves to a tall, spindly stalk offering seeds and a few tough, bitter leaves. Broccoli doesn't like the heat either; it quickly bolts to seed in hot weather. And peas just stop growing when the thermometer rises. Here are some basic veggies and the seasons they do well in:

Spring: broccoli, beets, Brussels sprouts, cabbage, cauliflower, celery, greens, kohlrabi, leeks, lettuces, onions, parsley, peas, potatoes, radishes, rosemary, sage, spinach, Swiss chard, thyme

Summer: beans (both green and yellow snap and beans to dry), beets, basil, cantaloupe, carrots, corn, cucumber, eggplant, leeks, onions, okra, parsley, peppers, potatoes, rosemary, sage, squash (both summer and winter), pumpkins, sunflowers (for seeds), sweet potatoes, thyme, tomatoes, watermelon, zucchini

Fall: broccoli, beets, cabbage, cauliflower, greens, kale, kohlrabi, lettuces, parsley, parsnips, peas, radishes, rosemary, sage, Swiss chard, thyme, turnips

I included a few popular herbs in the list because herbs are important for good nutrition and full-flavored foods. Just in case you aren't familiar with herbs, parsley is a biennial and will usually make it through the winter, but it will definitely bolt and go to seed the second year regardless of season or temperature. Sage is a tough perennial, rosemary is a very tender perennial (protect it over the winter), and basil and marjoram are annuals that turn tail and collapse at the first sign of frost.

Some things will grow fairly well in all three seasons, but they will taste different and be smaller or perhaps larger in differing seasons. For instance, kale and Brussels sprouts only become sweet after a frost. Let lettuces or broccoli get chilly and you have a taste sensation! In fact, the wider the range of temperatures your garden is subject to, the sweeter your produce will be. This is because the plant that has been subjected to both heat and cold has been forced to maintain a wide variety of enzymes, minerals, and vitamins in order to cope with differing stresses—all of which gives the flavor additional taste and "bouquet."

Although I didn't note it in the lists above, keep in mind the number of days a plant will need to develop to maturity. Corn or tomatoes planted in early August will not likely have time to develop edible ears in Michigan, though they might in Missouri or Colorado. Also, anything that flowers will need insects for pollination. You may manage to keep tomatoes or peas growing through the winter, but you might not have enough flying insects to pollinate; the result will be no fruit (farmers call everything a "fruit," including vegetables, grains, and seed). That's why most people just try to grow greens and cold crops when extending their growing season.

Temperature, Water, and Wind

The next thing you need when tending a spring, summer, or fall garden is a bit of intuition about watering. Watering in the summer is a lot different from watering in the spring or fall, and there are even more considerations if you're working in a greenhouse in winter. When deciding whether or not to water, the question to ask is, "How much respiration is going on?" You may not be a scientist, but you can make an educated guess and do pretty well. Respiration is the rate at which a plant is engaging in internal transactions that cause growth or the production of its fruit or seed.

If temperatures are in the 70s or 80s Fahrenheit, respiration is moving at a fast clip. Therefore, if there is no rain, water deeply once or twice a week rather than a little bit every day. Plant roots will be forced deeper into the soil to look for water and will be more resilient in hot, dry spells.

If temperatures are in the 50s or 60s, respiration is slow and steady. If the soil is damp on top, no watering is needed. If it looks dry, your watering should be just enough to rinse the dust off the leaves and give them a "small to medium" drink once a week.

If temperatures are in the 30s at night and the 40s during the day, watering should be minimal. It will usually be best to water lightly on sunny afternoons when activity is taking place. Sometimes that will only be every three weeks!

Too much water in any season will likely earn you all sorts of molds and mildew, but this is especially true in spring and fall because such organisms love cool, wet conditions. Too much water in winter will kill plants outright because the water will dilute the sugars in the plant—water without sugars in it will freeze much more quickly than water with sugars.

Extremes of any sort make gardening more challenging. If temperatures go above 85 degrees Fahrenheit, many vegetables shut down in order to conserve water. They close their pores to avoid losing moisture and simply rest. For this reason, if the plants are drooping visibly on a hot day, watering may not get you a quick response. Not until the temperature drops and activity picks up within the plant will it begin to straighten up. Sometimes it takes all night for a plant to drink its fill and stand up again. Plants will also shut down if the wind is blowing more than 15 miles per hour, simply because there is too much mechanical stress going on in the stems and leaves that are bending and waving wildly in the wind. Spring and fall are typically rather windy, so think about placing some form of fencing or maybe a few bales of hay in or around the garden to provide relief from wind.

Tools and Timing

The next thing you will need to consider when extending your garden season is tools and other items to have on hand. It's best if you till the garden in the fall and let it sit over the winter. That way you're ready to roll in spring and last year's weeds have composted. In the spring, the ground is heavy, dense, and more difficult to work with because the soil contracts in winter and does not expand again until temperatures rise. If you have a tiny garden, say 20x30 feet, you might want to turn the soil by hand. But if you have a large garden, perhaps a quarter acre or a half acre in size, you need something besides a shovel and your own back. Rent a tiller or hire someone with a small tractor to come in and till the garden for you. Renting a tiller for three or four hours will cost about $40. Hiring someone to come in with a small tractor will usually cost between $60 and $75 per hour, but it will only take an hour or less to get the job done.

If you have raised beds, you will want to have a good shovel to turn over the soil in the beds by hand. If you're planting in large pots on a deck or porch, you need a good hand trowel to loosen and turn the soil.

For a spring garden, you will need to start your seeds indoors. You can put them in anything from gardening flats to old pots to cut-off milk cartons. For a spring garden here in the north, I start seeds about the second week in February. Plants can go into the greenhouse beds or garden tunnels at the end of March. For a summer garden, I start seeds indoors about mid-April, and they are ready to go into the garden on Memorial Day weekend, which is a traditional planting weekend in our family. For a fall garden, I start seeds indoors about the first week in August, and they are ready to go in the greenhouse or garden in mid-September.

Pests

Once your plants are in place, you have to think about how to protect them. For a gardener, animals and weather are challenging forces to contend with. To protect your garden, you will need a roll or two of chicken wire and some pins to anchor it.

Over the winter, the local deer, rabbits, raccoons, and other four-legged creatures subsist on whatever they can find to eat in the field or the woods. If you plant a nice-looking spring garden of early cabbage, parsley, peas, and lettuces, they will see this as food from the gods and feast accordingly! To keep a spring garden from being eaten alive, we have tried everything—tunnels, lightweight frost cloth, pest deterrents, and chicken wire "tents" over the rows. Animals got into the tunnels easily and enjoyed their meals undetected and undisturbed. They chewed right through the lightweight cloth, and completely ignored the pest deterrents such as flapping strings or pieces of aluminum foil and scarecrows. Chicken wire tents over the rows are the only things that have worked fairly consistently, although deer have tried to push them out of the way.

We buy rolls of chicken wire that are 2 feet wide and 50 feet long, then unroll and bend them in half lengthwise to form a tent and set them over the young seedlings. We close the ends by folding them in, overlapping them and using wire to secure the flaps. To anchor the wire tent to the ground, use the U-shaped pins that are usually used to put down weed barrier cloth and anchor it in place. These pins can be purchased from a greenhouse supplier, a landscaper, a seed company that sells gardening equipment, or sometimes your local home improvement store.

By summer, many green things are growing and available, so local critters may not be as voracious, but they're still there and will wander through, grazing as they do. We try to plant enough for us AND the local animals. This fosters a gift mentality and honors the whole community of beings, both two-legged and four-legged. By autumn, the local animals are usually fairly well-fed and you may get a bit of relief … but now you have to be ready for freezing weather.

Frost

You'll want several large frost cloths, a tarp, some short stakes to hold up the tarp, six to eight large rocks or bricks, a shovel, and some wood to make a small fire. To counter freezing weather, we have used frost cloth in single, double, and triple layers depending on how cold we think it will get. A freeze in spring is usually more serious than a freeze in autumn; there is still a small amount of summer heat coming from the soil in autumn but very little in spring. One layer of cloth will offer a couple of degrees of frost protection. Two or three layers will offer much more, sometimes as much as 10 degrees if you don't put it down too smoothly. In other words, leave it looking kind of crumpled and messy, with lots of air pockets, and you will get much more protection out of it.

A low tunnel is also great protection for spring and fall gardens, but this is much more expensive and a little harder to get into when you want something from the middle of a 50-foot row. You have to be careful that you don't destroy your tunnel when you're trying to get something out of it.

We have also used a plastic-tarp-and-heated-rock combination to provide protection during severe cold snaps. The tarp is supported by 2-foot-high stakes at the corners of the garden, midway down the sides, and one or more in the center. Put the stakes in place before cold weather sets in—no one likes to be dragging tools and equipment into a freezing garden in bad weather! Once the stakes are in, put the tarp in a handy place so you know where it is. When the weather forecast predicts a sudden and severe drop in temperatures, start a small fire in a pit and put the rocks or bricks around it to heat them up. When the fire has burned down and cooled a little, use a shovel to pick up the rocks and place them throughout the garden. Drape the tarp over the stakes, making sure it reaches all the way to the ground on all sides. If the rocks aren't ungodly hot, you can even put frost cloth directly over the plants and rocks, then put the tarp on the stakes to cover all. Stake or pin the edges of the tarp if it is windy.

Using this method for avoiding hard freezes is one instance where thinking about the size and shape of your garden before planting pays off. It is much harder to keep a long, skinny row of something protected during a freezing spell. A garden planted in small squares or rectangles is much easier to keep covered and warm. Simply put all your cold-loving veggies in one area. And a small greenhouse is worth its weight in gold because you can use the frost cloth and hot rocks technique to keep things growing all winter.

Be aware that if you try to grow things through the winter, lettuces, cabbages, kale, and other greens can often freeze at night and thaw out during the day—don't touch them when they are frozen! If the sun comes out and the temperature rises, they will thaw and keep growing. If you touch them, the spot where you touched the frozen plant will turn to brown and green slime when the temperature rises and the plant thaws. If a plant freezes solid for more than three or four days, it is probably lost for the season.

There is nothing as healing as fresh vegetables, no matter the weather. If you have a hankering to try your hand at gardening, don't let the season get in your way—try a spring or a fall garden and save the summer for vacationing or travel!

About the Author

Penny Kelly is the owner of Lily Hill Farm and Learning Center in southwest Michigan. For thirty years she has been studying, researching, teaching, consulting, and writing about consciousness, perception, and intelligence. She is also a Naturopathic physician who gardens organically and teaches courses in organic gardening that are designed to increase sustainable living and food security in Kalamazoo, Michigan. Penny is the author of five print books, the lead author of fourteen e-books on self-development, and runs two small publishing companies. She lives and writes in Lawton, Michigan. www.pennykelly.com

Ale Gardens

Charlie Rainbow Wolf

Magazines at the home improvement stores are very quick to tell us how to create a water garden or an herb garden, but I wonder how many people have ever thought about growing a garden for the purpose of brewing ale? We are seeing a resurrection of many traditional skills as numerous people return to a more natural and connected way of life. Farmers' markets are expanding into previously devoid areas, making it easier to obtain the ingredients needed to create culinary delights. This involvement often sparks within us a desire to grow our own produce and forge an even stronger connection with Mother Nature. From baking bread to curing lye soap to fermenting and brewing—we're learning, experimenting, and experiencing.

It doesn't take a lot of room, or a lot of expertise, to be able to successfully grow things. Anyone who has battled weeds will readily appreciate that nature is persistent! Visit abandoned farms or homesteads, and the remnants of gardens and orchards can still be seen—sometimes with their original patterns or designs intact. Nature *wants* to thrive.

We can start to grow things in even the smallest area. Whether it is a large garden or some herbs in pots on kitchen window-sills, the connection is still the same. We nurture the plants in order that later they might nurture us. This all strengthens the relationship between ourselves and nature, as well as enhances our kitchen experiences, and helps us to create something truly unique.

It seems only natural that the next step from growing our food might be to make our own beverages. We can preserve leaves and flowers for tea. Cordials can be made by soaking fruit in appropriate spirits, such as vodka or brandy. Wine can be made from fruits and herbs, and so can beers and ales.

Most people don't think about growing ale when they think of gardens, but it's not only feasible, it's easy and enjoyable! Plants have long been fermented for medicinal use and used in the making of wines and other beverages. Growing and using plants for ales isn't that difficult, and with a bit of practice, it's possible to become quite proficient at it.

Hops?

Think of beers and ales, and most of us will immediately envision hops; however, most traditional ales will not include hops at all. Hops were only added as a standard ingredient in recipes about four hundred years ago. Hops are used to add bitter flavor and aroma to the beer, and this will vary, determined by when they are added. The addition of hops also helps to preserve the finished beer.*

* Fisher, D., and J. Fisher. *The Homebrewer's Garden: How to Easily Grow, Prepare, and Use Your Own Hops, Malts, Brewing Herbs.* Storey Publishing LLC, 1998.

Hops are easy to grow, and—like any plant—the subtle differences in the variety will affect the flavor of the ale in different ways. They do take a lot of room to grow, though, and they are not necessary for the beginner. Hops can be purchased from any reputable home-brewing shop should they be desired, but there are many traditional, easy-to-make ales that do not use them.

Flavor Additions

The basic ale recipe is a matter of choice, as there are many traditional recipes that will produce a wonderful brew; it all comes down to palate and preference. My husband is partial to a ninth-century Saxon ale that consists of malt extract, honey, cracked malt, tea, lemon juice, water, and yeast.[*] To this, he then adds produce from the garden to tweak the recipe and give each batch a subtle difference in flavor and body. In the past, we have added both herbs and fruits to the ales. As in all things, some results have been better than others! Raspberries were a howling success, giving the ale both a sweet and fruity flavor, and a rich color. Woodruff (*Gallium odoratum*) was a completely different story, indeed! Many of the additions to ales can be readily found, without the need for planning a specific garden. Some—like spruce or dandelion—can be found growing wild in wooded areas or meadows. Other additions might come from existing flower or herb gardens.

My herb garden starts with a big rose hip bush (*Rosa rugosa*) next to the driveway. This is a hardy, spreading shrub rose that can grow up to 6 feet tall and 6 feet wide in all but the coldest of climates. The bush is covered with sweet-smelling flowers in the spring. In the summer, fruits—called hips—appear until the first frost. The hips, which look like small orange crabapples and are full of seeds, are used to make jam, jelly, cordial, and syrup, and

---

[*] Ball , I. *Traditional Beer and Cider Making*. Surrey, UK: Elliot Right Way Books. 1984.

they can be added to ales to impart a rich amber color and a citrus flavor.

Another of the main staples in my garden is mint. We live in USDA growing zone 6, and mints are hardy perennials here. I have several different types of mint growing in various different areas. Many of my friends seem frightened of growing mint, because of the way that it takes over the area. For me, this is an advantage. It saves me having to weed, and the deer and other garden nuisances don't seem to like it. Left untrimmed, it will flower and attract many bees and other beneficial insects. There are three mints that we cultivate specifically for culinary purposes.

Lemon balm (*Melissa officinalis*) is very easy to grow. Lemon balm will reach approximately 2 feet in height and will spread, as will all mints. When rubbed between the fingers, it releases a strong, sweet smell not unlike lemon candy. Added to a pale ale recipe, it will impart a light, fresh flavor.

Anise mint (*Agastache foeniculum*), also called anise hyssop, is another one of the mints we have grown to use in ales. As the name suggests, this mint has a light anise or licorice flavor. It is native to moist woodlands and can grow to a height of over 3 feet. Used in moderation, it gives a very unusual and interesting aroma and taste to dark ales. We have added it to root beers with some success and are keen to try it in mead.

The third mint I have grown specifically for use in cooking and brewing is chocolate mint (*Menthe piperita chocolate*)—yes, it does smell and taste exactly how it sounds! The small, dark-green leaves are just bursting with a chocolate-mint flavor and scent. This makes a great addition to a heavy ale like a chocolate oat stout, but be careful: the minty flavor can be strong, and no one wants to drink ale that tastes like toothpaste!

These three mints are not as hardy as some of the other mint varieties, such as peppermint or spearmint. Care needs to be taken that they do not get too cold in the winter or too dry in the summer if they are to be treated as permanent features of the ale garden. To prevent them spreading, they can be planted in big pots dug into the ground. We've never had that problem though. We grow them where we can get through them with the lawn-mower; any unwanted growth is sheared, releasing a delightful smell in the process.

Lavender is another favored addition to the herb garden that can be used for brewing. There are many different types of lavender (*Lavandula*); the one we have growing in our garden is commonly known as English lavender (*Lavandula angustifolia*). Lavender is another plant that needs a bit of coaxing sometimes, and it doesn't like to be too cold nor too dry. Next time lavender is in bloom, carefully taste one of the small flower buds; it does not taste the way that it smells! In brewing, lavender will impart a bitter taste to the ale.

Next to our lavender is the rhubarb patch. Rhubarb (*Rheum rubarbarum*) seems to be one of those flavors that is either loved or loathed. It is easy to grow in all but the extreme climates and can reach quite a size. The leaves are toxic if ingested but make a wonderful vegetable dye. It is the long, fleshy stalks that are prized for their flavor. They are best picked in spring or early summer, before the plant starts to flower (any flower stalks should be removed to encourage leaf production). Although technically a vegetable, rhubarb is usually prepared as a fruit dish. Just as it has an unmistakable taste in pies and other desserts, rhubarb also adds a truly unique flavor to fruit ales.

We have a large spruce tree (*Picea*) in the middle of the garden, and we have had great success adding it to home-brewed ale. Adding new shoots to a porter-type recipe made lovely soothing ale for chilly autumnal evenings. There are many different types of spruce trees, and fresh growth from any type would work just as well. Leaves and berries from the juniper family (*Cupressaceae*) may also be used. Juniper has long been used to make gin and gin-like wines, and it will give the ale a very unique scent and flavor.

Annuals

I also plant some annual flowers in among the perennials and the vegetables. These are flowers that are short-lived and will die off when the autumnal frosts arrive. They can be raised from seed or purchased from a garden center. Not only do these add color, but they also help with pest control, pollination, and general productivity.

I think my favorite annual in the ale garden is the humble nasturtium (*Tropaeolaceae*) family. These come in many different colors and species, and they can easily be raised from seeds. The leaves are large and nearly round, and the flowers come in all shapes and sizes. Some nasturtiums are bushy and upright, while others will spread or trail for more than 3 feet. All parts of the nasturtium are edible and have a slightly peppery taste. They add a warm, peppery note when added to home-brewed ale.

We also grow a lot of marigolds (*calendula*), but not as an ingredient in the home-brews. Just as there are many different types of nasturtium, there are also many different types of marigolds. They are related to daisies, and like daisies, the blooms on marigolds are usually warm yellows and oranges, whites, and the petals are sometimes tinged with red. These plants not only bear colorful flowers, but they are also great garden companions: they attract beneficial insects, helping the rest of the ale garden to flourish. Marigolds have a very distinct odor; it is part of what helps them to deter the pests around other plants. Again, this is a companion plant only—we certainly don't want our ale smelling of old socks!

Fruits

Fruit beers and ales are gaining popularity on the supermarket shelves, and there is no reason they cannot be made at home, either. Adding fruit when brewing ale is nothing new. Using whole fruits at the onset of a recipe can produce a much richer product than just adding a fruit extract at the end of the fermenting process. We grow several different kinds of fruit, but it is blackberry, raspberry, and elderberry that are the key ingredients in our ale garden.

Raspberries can be found in many different varieties. Black raspberries can often be found growing wild in hedgerows, but we are partial to the cultivars named 'fall red,' and 'fall gold.' Most raspberries belong to the genus Rubus, which is a member of the rose family. The 'fall red' and the 'fall gold' are ever-bearing, meaning that we get fruit from late spring right through until early autumn. Raspberries will spread rapidly in all directions if the old growth is not removed. They need a part of the garden that has good drainage and lots of sunlight. Half a dozen canes will turn into a huge raspberry patch with heavy yields of fruit if just a little care and attention is paid to them. Red raspberries added to ale during the initial brew will turn it a lovely dark red and give it plenty of sweet berry flavor and aroma. I cannot comment on a golden raspberry recipe; we tend to eat them as fast as we pick them!

Blackberries (*Rubus fruticosus*) are another popular fruit to add to home-brewed beverages. Blackberries are also a member of the rose family, and their growing habit is very similar to that of raspberries. We have a cultivated 'Cherokee' blackberry, but they also grow wild in many hedgerows. Like raspberries, they are a long-time favored addition with brewers. Blackberry seems to do nicely in wheat ales, giving them a good "nose" and a nice berry flavor.

The third berry that is a staple in our ale garden is the elderberry. Elder has long been prized for wine, jam, jelly, pie, and other culinary pursuits. Two types are needed for cross-pollination, and we have grown *Sambucus canadensis* 'Johns' and 'Adams.'

Elderberries are hardy in all but extreme climates, and they are quite easy to grow as a small tree or—as we have done—a bush, which can spread up to 12 feet tall and wide. The bark and the leaves of elder is toxic if ingested, so be diligent when gathering the flowers and the fruits. In the spring the foliage is covered with large umbrella-like clusters of small white flowers. These are very fragrant and

can be added to ales for their bouquet. Leave the flowers, though, and soon small purple berries will be ripe for picking. Separate them from their stems with a fork, and add them at the initial brewing stage. Elderberries will bring a dark color and a dry flavor to the finished ale.

These are not the only fruits that can be used in home brewing, though. A bit of research will uncover plenty of recipes, some traditional and some modern, which involve using a wide variety of fruits. Another addition to the ale garden might be some kind of currant. *Ribes nigrum* (blackcurrant) or *Ribes rubrum* (redcurrant) are possibly the two most renowned. Blackcurrant is popular in cordials, while redcurrant is often used to make a sweet-tart sauce similar to cranberry jelly. Both will give a thick and rich fruity flavor when added to dark ales.

"Weeds"

Not everything that is appropriate for adding to home-brew needs to be a specifically grown cultivar, though. There are many humble weeds that will add flavor and interest to ales. One of

the first recipes we ever tried was a medieval dandelion and burdock recipe. The first attempt wasn't particularly rewarding, but
the second, slightly more complex version was quite successful,
indeed.

The humble dandelion (*Taraxacum officinale*) needs little introduction. We might think of it as a weed, but actually it is an
herbaceous perennial with many uses, including traditional dandelion wine. When gathering dandelions, make sure that they are
picked early in the spring and early in the day. Dandelions have a
very acrid flavor, but the earlier in the spring dandelions are gathered, the milder their flavor will be. They should be pulled out by
their long taproot, and the entire plant is used in brewing. Avoid
collecting them where the area has been exposed to chemical
fertilizers or herbicides. Not surprisingly, dandelions add a bitter
taste to ales, so they should be used in moderation.

Burdock is another plant that some consider a weed, but that
we prize in our ale garden. Burdock is a member of the Articum
genus and, like dandelion, is an herbaceous perennial, with large
heart-shaped leaves. It flowers through late summer into autumn,
and then the flower heads produce the "burrs" that become a
nuisance later in the season. Like rhubarb, it is best if the plant
can be kept from flowering, simply because it is less of a nuisance
that way! Burdock can grow several feet tall and nearly as wide,
with long roots that go very deep into the soil—it is the root that
it typically used in brewing. This also lends a very bitter taste to
the ales, and needs to be used in moderation.

Last but not least, the third weed that we have decided to stop
trying to fight quite so hard is the rather striking milk thistle (*Sily-
bum marianum*). It really is stunning, with its amethyst blooms
sitting high on a dark green stalk, but it needs careful handling
because of all the spines that cover the edges of the leaves. Left
unencumbered, this striking plant can grow to over 6 feet in
height, with blossoms up to 5 inches wide. The seeds are gener-

ally the component used in brewing. Milk thistle is another bitter-tasting herb, and care needs to be taken when calculating the amount to be added to the ale. It is well worth letting it grow just for the beauty it can add to the ale garden, though.

. . . .

Whether a structured and formal look is sought, or whether—like us—it is something that just happens with experience, it is possible to plan the ale garden successfully without a lot of expense or upheaval. Simply research the flavor additions you find most appealing and organize them in a way that is pleasing to your eye. Never be afraid to experiment, either with what grows, or with what is added to the recipe. You never know when you are going to hit on something that might be destined to be a family tradition!

Further Reading:

Buhner, S. H. *Sacred and Herbal Healing Beers.* Boulder, CO: Brewer's Publications, 1998.

Riotte, L. *Carrots Love Tomatoes and Roses Love Garlic.* North Adams, MA: Storey Publishing, 2004.

Sarles, C. V. & VanNorstrand, J. *Alewife's Garden 7 Radical Weeds for Brewing Herbal Ales.* White River Junction, VT: Chelsea Green Publishing Company, 2002.

About the Author

Charlie Rainbow Wolf is happiest when she is creating something. Knowledgable in many aspects of healing, she is most keen on using meditation as medicine. Charlie is the Dean of Faculty at the Grey School, where she teaches subjects in most of the sixteen departments. She is drawn most to the Tarot, a subject that has captivated her for more than two decades. Charlie has a flair for recycling, and is keenly interested in organic gardening and cooking. She feeds her creative muse with writing, pottery, knitting, and soap-making. She lives in the Midwest with her husband and special-needs Great Danes.